— Barnaby

OTHER PEOPLE'S CHILDREN

What happens to those in the bottom 50% academically?

First Published 2018

by John Catt Educational Ltd,
12 Deben Mill Business Centre,
Old Maltings Approach,
Melton, Woodbridge IP12 1BL

Tel: +44 (0) 1394 389850

Fax: +44 (0) 1394 386893

Email: enquiries@johncatt.com

Website: www.johncatt.com

ISBN: 978 1 911382 539

Set and designed by
Theoria Design

Reviews

'For too long, our FE provision has felt like the Cinderella offer within our wider education system. In this strongly argued analysis, Barnaby Lenon has built on his best-selling book about high-performing state schools, *Much Promise*, with this heartfelt call to action to improve the status and quality of what is on offer for almost half of all pupils as they enter post-16 education. As a society, he argues, we need to value 'head, hand and heart', not just cognitive ability.

'In his characteristically thorough way, Barnaby Lenon summarises the key evidence in this important debate, starting with the early years, highlighting how educational disadvantage leads to a growing achievement gap and an unacceptably long tail of underachievement. His analysis forms the basis of an insightful critique of current reforms that leads to a series of powerful recommendations about how this important area of our educational system can be given the status and success it deserves.'

Andy Buck, CEO, Leadership Matters

'*Other People's Children* makes a grand sweep over the history of education, providing a fascinating description of years of policy failure to address a fundamental challenge that we have faced in this country for at least the last century, but probably for longer. The coverage and the depth of analysis is impressive and should make this book a must-read for any policy wonks in the field; it will certainly provide food for thought for any committed reader.'

David Hughes, Chief Executive, Association of Colleges

Contents

Introduction

There is a tendency of long historical standing in English educational thought (it is not nearly so visible in some other countries) to concentrate too much on the interests of the abler pupils in any group that is being considered and to forget about the rest.

Crowther Report, 1959

In 2017, three members of my family enrolled with a further education college. First was my 20-year-old nephew who dropped out of school when he was 17 for personal reasons but would have been capable of top grades at A level; he has enrolled to study computer science. It is further education that has invariably given second chances to people like him. Next there was a 16-year-old nephew who has autism and had struggled to cope with school, but who is clearly very intelligent and keen on engineering. These were the first members of my family not to go to university, but both are very able. Finally, I enrolled to take an adult education course at my local college. This book is about the system we found ourselves in; a system about which I knew little despite having spent my whole life in education.

The academically least successful 50% of young people in England face a number of problems. Some will have struggled at school since the day they started. They attended lessons day in day out from the age of 5 to 16, but the exams they took at the end of that 11-year slog might well have left them with a sense of failure. They might have passed some GCSEs, but at best their grades were modest.

The path trodden after GCSEs is clear enough for the more academically successful 50%. They go on to take A levels and a university degree – qualifications which the whole population understand and recognise, qualifications which have been around for many years. But for the less academic the way ahead is much less clear.

Whereas their fathers or grandfathers, and even their mothers and grandmothers, quickly picked up employment at the age of 16 or younger, for them life will be less straightforward. Jobs in manufacturing and services, which formerly supported many towns and cities in the Midlands and north of England, have gone. Some of the jobs that remain – in the large construction sector, for example – have been filled by immigrants from Eastern Europe.

Their situation is made all the more difficult because of their family background. Many will have had few books at home. Some will not have had a father in the house when they were being brought up. A disproportionate number will have been on free school meals at school. Many will be boys. Some will be from minority ethnic backgrounds, which, for a variety of reasons, makes the transition to a good job more difficult. Some will be disabled or have other special needs.

They are not a small group. They are half of all young people, most of whom are mentally and physically able to do a good job if trained and given the opportunity.

In England, our A levels and our better universities are as good as any others anywhere on the planet. But every international study tells us that the gap between the top 50% and the bottom 50% of pupils is wider in England than in almost any country in the developed world. So this is where we have the greatest capacity to improve. This is where we would now expect any sensible government to focus its attention. Not on grammar schools but on further education colleges. Not on A levels but on apprenticeships.

In the past the unskilled bottom 50% were a huge asset. They found work because there were jobs available for those who were unskilled or who could be easily trained on the job. Some of these jobs still exist, but in diminishing numbers. If we are to be a grown-up standalone nation then we need to become more like other standalone countries, like South Korea or Japan, where very few pupils are allowed to fail at school and where the less academic go onto carefully planned, high-quality training programmes which lead to work.

David Goodhart (2017) makes the point that in recent years people have been judged more and more by their exam qualifications, their cognitive ability. The 'brightest and best' trump the 'decent and hardworking'. But a good society needs to balance the three Hs – head, hand and heart. We undervalue the skills of construction workers, engineers, artisans – those who work with their hands. And we undervalue those whose emotional intelligence makes them so important to the caring professions, such as nurses, early years teachers and those working in social care.

Post-Brexit, it is likely that immigration flow into the UK will fall, so upskilling the domestic population to fill positions that would otherwise have been taken by EU workers will become important. The current performance of many pupils at age 16 suggests that this will be difficult.

This book examines how we have got into this rather weak position and what we can do about it.

What do the terms 'higher education' and 'further education' mean?

In England, the term 'higher education' means university level, 'further education' means most things taught outside schools and universities to those over the age of 16. Vocational courses are part of what is taught in further education – skills needed for a job.

In recent years, the government has chosen to refer to vocational courses as 'technical education' because they think that 'vocational' has got a bad name.

Further education in England is quite complicated but it helps if you know two things:

1.   There is a distinction between the courses for 16- to 18-year-olds, which include large numbers doing basic English and maths as well as vocational courses, and the courses for everyone over 18 (adults), which are mainly vocational but include academic courses and 'developmental' courses for the community like pottery or learning English.

2.   There is a distinction between the qualifications on offer and the institutions that teach those courses. Both need to be good if the system is to work. Government-financed further education colleges are very important in terms of the teaching, but in fact many vocational courses are taught by private companies. The qualifications themselves are all devised and administered by private firms.

Who controls the vocational education and training system in England?

1.   *The Department for Education* together with the Treasury determine overall policy and funding. *The Education and Skills Funding Agency* manages the funding of further education. *The Department for Business, Energy & Industrial Strategy* (2017 name) helps to provide strategic guidance on skills shortages.

2.   *Ofsted* inspects schools, FE colleges and independent training providers and grades them. They monitor overall standards and assess the progress and impact of government reforms.

3.   The *Further Education Commissioner* assesses FE colleges if they are rated inadequate by Ofsted or fail to meet ESFA minimum standards. He helps support colleges that appear to be struggling, even though not yet graded 'inadequate'.

4.   *The Institute for Apprenticeships and Technical Education* manages what it says in its name. Employers have an important role in helping the Institute set up and run vocational courses and apprenticeships.

5. *The Federation for Industry Sector Skills and Standards* represents, promotes and supports *Sector Skills Councils* (SSCs) across the UK. SSCs are the employer-led skills organisations and they aim to reduce skills gaps and shortages and to improve productivity. The SSCs were, in the last few years, designers, as well as first-line accreditors, of most vocational qualifications. For example, ConstructionSkills is the Sector Skills Council for the construction industry.

   The Sector Skills Councils support 19 *National Skills Academies* which bring employers together with training organisations to develop skills training in areas like construction, environmental technologies, financial services, food and drink, health, nuclear, and railway engineering. Some opt for a permanent training centre in a fixed location, whereas others prefer training that is delivered in the workplace or online.

6. *Local enterprise partnerships* (LEPs) are voluntary partnerships between local authorities and businesses set up in 2011 by the then Department for Business, Innovation and Skills to help determine local economic priorities and lead economic growth and job creation within a local area. Each has a strategic economic plan. Each LEP bids for money from the government's Local Growth Fund.

   LEPs often undertake skills surveys and make recommendations for areas where existing vocational training needs to be strengthened. For example, in 2016 the Thames Valley LEP published a report identifying specific skills shortages in engineering, construction and digital technology.

7. *Metro mayors*, some of whom have control over the adult education budget. Skills Advisory Panels are integrated into Mayoral Combined Authorities and Local Enterprise Partnerships to inform the analysis that feeds into Local Industrial Strategies. The aim is that they will bring together businesses and education providers to determine local growth priorities.

8. *The Education and Training Foundation* helps colleges and teachers deliver vocational courses and functional skills qualifications.

9. *The Association of Employment and Learning Providers* (AELP) is the national trade association representing providers involved in skills and employment delivery. AELP members deliver the majority of apprenticeships, traineeships, and English and maths in the workplace.

Acknowledgements

I would especially like to thank Maggie Galliers, Chair of the Learning and Work Institute and former President of the Association of Colleges, who not only wrote chapter 9 but also introduced me to many of those leading further education in England today. This book could not have been written without her.

I am also very grateful to the following, all of whom gave generously of their time:

Phil Beach, Executive Director for Vocational and Technical Qualifications, Ofqual

David Corke, Association of Colleges

Di Batchelor, head of Abingdon & Witney College

Sir Clive Booth, former Vice-Chancellor, Oxford Brookes University

Mark Dawe, Chief Executive of the Association of Employment and Learning Providers

Stephen Evans, CEO of the Learning and Work Institute

Norman Gealy, Director, Network Exams Ltd

Julian Gravatt, Association of Colleges

David Hughes, Chief Executive of Association of Colleges

William Richardson, Professor of Education, University of Exeter

Frances Wadsworth, head of Croydon College

Charles Webster, emeritus fellow of All Souls College, Oxford

Andy Wilson, head of Capital City College Group

Alison Wolf, Professor of Education, King's College, London

Chapter 1

The bottom 50% at age 5

Too many children start primary school at the age of 5 without the basic skills they need to cope – they cannot speak well, they have little understanding of reading or numbers, they cannot manage simple tasks or respond to instructions. A high proportion of such children are from low-income homes and many are boys.

The 'Early Years Foundation Stage' is the slightly grim name the government gives to children from birth to age five. The EYFS defines standards expected of children when they are required to start school at the end of this period and are used to identify those who are already behind and may need extra help. The box below defines what is meant by a good (*ie* expected) level of development.

A good level of development

A 'good level of development' is defined as the expected level of development for children at the end of the Early Years Foundation Stage curriculum.

This is assessed at the end of reception year, when most children are aged five, through the Early Years Foundation Stage Profile (EYFSP).

This means that a child should, for example, be able to:

- · listen to, understand and follow instructions.
- · use the past present and future tenses correctly.
- · talk about their own and others' feelings.
- · read and understand simple sentences.
- · count and carry out simple addition and subtraction.

In 2016, 31% of children in England began primary school without this good level of early development, 46% of those on free school meals. Jane Waldfogel and Elizabeth Washbrook (2010) found that children from low-income families lagged behind their more advantaged peers by roughly 11 months at school entry. In a subsequent 2011 study, Waldfogel and Washbrook found, not entirely surprisingly, that parenting was the main reason for gaps in early development between children from low-income families and their middle- or high-income peers. The 2012 Sutton Trust *Social Mobility Report* found a 19-month gap in school readiness between the richest and poorest four- and five-year-olds in the UK. Parents from lower income homes speak less to their children, have a more limited vocabulary, are less likely to help them learn to read or count, are less likely to own books.

Once children are behind, it is hard to catch up. Bruce Bradbury *et al* (2015) found that more than half of the gaps in achievement at age 11 are due to inequality that was already present at age five.

This is true in most societies. University of Kansas researchers Betty Hart and Todd Risley (1995) entered the homes of 42 families from various socioeconomic backgrounds to assess the ways in which daily exchanges between a parent and child shape language and vocabulary development. Monthly hour-long observations of each family were conducted from the time the child was seven months old until age three. They found that children from high-income families were exposed to 30 million more spoken words than children from families on benefits over those years.

Reflecting differences in prosperity, young children in some parts of England are more successful than others. The proportion not reaching a good level of development in the EYFS in 2016 ranged from 25% in the best to 37% in the worst local authorities. In a town like Middlesbrough in north-east England, there are twice as many children starting schools at a low level of development than in Greenwich in London.

But these differences are not inevitable. Jon Andrews *et al* (2017) found the gap in attainment between disadvantaged five-year-olds and their more affluent peers ranged from seven months' equivalent of progress in expected development in Halton in Cheshire to zero in Newham in London.

Gemma Moss and Liz Washbrook's study (2016a) of Reception year pupils (four- and five-year-olds) was conducted at the University of Bristol using the Millennium Cohort Study data. The study found that each year a quarter of boys in England – 80,000 – start Reception aged four struggling to speak a single sentence or follow basic instructions. In 2015, 24% of boys were below the minimum level in early language and communication expected by EYFS, as were 14% of girls. So boys make up two-thirds of those who start primary school behind in their communication skills.

The gap between boys and girls was there irrespective of ethnicity or social class. Boys from wealthier homes reach a higher level but so do the wealthier girls, so the gender gap remains. Moss and Washbrook also found boys with lower early language and communication skills at age five:

- performed less well in Key Stage 1 reading assessments.
- were less attentive.
- read less often for pleasure.
- enjoyed school less.
- liked answering in class less.
- tried less hard in school.

This is why, once boys fall behind, they struggle to catch up. Children who do not achieve the expected standard of early language and communication at age five are over four times more likely to be below the normal target level of reading at age 11 than those who did.

According to Moss and Washbrook, two-thirds of the total gender gap in reading at age 11 can be attributed to the fact that boys begin school with poorer language and attention skills than girls. These boys go on to do badly at GCSE and struggle in life thereafter.

Again, this is not just a British phenomenon. In 2015, girls outperformed boys in reading at the end of secondary school in all 64 countries and economies in the OECD, the average gap being equivalent to an extra year of schooling.

In Alissa Goodman and Paul Gregg's 2010 study, the authors used the Millennium Cohort Study (MCS) and the British Cohort Study (BCS) to observe children at various points in time from early childhood onwards.

The Millennium Cohort Study (MCS) is a longitudinal study of approximately 19,000 children born in the UK in 2000/2001. The five surveys of MCS cohort members carried out so far – at age 9 months, 3, 5, 7 and 11 years – have built up a uniquely detailed portrait of the children of the new century.

The British Cohort Study aimed to recruit all children born in Great Britain in a particular week in April 1970. There have been six subsequent follow-ups (at ages 5, 10, 16, 26, 29 and 34), with information collected on a wide range of socioeconomic and other family background factors, attitudes and behaviours of parents and children, cognitive and non-cognitive test scores, educational attainment and subsequent labour market outcomes through a mixture of face-to-face, telephone and postal surveys.

Figure 1.1: Cognitive outcomes of children at ages three and five by socioeconomic background, sampled from the Millennium Cohort Study

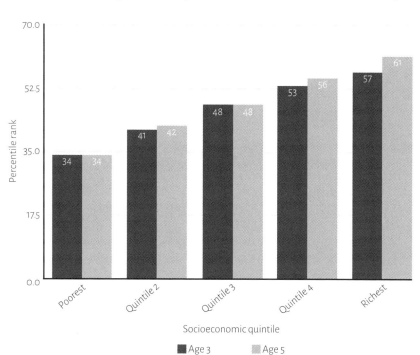

Source: Goodman and Gregg (2010)

By the age of three, there are big differences in the cognitive outcomes of poor children compared to those from better-off backgrounds, and this gap widens by the age of five. Children at age five living in the lowest income homes are the equivalent of eight months behind their peers. The reasons were thought to be related to the following factors:

- Physical disadvantages: poor children are born with a lower birth weight.
- Poorer mothers are less likely to breastfeed.
- Mothers from low-income homes were more likely to suffer from maternal depression.
- Family interactions, such as the closeness of the mother-child bond, were weaker in low-income homes.
- The quality of the home learning environment (see box) is less good;

for example there is less regular reading to the child. There is a strong intergenerational correlation between a wide variety of attitudes and behaviours – the probability that a parent reads to their child daily is 25% higher if they themselves were read to daily as a young child.

- Lower income homes had weaker discipline and fewer routines (such as regular bedtimes and mealtimes), compared to children from better-off backgrounds.

- More than 40% of children in the poorest quintile are in a lone-parent family at the age of three, compared to less than 2% of children in the richest fifth.

- Children in the poorest fifth typically have relatively young mothers, and are born into families with more brothers and sisters, compared to children from better-off backgrounds.

Questions used in the study to determine the quality of the home learning environment for five-year-olds

- *How often do you read to your child?*
- *How often do you tell stories to your child not from a book?*
- *How often do you play music, listen to music, sing songs or nursery rhymes, dance or do other musical activities with your child?*
- *How often do you draw, paint or make things with your child?*
- *How often do you play sports or physically active games outdoors or indoors with your child?*
- *How often do you play with toys or indoor games with your child?*
- *How often do you take your child to the park or to an outdoor playground?*

These findings are supported by Lindsay Richards *et al* (2016), who found that families where both parents are highly educated spend on average around 110 minutes a day on educational activities with their young children. Families where both parents have a low level of education tend to spend around 71 minutes a day. This compares with around 20-30 minutes a day in the 1970s, when there was no significant difference between these groups of parents.

Trying to improve

Given what we know – that differences in parenting have a huge impact on the school readiness of children – governments have tried to intervene to improve the situation for children from low-income families. Some schemes have shown a degree of success. For example, PEEP (Peers Early Education Partnership programme) is a birth-to-five intervention that aims to improve the life chances of children from a disadvantaged area of Oxford by raising their educational achievement through working with their families. It has been found to improve young children's cognitive development by providing parents with learning materials and supporting them in their use (Evangelou and Sylva, 2007). However, in general these sorts of interventions have proven to be very hard to roll out across the country on any scale, and often the children who need the help most do not access it.

The CANparent programme was developed by the 2010 coalition government as part of their effort to improve parents' capability. In a trial in three areas from 2012 to 2014, parents of young children were offered vouchers to access parenting classes. The trial was designed to stimulate the supply of classes at a cost that it would be reasonable to expect at least some parents to pay, and thereby evaluate the market potential for high-quality universal parenting classes to support the parenting skills of mothers and fathers of children under five years old. The trial was successful in stimulating a supply of providers of parenting classes, but overall the results were disappointing, with limited take-up and greater-than-expected cost (Lindsay *et al*, 2014).

Sure Start children's centres

In July 1998, Chancellor of the Exchequer Gordon Brown introduced Sure Start, aimed at providing good quality services for children under five years old and their parents.

Sure Start was originally designed to help the UK's poorest areas. In 2003, it was extended with the goal of reaching families with young children in all areas. But the main aim of Sure Start was always to enhance the life chances for young children growing up in disadvantaged neighbourhoods.

Children in these communities were at risk of doing poorly at school, having trouble with peers and agents of authority (parents, teachers), and ultimately experiencing compromised life chances (early school leaving, unemployment, limited longevity).

So the initiative's aim was 'giving children the best possible start in life' through improvement of childcare, early education, health advice and family support. It was based to some degree on the Head Start programme in the USA. Early learning and childcare was offered for a minimum of ten hours a day, five days a week, 48 weeks a year.

The impact of Sure Start has been examined by the National Evaluation of Sure Start (NESS) team at Birkbeck College London. They followed over 5000 seven-year-olds and their families in 150 areas, looking at the children when they were nine months, three and five years old. A group of non-Sure Start children and their families, against which the NESS sample was compared, was selected from the Millennium Cohort Study (MCS) cohort. They were living in areas with similar characteristics to Sure Start areas but which did not offer Sure Start services.

They found that, compared to their counterparts not in Sure Start areas, mothers in Sure Start areas:

- engaged in less harsh discipline.
- provided a more stimulating home learning environment for their children.
- provided a less chaotic home environment for boys.
- had better life satisfaction (this was true of lone-parent and workless households only).

However, these were only 4 out of 15 possible measures. On the other 11 measures, there was no obvious impact, at least in part because of the introduction of universal free early education for all children, whether in Sure Start areas or not. A 2012 NESS report found that Sure Start had made no impact on child cognitive or language development. One of the other problems with drawing conclusions from the Sure Start experience is that programmes were locally driven and designed, so there is a big variation between centres.

Early years education

Since 2004, free part-time pre-school provision has been available to every child aged three or four.

Early years provision for four-year-olds is largely found in the Reception classes of state primary schools, but most of the nurseries for younger children are in private, voluntary or independent centres.

Take-up of early years schooling has grown so that in 2016, 93% of three-year-olds went, as did 97% of four-year-olds. Take-up is lower among children from more disadvantaged areas and families, especially among three-year-olds. Because children become eligible for a place in the term after they turn three, autumn-born children can access five terms before entering reception class, spring-born children four terms, and summer-born three terms.

From September 2013, some two-year-olds became eligible for a free 15-hours-a-week early education place. Initially around 20% of two-year-olds were eligible (children meeting criteria for free school meal eligibility and those looked after by the local authority), extended in September 2014 to around 40% of the age group (to include children in families receiving in-work benefits, and those with special educational needs and disabilities). In January 2016, 68% of children estimated to be eligible had taken up their place, a long way short of full coverage (Department for Education, 2016a).

From September 2017, there was an extension of free early education places for three- and four-year-olds: children in 'working families' are eligible for 30 hours' provision each week rather than 15 hours. The problem with this reform is that many providers, particularly in the private or voluntary sectors, had found it difficult to deliver the free 15 hours because of the low rate of government funding, and relied on cross-subsidy from additional paid-for hours for younger children to cover it. Now the government-funded element has expanded to 30 hours, this cross-subsidy is no longer available.

The *quality* of early years provision matters greatly. The EYFS curriculum was introduced in 2008 to impose a degree of uniformity across all settings, including childminders. There has been a series of attempts to improve the qualifications of staff but it has been hard to attract high-quality candidates to work in early education and childcare, partly because of poor wage and career prospects. Only in state-maintained nursery schools do all three- and four-year-olds need to have a qualified teacher in the classroom.

Government spending does not reflect the importance of early years provision. The 2017 Institute for Fiscal Studies report (Belfield *et al*, 2017a), *Long-run comparisons of spending per pupil across different stages of education*, tells us that spending per secondary pupil in 2015-16 was £6300 compared to £1720 for those in early years.

The EPPE project (Effective Provision of Pre-school Education), which looked at 3000 children, found that at the age of seven, those who had attended pre-school did better than those who had not, and this was especially true of those on free school meals. Poorer children often receive less help from their parents so they benefit more from a good pre-school (Sylva *et al*, 2008).

Early years provision matters, but Willetts (2017) makes the point that the evidence for the success of pre-school programmes for children from low-income homes is mixed. He asserts that it is untrue to claim that if you do not intervene early, low-income children can never recover. There is plenty of neurological evidence that our brains continue to develop throughout our lives and money spent on early years is as well spent on school leavers. It is not true that our brains are shaped in our first three years of life.

Conclusions

Children from disadvantaged backgrounds are often well behind other children by the time they start school, both in terms of their vocabulary and their ability to carry out simple tasks. This is because of well-researched differences in the quality of parenting. Governments have attempted to remedy the situation, not least through the establishment of Sure Start centres and the funding of early years nurseries for two- to four-year-olds. These have had some effect but not sufficient to eliminate the disadvantages of weaker parenting.

Low-income families will always find it harder to improve their children's performance at school. They often work long hours and they suffer higher levels of stress, making it harder to spend quality time with children. They cannot afford access to the cultural capital enjoyed by richer families. So in the end, educational inequalities are caused by income inequalities. Nurseries and schools cannot completely make up for inequalities in society.

Those children who are behind at age five find it hard to catch up. 40% of the attainment gap between disadvantaged children and the rest at age 16 can be attributed to the gaps that were seen at age five (Hutchinson and Dunford, 2016).

Chapter 2

The bottom 50% at age 11

Primary schooling is very important. Research by Hans Luyten *et al* (2017) showed that pupils make more progress the younger they are. Learning gains decline as they get older, partly because younger children mature faster.

Of course, part of the learning gains during primary education occur independently of schooling. Children acquire knowledge and skills in the home. But Luyten *et al* found that 40% of the improvement in reading and maths of young children could be ascribed to the effect of school as opposed to home – a higher figure than had been previously thought. So primary schools matter greatly.

Attainment at age 11 (the end of primary school) is measured using Key Stage 2 tests in English and maths (they are called SATs). They show that poverty is a factor but is not deterministic: many poorer children do well if they have gone to a good nursery school and have a good home learning environment, regardless of low family income.

Nevertheless, on average the gap between poorer and better-off children is wide while they are at primary school. In 2017, 48% of disadvantaged pupils (see box for the definition) reached the expected standard in all of reading, writing and mathematics at age 11 compared to 67% of all other pupils (Department for Education, 2017a).

In 2017, disadvantaged pupils were defined as those who were registered as eligible for free school meals at any point in the last six years, children looked after by a local authority or children who left care through adoption or via a Special Guardianship or Child Arrangements Order. 32% of 11-year-olds were classed as disadvantaged in 2017.

Looking at the effectiveness of attempts to narrow performance gaps, Jon Andrews *et al* (2017) found that, over the period 2007-2016, by the end of primary school, the gap between disadvantaged pupils and their peers had narrowed by 2.8 months. This is a modest improvement; at the current rate of improvement it will take around 50 years for the disadvantage gap to close completely by the time pupils take their GCSEs.

Figure 2.1: Percentage reaching the expected standard in reading, writing and mathematics for different groups, England, 2017 (state-funded schools), Key Stage 2

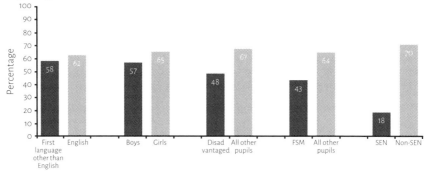

FSM = free school meals. 15% of 11-year-old pupils are known to be eligible for free school meals in 2017

SEN = special educational needs

Source: Department for Education (2016b)

Boys still struggle somewhat, except in maths. In 2017 Key Stage 2 SATs, 65% of girls achieved the expected standard in all of reading, writing and mathematics compared to 57% of boys.

Figure 2.2: Attainment by subject and gender, England, 2017 (all schools), Key Stage 2

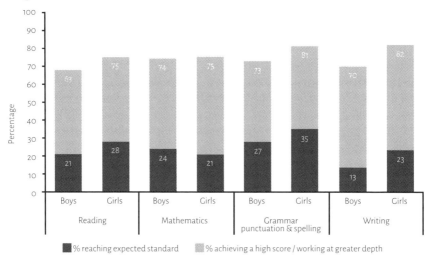

Source: Department for Education (2017a)

When looking at KS2 tests by ethnicity, Chinese and Indian ethnic groups are well ahead of other groups. Black Caribbean and Pakistani ethnicity groups come near the bottom of the table.

Causes of underperformance

In its 2017 report, the Commission on Inequality in Education, using test scores from the Millennium Cohort Study, found that the strongest influences on school performance were family income and the education of the child's parents (see Figure 2.3).

They also looked at *quality of parenting* by correlating various measures of parenting with verbal reasoning scores when the child was 11, controlling for parental income or education. They found that low verbal reasoning was related to:

- failure to attend parents' meetings.
- the child's assessment that the parents' interest in their school work is limited.
- the parent not ensuring a child has completed homework before doing other things (*eg* watching TV).
- the child being less likely to receive help with homework at home.
- failure to read to the child at age 5.
- children who do not read for enjoyment.
- not listening to or playing music outside school.
- not painting or drawing outside school.
- not having a regular bedtime.

Figure 2.3: Key predictors of progress between ages 5 and 11

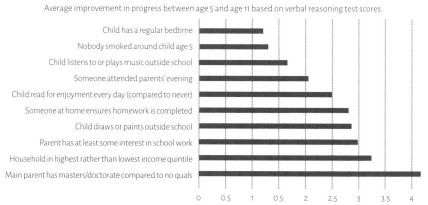

Average improvement in progress between age 5 and age 11 based on verbal reasoning test scores

Source: Clegg et al *(2017)*

Lindsay Richards *et al* (2016) looked at changing patterns of inequality (1969-2012), especially among children at primary school. They used multiple datasets, including the British Household Panel Survey, the National Child Development Survey, the British Cohort Study and the Millennium Cohort Study.

They found that, in some respects, gaps between richer and poorer children were narrowing over time with relation to:

- the incidence of rule violation such as truancy.
- the frequency of parents helping with homework.
- attendance at parents' evenings at school.
- the frequency with which mothers read to their 6- to 7-year-old children.

Improvements over time for disadvantaged pupils may reflect the fact that, in the past, many children could expect to gain jobs without school qualifications, but this is less true now. More parents of all social classes know their children need to do well at school and that is why more mothers are reading to their children and helping with homework.

What is more, the expansion of good education, including higher education, means that a greater proportion of parents are well educated than in the past. They appreciate the value of education and are more able to help their children.

In other respects, there was an *improvement in the position of disadvantaged children over time but the gap between them and more advantaged children had nevertheless widened.* This was true of:

- the amount of time that parents spend doing activities such as playing or reading with their children.

- the number of fathers reading to children. This is an example of an area where the middle-classes have taken the lead – with the gradual erosion of gender norms, middle-class fathers are reading more to their children. Working-class fathers have yet to catch up.

In some respects, the position of disadvantaged children *has worsened and the gap with more prosperous children has widened.* This was true of conduct problems, which are related to two other issues: emotional problems and hyperactivity. In 1969, low-income children were twice as likely to be in the highest 10% of conduct problems than high income, a gap growing to 3.5 times as likely by 1980, unchanged to 2012.

Richards *et al* (2016) were unable to explain this with any certainty. They do make suggestions, however:

We know that older mothers tend to have children with lower levels of behavioural problems and thus the changing patterns of the age of first birth may influence inequalities over time (middle-class mothers are having children later). Some studies have suggested that screen-time and computer games might be having a negative influence on children's attention and the modern diet may also be a factor (ADHD may be linked to diet). It is also possible that the conditions of life for families in more disadvantaged class situations are deteriorating, due to increasing economic insecurity, increasing debt and higher incarceration rates.

There are some interesting specific findings from this research. Families where both parents were highly educated spent much more time on educational activities with their young children than less educated parents did with theirs.

8% of children in higher professional families reported eating no meals together over the previous week, compared to 17% of those in families where no one is in work.

Around 21% of high socioeconomic status (SES) children reported hardly ever talking to their mother about things that matter, compared to 35% of low-SES children.

34% of children in low-income households did sport less than once a week compared to 13% of high-SES households.

84% of children from high-income homes went to art galleries compared to 51% from low-income homes.

The Effective Pre-school and Primary Education 3-11 Project (EPPE 3-11) was a large study of the developmental trajectories of approximately 2800 children in England from age 3 to 11 years (Sylva *et al*, 2008). The report showed that four things particularly determined the progress made by a child:

1. Attending a **good quality pre-school (often a nursery school)** had lasting benefits for both academic and social/behavioural outcomes, as well as pupils' self-perceptions. The benefits of pre-school were greater for boys, for pupils with special educational needs, and for pupils from disadvantaged backgrounds. Children who did not attend pre-school and those who attended a low-quality pre-school showed a range of poorer outcomes at age 11.

2. The **mother's highest qualification level**. More educated mothers had children that made better progress.

3. The **home learning environment**. Family income and being on free school meals were less powerful predictors of performance at age 11 than parents' qualification levels or the home learning environment. What is more, the home learning environment was only moderately associated with social class.

    What did they mean by a good home learning environment? A range of family members provide support for pupils' learning, and education is valued highly by the family as a means of improving life chances. The specific things measured in terms of home environment were:

    - Going to the library
    - Being read to
    - Learning activities with the alphabet
    - Learning activities with numbers/shapes
    - Learning activities with songs/poems/nursery rhymes
    - Playing with letters/numbers
    - Painting or drawing
    - Playing with friends at home
    - Playing with friends elsewhere
    - Visiting relatives or friends
    - Shopping with parent

- Watching TV
- Eating meals with the family
- Having a regular bedtime

4. **The quality of the primary school** unsurprisingly affected results achieved by pupils at age 11. Pupils who attended an academically more effective primary school had significantly better academic outcomes, whatever the child and family background.

Alissa Goodman and Paul Gregg (2010) used the Avon Longitudinal Study of Parents and Children (ALSPAC) cohort study that recruited around 14,000 pregnant women resident in the Avon area of England and whose expected date of delivery fell between the 1st of April 1991 and the 31st of December 1992.

The gap in educational attainment between the poorest children and children from better-off backgrounds grew rapidly during the primary school years so that, by age 11, only around three-quarters of children from the poorest fifth of families reach the expected level at Key Stage 2, compared to 97% of children from the richest fifth. Poor children who performed well at age 7 had all too often slipped back by age 11, while poor children who performed badly at age 7 were far less likely to catch up over the period.

They found that differences in attitudes and behaviours during primary school account for one-third of the differential progress that is made between rich and poor children between the ages of 7 and 11. Even after accounting for family background factors and prior attainment, children are more likely to perform well in tests at age 11 if:

their mother:

- has an external locus of control (*ie* believes that her own actions can make a difference, rather than things being determined solely by fate or chance).

- hopes that the child will stay in education beyond age 16, particularly if she would like them to go on to university. 81% of the richest mothers said they hoped their 9-year-old will go to university, compared with only 37% of the poorest mothers. Such adverse attitudes to education on the part of disadvantaged mothers are among the most important factors associated with lower educational attainment at age 11.

- found school valuable herself.

the child:

- has strong beliefs in his or her own ability.
- believes that school results are important.
- has an external locus of control.
- is less likely to engage in antisocial behaviour (such as fighting or stealing).
- does not suffer from hyperactivity or conduct problems.
- has not experienced bullying.

Mothers and children from better-off homes are more likely to have these attributes.

In his 2010 study, Professor Steve Strand looked at how well different schools achieved pupil progress from age 7 to 11 in relation to prior attainment, ethnicity, free school meals (FSM) and gender using an English national dataset of 530,000 pupils attending over 14,200 primary schools.

He found that no school appeared to eliminate or reverse the typical within-school attainment gaps in relation to FSM pupils, Black Caribbean or White British pupils. Some schools were much better than others in terms of the results achieved on average by all pupils but **the gap remained the same whatever the school**.

Strand concludes that the same schools that are most effective for White British pupils, boys or pupils on FSM are also the most effective for Black Caribbean pupils, girls and those not on FSM. In short, there was no evidence of differential school effectiveness for different pupil types.

In a 2016 study, Professor Strand analysed the national test results at age 7 and 11 of over 6000 pupils attending 57 mainstream primary schools over three successive years in a socially and ethnically diverse inner London borough.

The pupil groups with the poorest progress were White British pupils on free school meals (FSM) and Black Caribbean pupils, both those entitled and those not entitled to FSMs. Differences between schools in average pupil progress were large, but again there was no evidence of differential school effectiveness in relation to closing gaps linked to FSM, ethnicity or gender. All pupil groupings benefited from attending the more effective schools to a broadly similar extent.

So more effective schools 'raised the bar' but did not 'close the gap', suggesting that differences between schools in terms of quality plays little role in equity gaps.

Why is it that attainment gaps between rich and poor, black and white, boy and girl remain the same whether the school gets good results or bad results? The answer may be that the attainment gap has little to do with the school. It is a product of the family background. Or the answer may be that schools do things which limit their ability to close the gaps, like setting – which places the more disadvantaged children in lower sets, reducing motivation. Whatever the reasons, the conclusion is that 'failing schools' are not responsible for attainment gaps, they are merely responsible for all-round low attainment.

Selective education: not going to grammar school

The bottom 75% do not get into grammar schools in local authority areas with selective education. This damages them. The academic results at age 16 of this 75% are worse than they would have been had they been educated in a non-selective area.

Natasha Porter and Jonathan Simons's research for Policy Exchange (2014) showed that very few students from low-income backgrounds make it into grammar schools, so it cannot be argued that grammar schools help social mobility. The reason is that so few pupils on free school meals (FSM) are in the top 25% academically by the age of 11. And middle-class parents employ tutors to prepare their children for the entrance exams. Andrews *et al* (2016) found that 2.5% of pupils in selective schools are eligible for FSMs, compared with 13.2% across all state-funded secondary schools. 13% of grammar school pupils went to private schools before they moved to the grammar and 85% had private tutoring to prepare for the 11+ exam.

Chris Cook's research (2013 and 2016) shows that in local authority areas with grammar schools, a minority of students in the area go to the grammar schools and they do better than they might have done in a comprehensive, but the majority left in the comprehensive schools do worse than they would have done had the grammar schools not existed. Cook's research into Kent and Medway, an area with grammar schools, shows that poorer children lag further behind than they should do, while richer children move further ahead – but the losses at the bottom are much larger than the gains at the top.

The reason that comprehensive schools do less well in areas with grammar schools nearby is that all the brightest pupils have been stripped out. This makes it harder to push pupils towards the top marks and harder to attract good teachers. Those who have been rejected by the grammar schools (the great majority) are demotivated.

Simon Burgess *et al* (2017) showed that the average chance of getting into an existing grammar school in selective areas is low for almost all families. Only the most affluent families – the top 10% by socioeconomic status – have a 50% or better chance of attending a grammar.

Figure 2.4: Percentage of children at grammar school in selective areas by percentile of SES distribution

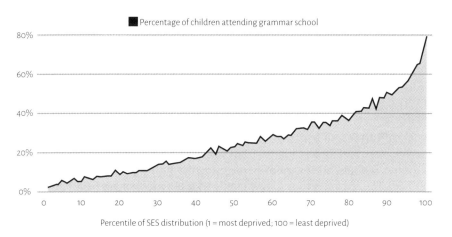

Source: Burgess et al *(2017)*

But maybe this is because the children from the richest families are simply the most able?

No. If you look at look at two children, one from the poorest quintile and one from the least-deprived quintile and both performing at the 80th percentile in the Key Stage 2 tests, despite the same level of academic attainment, the most deprived pupil has only a 25% chance of attending a grammar compared to a 70% chance for the least deprived pupil.

Even children from disadvantaged backgrounds who perform very well at primary school have less chance of getting into these schools than affluent children who perform moderately well.

What about the influence of house prices on selection? Good schools push up the prices of property around them. Schools select by geographical catchment, so good schools soon become middle-class schools. As the Sutton Trust has shown (Cullinane *et al*, 2017), most of the class segregation by schools in England is caused by house prices keeping lower-income families out of the catchment area of the best schools. That is why some people argue that we should get rid of proximity to the school as a basis for admissions but should instead use admissions lotteries for schools that are oversubscribed.

The relative importance of income, ethnicity and geographical region

The Commission on Inequality in Education (Clegg *et al*, 2017) looked at the relative impact of income, ethnicity and the region you live in on educational attainment. These three variables are not independent of each other. For example, if you are black, your family income is likely to be lower. If you live in the north-east of England, you are more likely to be white and on a lower income. So simply saying 'children in the north-east get lower test scores' does not tell you if the main factor operating here is income, ethnicity or geography.

Regression analysis tells us which of these three factors is more important. Looking at verbal reasoning scores from tests given to children aged 11, the Commission looked at children born in 1970 and those born in 2000. In their scoring system 0 means average score, -1 is the lowest score, +1 the highest score.

They found that income was the most important factor for both the 1970 and 2000 children. After taking into account the effect of region and ethnicity, they found that being in the top income decile rather than the lowest income decile took a child from being average to being high scoring. For children born in 2000, doubling family income added 0.3 to the expected score.

Ethnicity came next. Chinese ethnicity raised the score for those born in 2000 by 0.5 points above those of a white child of similar income and region.

Regional differences were less important, but differences in test scores in different regions were greater for children born in 2000 than for those born in 1970. For two otherwise identical children, the scores for those born in 2000 and living in London were 0.3 above those from Yorkshire. So location is least important, but becoming more so.

Special needs

Only 18% of 11-year-old pupils with special educational needs reached the expected standard in all of reading, writing and mathematics in 2017 compared with 70% of pupils with no identified SEN – a huge gap, the biggest of all gaps.

At primary level, almost 18% of boys and 9% of girls were identified as having special educational needs and/or disabilities. 27% of pupils who had special educational needs and/or disabilities were eligible for free school meals, compared with just over 12% of pupils who have no special educational needs or disabilities.

What are special educational needs (SEN)? The term means...

1. Struggling with behaviour or ability to socialise, sometimes caused by autism.
2. Struggling with reading and writing, often due to dyslexia.
3. Struggling to understand things.
4. Inability to concentrate, such as is caused by ADHD – Attention Deficit Hyperactivity Disorder.
5. Physical difficulties.

In 2016, 14% of all pupils in England were classified in that year as having special educational needs and/or disabilities; that is 1.2 million pupils. But if you look at pupils all the way from age 4 to 16, at some point a huge 39% had been identified as having a special need (Hutchinson, 2017). On average, this group struggles at school.

There are two types of support:

1. Special educational needs support. In schools this will be the responsibility of the SENCO – the Special Educational Needs Co-ordinator. Most SEN pupils are supported in this way, the largest group being those with a moderate learning difficulty.
2. Statement of special educational needs or an Education, Health and Care (EHC) plan for those children and young people up to the age of 25 who need more support than is available from special educational needs support. They get a personal budget that allows parents to decide how the money is spent. 3% of pupils come into this group, the largest number being those with autism. A high proportion of pupils who have statements or EHC plans are eligible for free school meals: almost a third.

There are over a thousand state-funded and private special schools in England for pupils with special needs.

Increasing school autonomy, which in some cases has fostered innovation and beneficial arrangements for SEND students, has often also left support up to the individual school's discretion. A system which used to be co-ordinated by local authorities has become more fragmented.

Measuring potential

If we think that talent is wasted because pupils are being held back by background, it is important to try and measure *potential* using methods that are independent of that background. That is what VESPARCH does: verbal and spatial reasoning tests for children, developed by the Oxford Group for Children's Potential.

The VESPARCH tests try to limit the extent to which the superior literacy of children from advantaged backgrounds guarantees them high scores in tests of general ability. It uses spatial as well as verbal tests; instructions are delivered through headphones rather than in writing; where there is writing, the vocabulary is simple; it uses practice questions with detailed feedback, so children with limited experience of tests learn how to do them; it uses multiple-choice questions; and it is untimed (to reduce anxiety).

VESPARCH is an antidote to exam targets set by schools based on previous tests scores – for example, GCSE targets based on the results of Key Stage 2 tests – because these tend to be self-fulfilling prophecies. A child with poor SATs results will be given low target GCSE grades and this results in low academic self-confidence.

VESPARCH is used in some primary schools. It identifies pupils who are underachievers at school, such as poor readers who are actually quite intelligent. When the results are given to the school, generally the school is unsurprised by half the names of intelligent underachievers (many of whom have behavioural difficulties) but is surprised by the other half. So the aim is for schools to focus on these intelligent underachievers in the knowledge that, with a bit more effort on both sides, significant improvement is possible. Correlating those in the top 20% of VESPARCH with GCSE results shows that only about half the pupils score highly in both tests. Many pupils with potential in terms of cognitive ability do not fulfil that potential when it comes to public exams.

Summary

By the age of 11, significant gaps in attainment between different groups are apparent. Boys do less well than girls, those from poorer homes do less well than others, and those with diagnosed special educational needs are often far behind. Less important, but still measurable, are the effects of ethnicity and geographical region. All schools, whether high- or low-performing in terms of Key Stage 2 results, have these attainment gaps.

In terms of overall performance at Key Stage 2, the home environment continues to play an important role, as does the education and attitudes of the mother and the quality of primary school attended.

Chapter 3

The bottom 50% at age 16

Between the ages of 11 and 16, the achievement gaps between the more and less able and between those from better-off and lower-income families widen. Some children appear to learn little at their secondary school, their behaviour worsens, mental health problems become more apparent. While the top 50% are moving steadily towards acquiring GCSEs and then A levels or BTECs, the bottom 50% are heading towards a more uncertain future.

The way that gaps grow is illustrated by this description from an Ofsted report (2012), *Mathematics: Made to Measure*:

> The disparity in children's pre-school knowledge of mathematics grows so that by the time they leave compulsory education at 16 years, the gap between the mathematical outcomes of the highest and lowest attainers is vast. The 10% not reaching the expected level at age 7 becomes 20% by age 11 and, in 2016, 30% of 16-year-olds did not gain grade C at GCSE. Pupils known to be eligible for free school meals achieve markedly less well than their peers and increasingly so as they move through their schooling.

If you do poorly at age 11, are you doomed to fail your GCSEs? Research by Tom Benton and Tom Sutch (2013) tells us that the correlation between a pupil's Key Stage 2 (age 11) test scores and GCSE results is quite strong:

> On the basis of this evidence we may conclude that KS2 is neither a terrible nor an excellent predictor of likely success at GCSE. Correlations for the vast majority of subjects are between 0.4 and 0.7 indicating a strong relationship but hardly a definite means of predicting attainment at either individual or aggregate level.

(On this scale 0 = no correlation, 1 = a perfect correlation.)

This is the result one might expect. It would be improbable if there was no relationship between tests taken at the ages of 11 and then 16, but the fact that the relationship is only 'quite strong' means that, for many pupils, there is scope to improve or decline relative to others.

The Key Stage 2 tests are in English and maths, so what is the correlation between these tests and GCSE results in the same subjects? It is strong:

Correlation coefficient KS2 test scores vs GCSE grade, 2011

English 0.71

Mathematics 0.76

But for other subjects the correlation with the age-11 English and maths tests is weaker:

Physics 0.47

Geography 0.67

So what this tells us is that a child who does badly in the tests at age 11 may struggle with GCSEs at age 16, but most particularly in maths and English. In other subjects there is scope to do better – or worse.

In 2016, 43% of disadvantaged children achieved A*-C in both English and maths GCSEs compared to 71% of their non-disadvantaged peers. But over 75% of those who failed to get five GCSE passes including English and maths were NOT on free school meals. **So it is a mistake to assume that poor academic performance is all about poverty.**

Over time, the performance gap between boys and girls grows. In 2016, 62% of girls achieved five good GCSEs including English and Maths compared to 52% of boys. Looking at all GCSE entries, in 2017, 71% of female entries were awarded at least a grade C/4 compared with just 61.5% of their male counterparts.

The performance of White British pupils falls compared to other groups. 24% of white working-class boys achieved five or more GCSEs A*-C in 2016, compared to 69% nationally.

Most of these effects are due to things that began years before – many of the children who do poorly at 16 were already behind at the age of 3. Furthermore, some pupils are more intelligent than others and it seems that the impact of genetic endowment gets greater the older the child becomes.

Progress age 3-14

In 2012, Kathy Sylva and colleagues tracked about 3000 children from age 3 to 14. They found that attainment at age 14 in English, maths and science tests was strongly linked to circumstances ten years earlier, when the children were aged 3-5 (Sylva *et al*, 2012):

- High-quality pre-school education (age 3-5) still showed beneficial academic, social and behavioural outcomes even after ten years. Pre-school quality seemed particularly important for low socioeconomic status boys: all those who attended excellent pre-school settings went on to succeed above expectation at age 14.

- The academic effectiveness of their primary school continues to predict outcomes at age 14. Those who went to good primary schools stayed ahead.

- Positive parenting experiences, especially the age 3-5 home learning environment, were related to better longer-term outcomes. Between the ages of 11 and 14, parents of the more successful pupils helped through 'active cultivation'. They valued learning, provided emotional support, and had high aspirations and standards of behaviour. They provided practical support by encouraging participation in extracurricular activities.

- However, differences in academic attainment and social-behavioural development related to background emerged early (at age 3) and remained fairly constant to age 14. Students who experienced multiple disadvantages in the early years had an increased risk of poorer social and behavioural development as well as lower attainment at age 14.

- Students' academic attainment and progress are strongly influenced by the education level of their parents, especially the mother. Low family income and FSM status are significant predictors of poorer outcomes but with less strong effects than parental education.

- At Key Stage 3 (age 11-14) there was an increasing, though not strong, neighbourhood effect. Higher levels of deprivation amongst children aged under 16 in a local area predicted poorer attainment and social behaviour for other children in that area.

- At Key Stage 3, time spent on homework was a strong predictor of better attainment and progress in all three core academic subjects as well as influencing better social-behavioural outcomes.

- Children who made poor progress, or who were not seen as clever, developed a negative self-image, which led to, or reinforced, poor motivation.

Performance gaps

Socioeconomic group

John Jerrim (2017) plotted the 2015 PISA scores for English 15-year-olds by socioeconomic quintiles. The lines on the graph on the next page (for reading, maths and science) kink up for the richest 20%. In other words, the gap between the socioeconomically top 20% and the rest is quite great.

Compared with the middle group (Q3), the top quintile is the equivalent of two years of schooling ahead. Poor children not only start school at a lower base, but also make less progress while they are there. The attainment of wealthier children accelerates during their school years, while it stalls for the poorest. This link between school results and income is greater in England than most countries.

Figure 3.1: PISA 2015 results in reading, maths and science by socioeconomic status

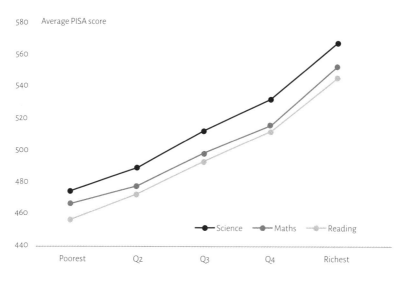

Source: Jerrim (2017)

Andrews *et al* (2017) found that the gap between disadvantaged 16-year-old pupils and their peers only narrowed by three months of learning between 2007 and 2016. In 2016, the average gap at the end of secondary school was still 19.3 months. Disadvantaged pupils fall behind their more affluent peers by around 2 months each year over the course of secondary school. For pupils who had been on free school meals for 80% or more of their school lives, the 2016 gap in attainment at age 16 was the equivalent of two years of learning.

In 2016, the DfE used a new measure, Attainment 8, based on the scores of the best eight GCSEs taken by pupils. The gaps between groups of different pupils can be seen here:

Figure 3.2: Average attainment 8 score by pupil characteristics, England, state-funded schools, 2017

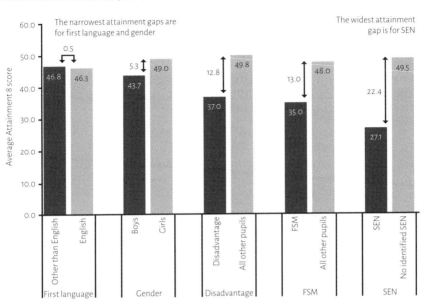

In Attainment 8 a top grade in reformed GCSEs is scored 9, the second highest is 8 (the equivalent of the old A*) and so on. The average 2017 Attainment 8 score in state schools was 46.3.

Pupils are defined as 'disadvantaged' if they are known to have been eligible for free school meals in the past six years (from year 6 to year 11), if they are recorded as having been looked after for at least one day or if they are recorded as having been adopted from care. In 2017, 27% of pupils at the end of key stage 4 were classified as being disadvantaged.

Source: Department for Education (2017b)

Mike Treadaway (2017) showed that amongst free school meals pupils, the longer a child was eligible for free school meals the lower their educational attainment. Some pupils only qualify for free school meals for one year, others for their whole school career. Even those on FSMs for only one year have lower average attainment than those never on FSMs and this effect is more pronounced in secondary than primary school.

Since 2008, GCSE attainment has been improving for those that are FSM-eligible for less than 60% of their time in school. But the improvement has only been small for pupils who were FSM-eligible for between 60% and 90% of the time. For pupils who were FSM-eligible for 90% or more of the time, their attainment relative to the national average has actually been *falling* since 2008.

Those who do very badly in their GCSEs face an uphill battle thereafter. According to the Wolf Report (Wolf, 2011), as many as 20% of Key Stage 4 completers are not able to start a level 2 course, a percentage which is significantly higher than in comparable countries. Young people with these low achievement levels at age 16 have historically been offered training schemes or 'experiential' programmes which provide little or no opportunity for progression.

There may be, amongst those 16-year-old pupils who have taken GCSEs, some who could have benefited from taking A levels but they are denied the opportunity. There are two reasons for this:

- First, most schools are anxious to achieve good A level results because of accountability regime, as well as the way in which league table position is used to market the school. They will not permit students to take A levels if they are unlikely to achieve good grades. They impose a minimum GCSE score for entry to the A level programme (in the range from five grade 4s (Cs) to five grade 7s (As)). They impose specific entry requirements for individual A level subjects (typically a grade 7 or better at GCSE in maths if you wish to take maths A level and something similar for the sciences). Finally, many schools require pupils to leave or change courses at the end of year 12 if their progress is not good enough.

- The comparable outcomes approach to grading imposed by Ofqual means that the weaker students cannot obtain a good A level grade however well they do, if other students have done better. The number of higher grades awarded is rationed.

This is why many pupils, especially from lower-income homes, have been persuaded to take BTECs rather than A levels. Those same students in private schools might have taken A levels, which are higher quality, and they achieve good results with weaker pupils by providing better or extra teaching.

Some schools are better than others, but inter-school differences are less important than the background of children. Clifton and Cook (2012) explored the role that schools can play in tackling the link between educational achievement and family income. They note that previous academic studies found that about 20% of variability in a pupil's achievement is attributable to school-level factors, with around 80% attributable to pupil-level factors (Rasbash *et al*, 2010).

Clifton and Cook found that pupils from deprived areas in England are more likely to attend a school rated 'requires improvement' or 'inadequate' by Ofsted, and pupils from wealthier areas are more likely to attend a school rated 'outstanding'. *But even if every pupil in the country attended an 'outstanding' school, the achievement gap between the poorest and wealthiest pupils would only be cut by a fifth.* If the education gap between advantaged and disadvantaged pupils is to be closed, we need more focus on interventions such as one-to-one tuition and pre-school programmes.

Robert Plomin, professor of behavioural genetics at King's College London, found that nearly all of the variance in children's GCSE results can be explained by prior educational attainment, socioeconomic status and general cognitive ability, with only 0.5% of the variance due to whether they attended an independent school, a grammar or a comprehensive once these other factors are controlled for (Young, 2017). School quality matters less than we think but politicians seem to ignore this. As Chris Woodhead said: 'Politicians have convinced themselves that they can make all children brighter than God made them'.

The same team at King's found that individual differences in educational achievement at the end of compulsory education are not primarily an index of the quality of teachers or schools: much more of the variance of GCSE scores can be attributed to genetics or family environment. By measuring whether identical twins are more similar than nonidentical twins on any human trait, one can estimate the degree to which that trait is influenced by genes.

In a national sample of 11,117 16-year-old twins, they found that heritability was substantial for overall GCSE performance for compulsory core subjects (58%) as well as for each of them individually: English (52%), mathematics (55%) and science (58%).

They found that the overall effects of shared environment, which includes all family and school influences shared by members of twin pairs growing up in the same family and attending the same school, accounts for only about 36% of the variance of mean GCSE scores (Shakeshaft *et al*, 2013).

The Education Endowment Foundation (2018) makes a related point: similar gaps in achievement between disadvantaged and non-disadvantaged pupils remain regardless of whether the school is graded 'outstanding' or 'inadequate' by Ofsted (see graph on next page).

Figure 3.3: GCSE Attainment 8 scores for disadvantaged and non-disadvantaged pupils, by school overall effectiveness judgement

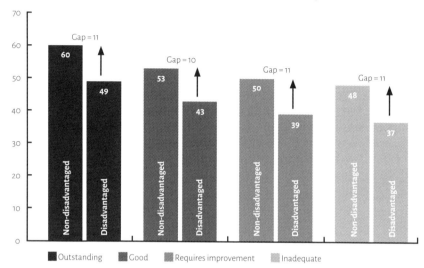

■ Outstanding ■ Good ■ Requires improvement ▦ Inadequate

Source: Education Endowment Foundation (2018)

Having said that, research consistently shows that the **effect of schools** is greatest for disadvantaged students, both positively and negatively. A good school can hugely improve the prospects for pupils with a poor background. Pupils from more prosperous homes tend to do quite well regardless of the quality of their school (Coleman *et al*, 1966). The Coleman Differential Effect can be summarised as *'school quality affects disadvantaged children twice as much as advantaged children'*.

Are children predestined to fail?

Goodman and Gregg (2010) used data from the Longitudinal Study of Young People in England (LSYPE), a study of more than 15,000 young people in England who were aged 13 and 14 (Year 9) and born in 1989/90.

After controlling for family background factors and prior attainment, the study found that young people are more likely to do well at GCSE if:

their parents:

- think it likely that they will go on to higher education. Four out of five parents in the top socioeconomic quintile think that their child is likely to apply to university, compared to just over half of parents in the bottom socioeconomic quintile at age 14.

- spend time sharing family meals and outings.
- quarrel with their child relatively infrequently.
- devote material resources towards education including private tuition, computer and internet access.

the child:

- has a greater belief in his or her own ability at school.
- believes that his or her own actions make a difference and that he or she can control events that affect him or her (captured in this study by having an 'external economic locus of control').
- finds school worthwhile.
- thinks it is likely that he or she will apply to, and get into, higher education.
- avoids risky behaviours such as frequent smoking, cannabis use, antisocial behaviour, truancy.
- does not experience bullying.

Parents and children from more prosperous families are more likely to exhibit these characteristics.

However, Goodman and Gregg found that these behaviours and beliefs only explain a quarter of the difference in GCSE results between wealthier and poorer children. Differences in **prior attainment** at age 11 and 14 explain about 60% of the gap – so once you are ahead academically, you tend to remain ahead irrespective of other circumstances.

Using data collected on the children of the British Cohort Study, their study found that parents from poor families tend to have lower cognitive outcomes and this is passed on to their children, partly through genes and partly through their attitudes and behaviours. This is one reason why poverty passes down the generations of families. Del Bono and Ermisch (2010) found that 79% of children from degree-educated parents obtained at least 5 GCSEs at A*-C grades compared with 33% of children whose parents left school without any O-levels or equivalent qualifications.

The link between low income and academic outcomes is not deterministic and can be exaggerated. Most of those doing badly at GCSE are NOT on free school meals and many of those on free school meals do well at GCSE, especially if they live in London. Of those who failed English and maths GCSEs in 2016, 44,000 were on free school meals but 156,000 were not.

Mary-Claire Travers (2017) researched the educational trajectories of white working-class boys and found that many had their aspirations dampened by being placed in a lower set in school. They feel written-off and looking at the teaching did indeed suggest that lower sets were treated very differently to higher sets – less homework, less discussion, less feedback, more repetition. There is strong evidence that being put in a lower set becomes a self-fulfilling prophecy: members of that set are doomed to do badly.

Bart Shaw *et al* (2017) found that low-income pupils make less progress at secondary school than their peers. This is even true of low-income pupils who made more progress than others at primary school. Compared to all pupils with similar prior attainment at KS2, FSM pupils make between 0.26 and 0.35 of a GCSE grade less progress, depending on which subjects are considered. Meanwhile, non-FSM pupils make between 0.06 and 0.09 of a GCSE grade more progress.

Shaw found that differences between secondary schools account for only 12% of the variation in how much progress pupils make between KS2 and KS4. The rest of the gap in progress between low-income pupils and their peers stems from differences in achievement between pupils in the same school, rather than differences between schools. **Focusing too much on differences between schools (such as school type) is therefore a policy mistake**.

What are the reasons for this deterioration in the relative performance of low-income pupils?

1. **Factors to do with the children themselves.** Some children, especially boys, develop a less positive view of education. They are less likely to see merit in going to university.

    Behaviour deteriorates, especially amongst boys. More are excluded from school: pupils eligible for FSMs have an exclusion rate four times higher than their better-off peers. Boys are three times more likely to be excluded than girls (Department for Education, 2017f).

    Mental health and wellbeing problems increase among pupils between the ages of 11 and 15, especially among children from poorer homes (The Children's Society, 2016). Looked-after children have especially high levels of SEND, mental health and behavioural problems.

2. **Factors to do with their families.** Parents from low-income families are less likely to be able to support children in secondary school. The work is more advanced than it was in primary school. Parents have less direct contact with the school than was the case with their child's primary. Teenage pupils are less receptive to help from parents. Homework is a key factor in progress at secondary school relative to primary school, with more time on homework strongly predicting better progress between KS2 and KS4, even when other factors are taken into account (Sammons *et al*, 2015). Pam Sammons found that progress at secondary school was greatest for those completing two to three hours of homework per night.

Low-income ethnic minority parents provide good educational support at home, particularly those parents who have migrated to the UK, and this is why ethnic minority pupils make better progress than White British pupils.

Wealthier parents are much more likely to employ tutors.

An estimated two million children in the UK live in 'difficult family circumstances', which means such things as domestic violence, drugs, alcohol and mental health issues in the home. Such children are much more likely to have high rates of absenteeism and much less likely to be able to concentrate in school.

Family support structures have broken down as families have broken down. The proportion of families headed by a lone parent rose from 8% in 1970 to 30% today. 40% of births take place outside marriage. On average, only half of children in England are living with both birth parents at the age of 16, but this proportion is much lower among less-affluent and less-educated families.

Charles Murray (2012) shows that being married is now as important as race, education or employment in determining the likelihood of Americans being poor. In 1960 it was not that important – most people got married and poor people were only 10% less likely to be married than those who were college-educated. Today the gap between these two groups is 35% – being married or not has become a fault line dividing classes. Getting married produces better outcomes for people than being single, divorced or cohabiting because marriage motivates people to work hard and save in a way that cohabitation does not. All other things being equal, people who get married are more likely to be healthy, happy and earn more. At the other end of the spectrum, being a single-parent household drives people into poverty.

3. **Factors to do with their schools (least important).** Teachers have lower expectations of boys, those from poorer homes and those in lower ability sets. Strand (2015) found lower progress for Black Caribbean 11- to 14-year-old boys, which he suggests is linked to lower teacher expectations for boys from this ethnic group. Pupils put into lower sets lose motivation.

    Many schools place more emphasis on Key Stage 4, giving less good teachers to Key Stage 3 classes and tracking the pupils less thoroughly. We know that pupils from disadvantaged homes are more affected by the quality of teacher than their better-off peers. This is why FSM pupils fall behind in Key Stage 3.

4. **Factors to do with the area in which they live.** Pupils in cities, especially London, do better than pupils in rural areas. This is because there are more ethnic minority pupils in larger cities and they prioritise educational achievement more than White British families. In cities, there are a greater range of jobs available and the relationship between school achievement and career success is more obvious. In places with few jobs or a narrow range of jobs, motivation to do well at school is reduced.

Previous research by Andrews *et al* 2016 (quoted above) showed that by the age of 16 the attainment gap between advantaged and disadvantaged children equates to 19 months (two school years) of teaching. Hutchinson and Dunford (2016) showed that this gap at age 16 can be broken down as follows:

● Two-fifths of the gap was already present by the age of five (the gap for those who will be on free schools meals the whole time between age 5 and 16 is the equivalent of 6 months' teaching).

● One-fifth develops during the course of primary school (for those continuously on free school meals the gap is now 12 months' teaching).

● Two-fifths develops during the course of secondary school (for those continuously on free school meals the gap is now 24 months).

So there is a slowly evolving pattern of disadvantage for children from low-income families – bad at age five, slightly worsening at primary school, accelerating in secondary school.

Bright but poor

Another way of looking at the deterioration in the relative performance of poorer children is to look at what happens to children from low-income families who do very well in the age-11 tests. Becky Allen (2015) looked at 7000 pupils (including 943 boys and 614 girls who were disadvantaged) who scored in the top 10% nationally at the end of primary school but who received a set of GCSE results that placed them well outside the top 25%.

Over a third (36%) of the bright but disadvantaged boys seriously underachieved at age 16. Clever but poor girls were less likely to underperform, with just under a quarter getting disappointing GCSE results. These figures compare with 16% of boys and 9% of girls from better-off homes who similarly underperform at age 16 compared to their KS2 results.

Sammons *et al* (2015) tracked the progress of 349 bright children (those who had achieved level 5+ in Key Stage 2 tests) from disadvantaged families. Key Stage 2 tests were taken at age 11 and the 'expected' level was 4. Pupils reaching Level 5 achieved the standard expected of an average 14-year-old.

So these 349 children did very well at age 11. Why?

They were three times more likely than other disadvantaged children to have a mother with a university degree. They were twice as likely to have experienced a good home environment. They were twice as likely to have enjoyed a reasonable number of enrichment activities such as visits to libraries and playing sports. They were twice as likely to have read books at home. They were twice as likely to have attended a pre-school and more than twice as likely to have gone to a good primary school with high value-added in English.

Those who went on to get the best GCSE results had certain characteristics. They were the ones who engaged in school enrichment activities such as outings and who read at home. They attended secondary schools which they liked because there was an emphasis on learning, the students were valued, the headteacher was involved in school activities, and the relationships between students and teachers were good. There was a high level of teacher monitoring of their work. Time spent on homework was also a good predictor of success.

These pupils were significantly more likely to gain three or more good A levels where they attended a secondary school rated 'outstanding' by Ofsted for the quality of pupil learning and where they experienced academic enrichment at home. Time spent on homework was still a good predictor of success: completing two to three hours of homework a night rather than none increased the likelihood of getting three A levels nine times.

Facilitating A level subjects are those listed by the Russell Group of top universities as those which 'keep most options open' for entry to their universities. Nearly twice as many 'bright and advantaged' as 'bright and disadvantaged' students took one or more facilitating subjects at A level.

So the study concludes that bright children from disadvantaged homes greatly benefit from:

- going to a pre-school.
- encouragement to read at home.
- school trips and other enriching activities.
- homework.
- frequent teacher feedback on their work.
- encouragement to take facilitating subjects at A level.

Poor and white

The House of Commons Education Committee (2014) undertook a survey to establish the reasons that white working-class children had fallen behind other groups. PISA data shows that the relationship between social class and exam results is stronger in England than in most countries.

The gap is already wide by the age of four. The gap is wider at Key Stage 2 (age 11) and wider still at GCSE. Other ethnic groups on FSMs are doing better. White working-class girls do better than white working-class boys but the gap in achievement between FSM and non-FSM girls is just as wide as with the same boy groups, so this is not a 'boy' problem.

What did the report suggest causes this underperformance?

1. Lack of aspiration in white working-class homes. Some witnesses suggested that it was not lack of aspiration that was the problem but lack of confidence – if, for a variety of reasons, a pupil does not succeed in the early years at school, they feel that there is little point in trying.

2. Social capital. Parents who did not themselves succeed at school lack the knowledge to help their children and give them good advice. Parental engagement with the school and with schoolwork is important and often low among white working-class families.

3. Parenting skills. Children without stable and secure homes are less likely to succeed at school. Many parents have a much more limited vocabulary and this is passed on to their children. They are less likely to own books, less likely to read to their children.

4. White working-class children have higher rates of absenteeism.

5. Culture. Based on a two-year research project on working class families in Bermondsey, South London, Gillian Evans's book *Educational Failure and Working Class White Children in Britain* (Evans, 2007) argues that white working-class boys are often pressured to uphold a stereotypical tough 'street' reputation linked to concepts of masculinity. This leads to poor behaviour and a failure to work at school.

6. Employment prospects. The exam results of white working-class children are worst in those parts of the country with high unemployment. In some areas, the link between success at school and getting a job may be broken.

7. Genetics. Professor Robert Plomin (Professor of Behavioural Genetics, Kings College London) concluded that 50% of the variation in children's individual educational *achievement* was the result of genetic factors (Plomin *et al*, 2013).

8. School quality. The proportion of Ofsted 'good' and 'outstanding' schools is lower in those parts of Britain with more white working-class children.

Gender

In 2017, **the Progress 8 score for boys was -0.24, for girls +0.18**. Only 26% of White British boys on free school meals gained five good GCSEs.

Girls mature faster. In the classroom, they seem to be keener to please the teacher than boys. They score higher marks because they work harder and are dissatisfied with themselves if the quality is low. 85% of primary teachers are female, as are 62% of secondary teachers. If you give boys and girls a test, boys tend to overestimate how well they have done, while girls underestimate. So girls will feel the need to work hard more keenly than boys.

Figure 3.4: Performance in key measures by gender, England, state-funded schools, 2017

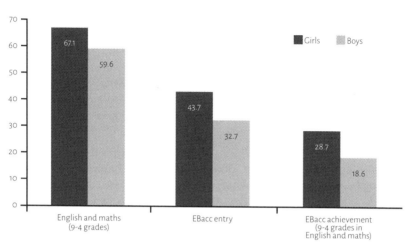

Source: Department for Education (2017b)

Leonard Sax, an American doctor, has written extensively about the issue of boy underachievement including *Why Gender Matters* (2017) and *Boys Adrift* (2007).

He claims that research in the past 20 years – made possible by Magnetic Resonance Imaging – has shown that the brains of boys and girls are different from the moment they are born. These genetic differences lead to differences in the ways boys and girls learn. Boys simply cannot learn to read at such a young age as girls, so pushing children to read at a young age establishes male inferiority. Young boys quickly gain a sense of failure at school.

The brains of girls develop quicker than the brains of boys. At 20 months old, girls have twice the vocabulary of boys. Girls are fully mature by the age of 22, boys at the age of 30, and the differences between the two is greatest when they are about 15, as any experienced parent knows.

Another explanation is the astonishing fact that the sperm count and testosterone levels of boys are now half that of their grandfathers. This is partly due to residues from plastics absorbed from drinking bottles – bottles that all children use from the earliest age – chemicals that make your drink taste a bit plasticky. These residues are making girls reach puberty earlier because they mimic female sex hormones. But they also act to reduce testosterone levels and this disproportionately affects boys, because testosterone is what produces motivation in males.

Parents seem to find it harder and harder to discipline their children and the impact of this is greatest on boys because boys are born with a greater propensity to take risks and be aggressive. They need discipline. Most of us welcome the fact that the gap between the generations has narrowed – but over the past 50 years, authority has been transferred from parents to children, and boys are paying the price.

Ethnicity

In 2015, the Department for Education published another research report by Professor Strand – *Ethnicity, deprivation and educational achievement at age 16 in England: trends over time*. This looks at GCSE results in terms of ethnic group, entitlement to free schools meals and gender. He showed that achievement gaps between different ethnic groups have narrowed substantially over the past 20 years – much more than gaps based on FSMs or gender.

In 2004, the average gap between ethnic minority students and White British (based on proportion gaining five GCSEs grade A*-C including English and maths) was 18%, compared to a 7.7% gap between girls and boys and a 28% gap based on FSMs. By 2013 the ethnicity gap had fallen to 7.2%, the gender gap had risen to 10.1%, and the FSMs gap was 26.7%.

Several studies have shown that ethnic minority parents are more engaged in their children's education than their White British peers. Professor Strand found that Indian students are much more likely to complete homework five evenings a week compared to those from White British backgrounds, and Indian parents are more likely to have a home computer or pay for private lessons (Strand, 2011).

Looking at individual ethnic groups, since 2004:

- Indian and Chinese students have moved way ahead of White British.

- Bangladeshi students have moved from well below to above White British despite being amongst the most socioeconomically deprived.

- Black African students have moved from below White British to being better.

Black Caribbean and Pakistani students have nearly caught up and are now quite similar to White British, a bit below for those not on FSMs, a bit above for those on FSMs.

If you just look at pupils entitled to FSMs, all ethnic groups do better than White British and the gap is growing. This is true with both the Key Stage 2 results at age 11 and GCSE results at age 16. The figures for 2017 Attainment 8 (the best eight GCSEs taken) are shown below:

Figure 3.5: Average Attainment 8 score for FSM-eligible pupils from selected minor ethnic groups, by gender, England, state-funded schools, 2017

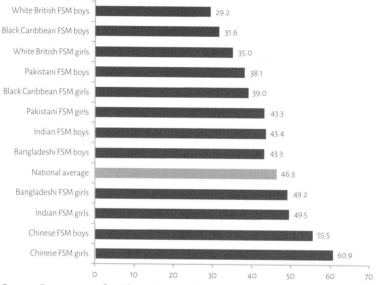

White British FSM boys — 29.2
Black Caribbean FSM boys — 31.6
White British FSM girls — 35.0
Pakistani FSM boys — 38.1
Black Caribbean FSM girls — 39.0
Pakistani FSM girls — 43.3
Indian FSM boys — 43.4
Bangladeshi FSM boys — 43.3
National average — 46.3
Bangladeshi FSM girls — 49.2
Indian FSM girls — 49.5
Chinese FSM boys — 55.5
Chinese FSM girls — 60.9

Source: Department for Education (2017b)

On the 2017 GCSEs Progress 8 measure in England, all Chinese pupils scored an average +0.93, Black pupils +0.16, White pupils -0.11 (the average of all pupils being -0.03).

Black children, especially boys, also underperform. Shaw *et al* (2016) showed that, despite starting school with performance largely in line with national averages, black children fail to maintain this in later years. They are the ethnic group most likely to fail their maths GCSE and most likely to be excluded from school. Black boys do substantially less well than their black female peers, particularly at Key Stage 4.

Pupils with special educational needs and disabilities (SEND)

The biggest gaps in attainment are between those diagnosed with special needs (14% of those at Key Stage 4) and those not. The average Attainment 8 score in 2016 was 48.5; but for those with special needs it was 31.2, and for those without special needs it was 53.2. Given that many forms of SEND affect children's progress in school, this was not a surprising finding, but many of these pupils are able and much more could be done to help them pass GCSEs. Just 24% of pupils with identified SEND achieved an A*-C grade in their maths and English GCSEs in 2016, compared with 69.7% of mainstream students. Although those with an Education, Health and Care Plan can gain access to extra funding, special needs children without an EHCP may find support is limited.

Pupils in 'alternative provision'

15,000 pupils are educated in alternative provision, mainly Pupil Referral Units but also academies and free schools set up for this purpose. Most of the pupils have been permanently excluded from school and almost half are in Year 11. 70% have special needs and many are on free school meals. Many have mental health problems and a high proportion will end up in prison. A 2017 study by the Institute for Public Policy Research estimated that of the 86,000-strong prison population, more than 54,000 were excluded when at school.

Despite very small class sizes, only 1% of those in alternative provision achieve passes in five GCSEs including England and maths.

Pupils in care

For many of the 72,000 children in care in England, their life chances are significantly worse than for young people as a whole.

Those who have been in care between the ages of 10 and 17 are five times more likely to be convicted of a criminal offence or subject to a final warning or reprimand. Children in care are also five times more likely to have been excluded from school. Overall, they face a much higher risk of homelessness, teenage pregnancy and unemployment.

Looked-after pupils make less progress at secondary school than their peers. 37% make expected progress in English, while fewer than 29% make expected progress in maths (Department for Education, 2016c). Only 6% of young people with experience of the care system attend university, compared to almost 50% of the general population.

Figure 3.6: Why are children in care?

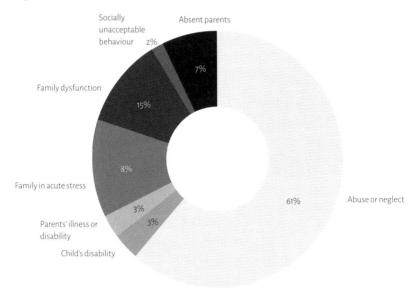

Socially unacceptable behaviour 2%
Absent parents 7%
Family dysfunction 15%
Family in acute stress 8%
Parents' illness or disability 3%
Child's disability 3%
Abuse or neglect 61%

Source: Department for Education (2017c)

Vocational equivalents

One of the key pedagogical arguments of the past two decades has been whether children should be required to follow an academic curriculum. In the period 2000-2010, there was an explosion in the number of vocational courses taught in schools at Key Stage 4. These were taught as an alternative to GCSEs and were made possible by the fact that the government agreed a set of 'equivalences' whereby a vocational course would count as equivalent to one or more GCSEs in accountability measures applied to schools. These courses were often not as demanding as GCSEs. They were taken by less-academic pupils and were seen as an example of dumbing-down.

The vocational equivalents were withdrawn after 2011 by the Coalition government because the Wolf Review (Wolf, 2011) showed that many vocational qualifications had no market value. The Coalition ministers believed that schools were encouraging pupils to take vocational equivalents when they were quite capable of taking academic GCSEs. This was especially true of pupils from low-income homes. The introduction of the EBacc league table measure, which recorded the proportion of pupils taking maths, English, sciences, history or geography and a modern language, nudged schools in the direction of academic qualifications. The Progress 8 measure, which started in 2016, reinforced this direction of travel.

Summary

In England, we have a long tail of pupils who leave school with poor results. 17% leave functionally illiterate and 22% functionally innumerate.

In part, this reflects the lower IQ of the bottom 20% of the population. Other countries with a similar IQ profile do not have the same tail of underachievement (Lenon, 2017), but intelligence matters. In a five-year longitudinal study of 70,000 children in England, the correlation between psychometric intelligence measured at age 11 and GCSE results at age 16 in 25 academic subjects was 0.81 – very strong (Deary *et al*, 2007).

Figure 3.7: IQ Score Distribution

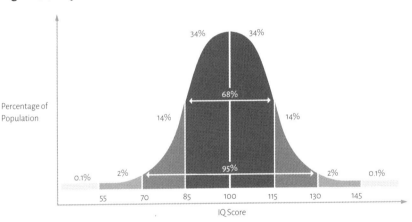

Prior attainment has a big influence on GCSE results. Many of those who did badly at age 11 do badly at age 16.

Low-income children do least well in GCSEs and their relative position worsens while they are in secondary school. The main influences on low-income children are their family background, their attitudes and behaviour. Differences *between* schools account for only 20% in the variation of children's performance at GCSE.

Gender and ethnicity have a big influence on GCSE results, but not as big as income.

Children with special needs or disabilities, those in care and those being educated in 'alternative providers' do especially poorly at GCSE.

Focusing too much on gaps in attainment between sub-groups tends to obscure an arguably more important fact – that the standards we expect at GCSE are quite low compared to some other countries. This is discussed further in chapters 6 and 8.

Chapter 4

The bottom 50% after the age of 16

What do young people do between the ages of 16 and 18?

Almost all young people in England are in regular education, employment or training in the year after taking GCSEs. School sixth forms are the most common destination (39%) with further education colleges the second most common (38%) followed by sixth form colleges (13%) (Department for Education, 2017d).

Pupils from more prosperous homes and those with good GCSEs tend to stay at school to do A levels. Those with less-good GCSEs, those who had been on free school meals and those with special needs are more likely to go to an FE college. They are more likely to do level 1 and 2 courses or, if level 3, more likely to do BTECs (a level 2 course is the level of a GCSE pass; level 3 an A level). Only 36% of young people from an FSM background who enter some form of education post-16 progress to a level 3 qualification by age 19, compared to 60% of non-FSM students.

Claudia Hupkau and Guglielmo Ventura from the London School of Economics tracked the decisions made by all students in England who left compulsory education after having taken GCSEs at age 16 in 2010 (Hupkau and Ventura, 2017). The table below shows what all 17-year-olds in England who were in education a year after they took GCSEs were doing. 60% were doing A levels or an equivalent level 3 course (those doing Applied Generals or Tech Levels often having weaker GCSE grades). 13% were doing level 2 courses. 11% were taking courses below level 2 and 7% were taking apprenticeships.

What were 17-year-olds doing?

Level 3 qualifications

Mainly A levels	44.83%
Mainly applied generals	5.29%
Mainly tech levels	4.44%
Mainly KS/NVQ level 3	0.04%
Mainly other level 3	3.52%

Level 2 qualifications

Mainly tech certificates	1.79%
Mainly vocational qualifications at level 2	9.53%
Mainly key/functional skills level 2	0.48%
Mainly GCSEs	0.86%

Level 1 and entry level

Below level 2	10.84%

Apprenticeships

Apprenticeship level 2	5.61%
Apprenticeship level 3	1.26%
Apprenticeship level 4+	0%

Unknown qualification	5.48%
Not observed	6.01%

Total	574,967

So nearly a quarter of students aged 17 are undertaking educational qualifications at level 2 or below, the level they should have mastered at school when they were 16. These students are much more likely to be from disadvantaged family backgrounds than those undertaking higher levels of qualifications, and fewer than half progress to higher levels of education. So there seems to be limited progress made by those who do badly at school. For those pursuing a level 2 (GCSE or equivalent) qualification at age 17 and nothing higher, there is often no clear trajectory to higher levels of learning. Most do not progress any further up the education qualification ladder.

The life chances for a student who only just fails GCSE English, for example, and who is consequently debarred from taking A levels, seem to be much worse than those for a similar student who only just passes GCSE English. The cliff-edge effect is too great.

But that does not mean that those taking low-level courses are wasting their time. De Coulon *et al* (2017) looked at the 10% of school leavers in England who start low-level vocational courses (below level 2) at the age of 16 and found that even low-level qualifications can lead to better employment prospects and higher earnings four years later.

Here is similar data, but this time for all under-19s in the FE and skills sector. Most are level 2 and below, many retaking English and maths.

FE and skills participation in England 2013-14, under 19s

All FE and Skills Participation					
Below Level 2 (excluding English and maths)	English and maths	Level 2	Level 3	Level 4+	Total FE and Skills
247,600	403,100	469,500	523,200	2900	983,900

Source: Department for Education and Education and Skills Funding Agency (2017a)

One important observation by Hupkau and Ventura (2017) was of the complexity of the vocational options compared to the simplicity of A levels followed by a university degree. At level 3, students in England in the 16-18 age group can in principle undertake any of 3729 vocational qualifications (although students' choices will be limited by what's available locally). And there were 9835 qualifications at level 2 and below approved for such students.

Using the National Pupil Database, Individual Learner Records and Higher Education Statistics Authority data, Rebecca Allen *et al* (2016) looked at the choices made by students who took their GCSEs in 2010. They found:

1. FSM pupils are more likely to drop out of education at age 16 than non-FSM pupils, partly because they have worse GCSE results. But a third of the participation gap arises from differences in choices made – the FSM

pupils are more likely to drop out than non-FSM pupils in the same area and *with the same GCSE results.*

2. FSM pupils are much less likely to go on to study level 3 qualifications than non-FSM pupils in the same area and *with the same GCSE results.*

3. FSM pupils are less likely to go on to higher education than non-FSM pupils in the same area and *with the same GCSE results.*

4. Boys are more likely to drop out of education, less likely to take level 3 qualifications than girls in the same area and with the same GCSE results.

5. White British pupils are more likely to drop out of education and less likely to take level 3 qualifications than other ethnic groups living in the same area and with the same GCSE results.

6. Students who live in areas with no school sixth forms are less likely to take level 3 qualifications than students of similar ability who are able to go to school sixth forms.

Poor careers advice in a complex system

An enormous barrier to progress for those who do not take A levels is the poor quality of advice available to them.

A survey carried out on behalf of AllAboutSchoolLeavers.co.uk found that almost a third (31%) of schools leavers report that they do not know what they want to do after leaving school or college. In addition, 78% of young people say that their parents are their main source of careers advice.

Careers advice is poor because schools and colleges have not been able to fund it well or they choose not to give it the priority it deserves. Often careers advice is left to a teacher whose own knowledge is limited or out of date. Schools are driven by DfE accountability measures to focus on university success and are less interested in vocational routes to employment. Schools are not incentivised to give good vocational training advice to able Year 11s: for financial reasons, schools need students to stay on and take A levels, not go off to an FE college.

The House of Lords Select Committee on Social Mobility (2016) found:

> The current system for young people who do not follow an academic route is complex and incoherent, with confusing incentives for young people and employers. Careers advice and education are being delivered in a way which means that too many young people simply drift into further studies or their first job, which often has no real prospect of progression.

The Social Mobility Commission (2016) found that:

> Young people from low-income homes with similar GCSEs to their better-off classmates are one third more likely to drop out of education at 16 and 30 per cent less likely to study A levels that could get them into a top university. The complexity of the post-16 education and training system makes it particularly difficult for lower-income youngsters to translate their attainment at school into qualifications that are well rewarded in the labour market. There are nearly 16,000 qualifications available to 16- to 19-year-olds, but zero transparency on which produce the best outcomes. Nor is there a single point of entry for youngsters going onto further education, unlike those going into higher education.

The National Careers Service (NCS) for students aged 13 and above was launched in 2012. In 2017, research by consultants London Economics compared the progress of people who used the NCS with those who did not and found they could not identify a positive impact of the NCS on employment or benefit dependency outcomes, but there was some benefit in relation to the education and training of those who accessed the service (Lane *et al*, 2017).

Barriers to those of middle ability

There is a large group of quite able young people who have some GCSEs, do not take A levels and who find the process of obtaining a suitable job quite difficult. They are a third of the cohort. Young people from this middle group are often caught in part-time, low-paid, low-skilled and temporary jobs. After leaving school or college, they take on jobs such as kitchen and catering assistants or as serving staff in bars and restaurants. This is the group who should be doing more advanced training, developing what are often called 'intermediate skills'.

A 2014 UK labour market survey (UKCES, 2014) found that:

> Jobs with intermediate skills demands tend to have high shares of skills shortages. These include skilled roles in manufacturing, construction, wholesale and retail, and hotels and restaurants. This partly reflects longstanding shortages of skilled construction trades workers such as plumbers, electricians and carpenters, and skilled chefs within the hotel and catering industries.

What is the problem?

1. **Too many graduates**

    In 1999, Tony Blair set the target of 50% going to university. The cap on numbers of university places has recently been lifted, allowing universities to expand. The 2017 Higher Education Bill encourages private providers to set up universities.

The consequence of the explosion in the number of graduates is that many of them take jobs that used to be done by non-graduates. And the middle group who used to do those jobs is pushed out.

2. **Government policies**

   Successive governments have been to blame for paying less attention to the students in the middle. Attention has been focused on universities and on those at the very bottom – those not in employment, education or training.

3. **Recruitment practices**

   Employers prefer people with work experience, and this is a barrier for able young people who have simply not had the opportunity to do work experience. The UKCES 2014 Employer Perspectives Survey found that while 66% of employers think that work experience is critical when hiring young people, only 38% offer it.

   Small and medium-sized employers often recruit by word of mouth, and this again acts as a barrier to employment for young people. Employers often use school exam results as employment filter, such as those who only interview applicants with maths and English GCSEs, when in fact there are many young people who have great personal qualities as well as manual dexterity but who were weaker at school subjects.

4. **Ignorance of the options open to them**

   There are alternatives available to students of middle ability who do not quite have the qualifications necessary for direct university entry, but they often do not know about them.

   Foundation Years are offered by some universities for students who are not eligible for direct entry into their undergraduate degrees because they do not meet the entry requirements for their course of choice.

   Foundation Degrees are degree-level qualifications which combine academic study with workplace learning. Designed in association with employers, they are qualifications to equip people with the relevant skills, knowledge and understanding to achieve academic results as well as improve performance and productivity in the workplace.

Foundation Degrees focus on a particular job or profession. They are intended to increase the professional and technical skills of current or potential staff within a profession, or intending to go into that profession.

A Foundation Degree is the equivalent of two-thirds of a full honours degree and is a flexible qualification allowing students to study part-time or full-time to fit their lifestyle. A full-time Foundation Degree will usually take about two years to complete and can be taken at both universities and colleges.

Another option is a Higher National Certificate/Diploma (HNC/D), a level 4/5 qualification. The HNC is equivalent to the first year of a university degree programme. The HND is equivalent to the first two years of a full honours degree. Some HNCs allow direct entry into the second year of a degree programme, and some HNDs allow direct entry to the third year.

Helen Thorne, director of external relations at UCAS, said: 'These lesser-known pathways provide a different set of opportunities for students who may not be able to commit to a full-time degree by offering an approach to higher education which may better suit their circumstances'.

5. **Opportunity hoarding and the glass floor**

In 2015, the Social Mobility and Child Poverty Commission published research by Abigail McKnight from the London School of Economics (McKnight, 2015) suggesting that middle-class parents support their children in ways which mean that even less-intelligent middle-class children do quite well in life, reducing opportunities for able young people from lower-income homes.

Seventeen thousand children born in a week in 1970 took an intelligence test when they were five (British Cohort Study). When they were aged 42, their income was recorded. Less-intelligent middle-class adults were earning more than the more intelligent adults who had grown up in low-income homes.

In the post-war period, the number of good white-collar jobs grew faster than the size of the middle-class workforce and this enabled working-class children to obtain middle-class jobs. This is no longer happening, so for able working-class children to have upward mobility, some middle-class children will have to have downward mobility. The fact that middle-class children do not generally experience downward mobility is the 'glass floor'.

Dr McKnight suggests there are two main pillars supporting the 'glass floor':

1. More-advantaged parents secure educational opportunities to help their children overcome lack of ability by:

   ● investing time and resources in education to help children showing early signs of low attainment to recover and achieve good qualifications.

   ● providing good careers advice and guidance – this is likely to be important in explaining why parental education has such a big impact on their children's earnings after controlling for qualifications and schooling.

   ● placing a high value on polish and 'soft skills' such as self-confidence, decisiveness, leadership and resilience.

   ● researching and choosing the best schools, with more advantaged parents able to move house to be in the catchment area of a good state school, invest in private tutors to coach their children to pass the 11+ in areas with grammar schools, or give their children a private education.

2. More-advantaged parents secure advantages for their children entering into the labour market that are unavailable to less well-off parents by:

   ● helping their children into employment through informal social networks.

   ● securing informal and unpaid internships.

   ● investing in their children's 'soft skills', which are highly valued in employment recruitment processes.

The chair of the commission, Alan Milburn, said:

No one should criticise parents for doing their best for their children. That's what we all want. But Britain is a long way from being a meritocratic society when the less able can do better in life than the more able.

It has long been recognised that there is a glass ceiling in British society that prevents children with potential progressing to the top. This research reveals there is a glass floor that inhibits social mobility as much as the glass ceiling.

The Sutton Trust (2014) has drawn attention to the fact that many employers now offer unpaid internships and that having an internship is necessary if you wish to get a job – employers want people with work experience. Quite apart from the fact that employers may be exploiting young people by obtaining very cheap labour, unpaid internships are often only possible if the young people are supported financially by their parents. They are, therefore, a significant barrier to social mobility.

Being a young man

According to UCAS, in 2017 about 41% of young men applied to university by age 19 and 37% went, while 54% of young women applied by age 19 and 48% went (UCAS, 2017). This gap between the sexes is widening year by year and the gap is even wider when one looks at those who come from low-income homes, where women are over 50% more likely to go to university.

This phenomenon is quite recent. After all, the University of Cambridge refused to make women full members of the university until after the Second World War, in 1948. The number of women undergraduates only overtook men in the mid-1990s (Hillman and Robinson, 2016).

Figure 4.1: The gender gap: there are consistently more women than men applying to university

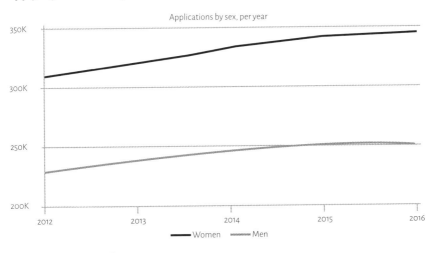

Applications by sex, per year

Source: UCAS (2017a)

The Sutton Trust report, *Believing in Better* (Sammons *et al*, 2016), showed that one reason so many more women go to university than men is that they are much more likely to believe in the importance of a university degree. Even in Year 9, 65% of girls said it was important to go to university compared to 58% of boys. And 15- and 16-year-olds with similar GCSE results were twice as likely to go on to do three A levels if they saw university as a likely goal for them.

Women outperforming men is a worldwide trend. In *Education at a Glance 2015*, the Organisation for Economic Co-operation and Development (OECD) found that women make up the majority of entrants into tertiary education in all OECD countries except Mexico, Saudi Arabia, Switzerland and Turkey (OECD, 2015). On average across OECD countries, 54% of tertiary education entrants are women.

Around five-sixths of higher education institutions in the UK have more female than male students. Yet, aside from initial teacher training, only two set targets for the recruitment of more male students in their 2016/17 Access Agreements.

Ethnicity

We have seen that at Key Stage 4, white pupils and black pupils do worse than pupils with Asian or Chinese ethnicity, especially boys.

At Key Stage 5 (age 16-18), black pupils are the ethnic group with the lowest outcomes. At university, black students are less than half as likely to get a first-class degree as their white counterparts and one in ten drop out in their first year.

After Key Stage 5, Asian Muslims do less well than they should do in terms of employment. Young people from Pakistani and Bangladeshi backgrounds are more likely than ever to succeed in education and go on to university, especially girls. Yet these outcomes are not yet being translated into jobs, with unemployment particularly prevalent amongst Bangladeshi women. Both Pakistani men and women are relatively unlikely to secure managerial or professional occupations (Shaw *et al*, 2016). Niven *et al* (2013) found that Bangladeshi families were more likely than other groups to expect their daughters to marry young and have children.

Special needs

2% of pupils complete Key Stage 4 in special schools for those with the most complex needs. Just over half of pupils from special schools stay in the special school sector after completing Key Stage 4.

The most common destination for SEN pupils with a statement in 2015 was further education (61%), while for pupils without special educational needs it was a school sixth form (Department for Education, 2017d).

In 2016, Ofsted reported on special needs students in further education:

In 2014/15, there were over 22,000 young people in England aged 16 to 24 with allocated places as learners with high needs attending further education (FE) and skills providers. In 2015 Ofsted visited a number of FE colleges and sought the views of 1600 students. They were not especially impressed. They found that the colleges often lacked the specialist resources, including staff with the necessary experience and expertise required to support learners with high needs. Careers advice was weak and there were inadequate efforts made to prepare the students for adult life. Attempts to improve English and maths skills were weak. There was little work experience. (Ofsted, 2016)

In 2012, the government started helping young people with learning difficulties and disabilities prepare for work using 'supported internships'. These are unpaid study programmes for 16- to 24-year-olds, lasting a year and based with an employer. They have on-the-job training backed by job coaches and complementary college-based courses. In January 2017, there were only 715 on such supported internships (Robertson, 2017). Remploy, which provides employment placements for disabled people, said that while 60% of those with learning disabilities want to work, only 6% are in fact employed.

So special needs students continue to struggle after they leave school. Whereas students in higher education have access to a Disabled Students Allowance, students in FE (where most of those with special needs reside) do not have access to such money.

NEETs

In 2017, the percentage of young people (16-24) in the UK who were not in education, employment or training (NEET) was 11%, with around 6.5%, or 465,000 young people, either not looking for work or not available for work and so classed as economically inactive (ONS, 2017a). The regions with the highest proportion of 16- to 24-year-olds NEET were the North East (18.6%), Yorkshire and Humber (17.5%) and the West Midlands (14.9%). The lowest proportion was the South East with 10.7%. Half are women, half men.

Compared to the population as a whole, NEETs have the following background characteristics:

- They have disabilities. 30% of those with disabilities were NEET compared to 9% of those without.
- They have poor GCSEs.

- 13% had Pakistani/Bangladeshi backgrounds. The lowest proportion was from Indian/Chinese/Other Asian backgrounds (8%)
- They have been on free school meals.
- They have a child.

Young men who are NEET between the ages of 16 and 18 are four times more likely to be out of work in the long term and five times more likely to have a criminal record.

Adult education

There are three main types of adult (over 18) education:

1. Skills development courses, including English and maths up to level 2 for those who need to improve their literacy and numeracy. These courses include all the professional and technical routes and traineeships described in chapter 7.

2. English tuition for immigrants who need to learn the language.

3. Community courses in such things as pottery, history of art or the University of the Third Age.

In the survey conducted by Hughes *et al* (2016), 75% of those asked why they took part in an adult education course said it was for their personal development. Adult education allows people to make friends and alleviate boredom as well as improve job prospects.

In addition, one should add apprenticeships, described on pages 174-183.

Types of adult education

Provider	Size of sector	Description
General FE colleges & tertiary colleges	Around 235 colleges serving 2.3 million learners (including 16- to 18-year-olds); government funding worth £2.3 billion.	Large institutions that offer a broad range of subjects for all adult learners (and increasingly for 16- to 19-year-olds as well). They deliver the majority of classroom-based courses for adults classified as 'education and training' by the SFA. These were historically run by local government but, following incorporation in 1993, were given self-governing status.
Independent providers	Around 600 providers have direct contacts with the SFA (although many more will operate as subcontractors). They serve around 950,000 learners and receive government funding worth £1.5 billion.	There is an extremely wide range of independent skills and training providers in England. The majority will be for-profit companies who provide skills training and apprenticeships for particular sectors and employers. The majority of adult apprenticeship (up to 75%) have their education component delivered by independent providers. Some employers will also receive government funding to deliver training to their staff.
Adult community learning providers	Around 250 community learning providers, including many local authorities. They serve around 360,000 learners and receive government funding worth around £300 million.	Local learning provision targeted towards helping 'hard to reach groups' engage in more formal education. They also deliver recreational learning (usually on a cost-recovery basis by charging fees to learners).
Specialist providers	Around 75 providers with government funding worth £200-£300 million.	There are number of providers which offer specialist provision - for example to learners with disabilities or learning difficulties; or to learners specialising in particular disciplines, *eg* agriculture and horticulture. This is a very disparate group of providers who deliver a small amount of adult FE in niche areas.

Source: Dromey and McNeil (2017)

There are many people who do less well at school but, later in life, discover that they could manage and benefit from further training. Of course, it is hard for this huge group because, by the time they are in their 20s or 30s, they may have a family to support and other financial obligations. Adult education has developed the expertise to offer non-qualification courses or bite-sized units that can successfully engage adults and offer stepping stones to success.

Hughes *et al* (2016) researched adult education using a literature review, an online survey of adults, focus groups, town hall meetings and telephone interviews. A significant proportion of respondents said that they faced barriers to starting and/or completing an adult education course, often due to finances and low confidence. Much seemed to depend on where you lived; in the east of England, for example, lack of transport was a significant barrier to attending college.

But adult education matters because people are in employment for much longer than they used to be, partly because of better health and because people are not able to draw a pension until they are in their 60s. With more people living longer and declining birth rates, almost three in ten workers in the UK are now over 50, compared to about two in ten in 1997. Many adults will need to retrain at some point in their long working lives.

Adult education has suffered in recent years because of the government's concentration on young people and apprenticeships at the expense of other types of adult education. There were 40% cuts in adult skills budgets from 2010 to 2017 and it therefore comes as no surprise that the number of adult learners in further education has fallen rapidly. The total number of people aged 19 and over who were registered as adult FE learners reached a peak of 3,750,000 in 2008-9 and then started to fall. Many attend part-time.

The number of adults aged 24 or older participating in level 3 and 4 courses fell from 400,000 in 2012 to 57,000 in 2014 (Hughes *et al*, 2016).

Advanced learner loans were first introduced in 2013 for learners aged 24+ at levels 3 and 4, expanded in 2016 to cover all learners aged 19+. Loans-funded education has had a very damaging effect on adult education numbers.

Figure 4.2: Adult Learner (19+) Participation and Achievement in Government-funded Further Education, England, 2010/11 – 2015/16

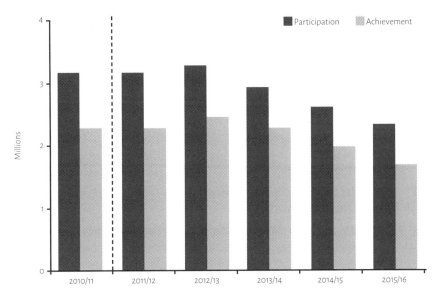

Source: Department for Education (2017e)

One other reason for the decline in adult education since 2012 is that there has been an increased emphasis on courses that were felt to help the economy and which resulted in a qualification. In a period where cuts had to be made, liberal, non-vocational adult education was inevitably going to be a target.

In the past, many adults of all ages attended 'night school' to improve themselves. This has become less common, but the need is still there. Many adults lack basic digital skills, preventing them from booking a doctor's appointment online or sending an email to their child's school; 5.9 million adults in the UK have never used the internet (Royal Geographical Society, 2015). Job structures are changing and in the future skills and qualifications will play a central role in determining individual employability, career progression and earnings potential.

The 2011 Skills for Life Survey undertaken by the UK government found that nine million adults in England lack basic numeracy and literacy, and this seriously impacts on their life chances.

In 2017, the government announced the creation of a National Retraining Scheme in England. The stated aim is that it will give adults the skills they need to thrive and support employers to adapt as the economy changes. A high-level advisory group – the National Retraining Partnership – will bring together the government, businesses and workers, through the Confederation of British Industry and the Trades Union Congress, to set the strategic direction and oversee implementation of the scheme.

Summary

1. Those who do not go on to take A levels or level 3 BTECs often receive poor advice about what to do next.

2. Provision for a large number of young people with special needs could be much better.

3. Many middle-ability young people could be doing more advanced courses than they are.

4. Young men and those who come from lower-income homes do relatively poorly after they leave school.

5. Adult education has suffered in recent years because of funding cuts and the government's concentration on young people and apprenticeships at the expense of other types of adult education.

Chapter 5

Failure in vocational education, 1800-2015

There has been no sustained period since 1867 when the Government has not fretted about the standard and availability of technical and vocational skills in England. Since 1960, there has not been a single year when the Government has not strained itself to improve what is usually perceived to be an uncompetitive situation. To little effect. Endless reports about the superiority of Germany particularly – but also France, Holland, Japan and the USA – have underlined our problem. Yet little has changed.

The history of technical and vocational education in England can make grim reading. By the end of the Second World War, such education was 50 years behind that of Germany or America, reflecting a century in which school and university education had been dominated by the influence of Oxford and Cambridge universities, public schools, the Church of England and the perverse influence of social class on the organisation of education.

It was not as if the country was unaware how weak was its scientific and technical education compared to much of continental Europe and America. Although Britain shone at the 1851 Great Exhibition, organised by Prince Albert in Hyde Park, 16 years later at the 1867 Paris Exhibition it was obvious that France, Italy, the USA and Japan were catching up – Britain won only 10 of the 90 classes.

The Samuelson Royal Commission on Technical Instruction, 1884, reported: 'The one point in which Germany is overwhelmingly superior to England is in schools ... the dense ignorance so common among workmen in England is unknown.'

The problem was not only poor technical education. Manufacturers were themselves failing to invest in research and knowledge development. The Balfour Committee on Industry and Trade, 1928-9, found: 'Before British industries, taken as a whole, can hope to reap from scientific research the full advantage which it appears to yield to some of their most formidable trade rivals, nothing less than a revolution is needed in their general outlook on science.'

The historical introduction to the Spens Report (Spens, 1938) – the Consultative Committee of the Board of Education on Secondary Education, 1938 – noted that between the many secondary schools set up since the 1902 Education Act, the most striking feature was the way they all followed the traditional grammar school curriculum: 'On a dispassionate retrospect of the history of post-primary education since 1900 we cannot but deplore the fact that the Board did little or nothing ... to foster the development of secondary schools of quasi-vocational type designed to meet the needs of boys and girls who desired to enter industry or commerce at the age of 16.'

The Report of the Independent Panel on Technical Education (Sainsbury, 2016) – the Sainsbury Review – in 2016 suggested little had changed:

> It is over a hundred years since the first report was produced which highlighted the failures of technical education in the UK, and since the Second World War there have been very many attempts to reform the system. These have all been unsuccessful because they tinkered with technical education, and failed to learn from the successful systems in other countries.

As a result we have today a serious shortage of technicians in industry at a time when over 400,000 16- to 24-year-olds are unemployed. It is hard to believe that none of these young people have the ability and motivation to train as technicians if given good opportunities to do so.

The UK has a long-term productivity problem. Although some sectors such as the automotive industry have enjoyed stronger productivity growth in recent years, in 2014 we had a productivity gap of around 30 percentage points with countries such as France and the USA, while the gap with Germany was 36 percentage points and UK productivity was 18 percentage points below the average for the rest of the G7 economies.

What went wrong?

1867-1944

In the century before the Second World War the economic success of the country may have blinded it to the relevance of technical education.

Britain gave the Industrial Revolution to the world and was the top industrial power from 1750 to 1850. This was achieved by on-the-job practical experience, not education. James Watt, developer of the steam engine, was a repairer of scientific instruments with limited education. Isambard Kingdom Brunel was taught by his engineer father and trained as a clock-maker. Richard Arkwright, inventor of textile machinery, did not go to school. So there seemed to be little link between education and industrial success. Employers in the 19th century did not value traditional formal education for their workforce; indeed, they were concerned that compulsory education until the age of 14 would deny them the children they needed to work on their farms or in their factories.

The 1868 House of Commons Select Committee on Scientific Instruction noted that owners and managers of industries had simply risen from the ranks: 'Any knowledge of scientific principles which they may have acquired is generally the result of solitary reading, and of observation of the facts with which their pursuits have made them familiar.'

Most of what we needed to be learnt could be learnt on the job. In a debate in Parliament setting up the 1868 Select Committee, the MP for Banbury, Bernhard Samuelson, noted:

> Now, it could not be denied that the instruction received by artisans in our factories was at least equal, if not superior, to the instruction received in the factories of any other nation in the world. Our manufactures had long carried off the palm among the industrial productions of nations; our manufactures had been renowned at a time when the Continent had even the rudiments of good workmanship to learn.

An MP for Manchester went on: 'There were many persons in this country who were continually undergoing a system of self-education, not being much indebted to school education, and to that class the manufacturers of this country owed more than to those who were deeply skilled in science and art.'

At the top of English society, there was a sense that subjects with practical application were second-rate. John Henry Newman, who led the Oxford Movement and was Rector of University College Dublin, had great influence in the 19th century promoting the concept of a liberal education – the primacy of philosophical knowledge over practical. In 1852, he published his lectures under the title *The Idea of a University* (Newman, 1959).

> The purpose of a university is to provide knowledge which is its own end, which I call liberal knowledge ... Liberal education makes not the Christian, nor the Catholic, but the gentleman. It is well to be a gentleman, it is well to have a cultivated intellect, a delicate taste, a candid, equitable, dispassionate mind, a noble and courteous bearing in the conduct of life.

> The University ... has this object and this mission; it contemplates neither moral impression nor mechanical production; it professes to exercise the mind neither in art nor in duty; its function is intellectual culture; here it may leave its scholars, and it has done its work when it has done as much

as this. It educates the intellect to reason well in all matters, to reach out towards truth, and to grasp it.

Knowledge is capable of being its own end. Such is the constitution of the human mind, that any kind of knowledge, if it be really such, is its own reward.

You see, then, here are two methods of Education; the end of the one is to be philosophical, of the other to be mechanical; the one rises towards general ideas, the other is exhausted upon what is particular and external. Let me not be thought to deny the necessity, or to decry the benefit, of such attention to what is particular and practical, as belongs to the useful or mechanical arts; life could not go on without them; we owe our daily welfare to them; their exercise is the duty of the many, and we owe to the many a debt of gratitude for fulfilling that duty. I only say that Knowledge, in proportion as it tends more and more to be particular, ceases to be Knowledge.

The purpose of education, according to Newman, was the creation of Christian gentlemen. Classics and theology were the means to this end.

Thomas Arnold, the influential headmaster of Rugby School 1827-1841, believed that religion was the most important subject of education. He wrote the following in a letter to a friend:

Rather than have physical science the principal thing in my son's mind, I would gladly have him think that the sun went round the earth, and that the stars were so many spangles set in the bright blue firmament. Surely the one thing needful for a Christian and an Englishman to study is Christian and moral and political philosophy.

The boys' main study at Rugby was the dead languages of Greece and Rome. That Classics should form the basis of all teaching was an axiom for Dr Arnold: 'The study of language seems to me as if it was given for the very purpose of forming the human mind in youth; and the Greek and Latin languages seem the very instruments by which this is to be effected.'

James Pillans, Professor of Humanity at Edinburgh University, wrote in his *The Rationale of Discipline*, published in 1852:

In the great schools of England – Eton, Westminster, Winchester and Harrow, where the majority of English youth who receive a liberal and high professional education are brought up – the course of instruction has for ages been confined so exclusively to Greek and Latin that most of the pupils quit them not only ignorant of, but with a considerable disrelish and contempt for, every branch of literature and scientific equipment, except the dead languages.

The Clarendon Royal Commission, 1864, a report on nine 'great' public schools (Harrow, Eton, Westminster, Winchester, Charterhouse, Rugby, St Paul's, Merchant Taylors' and Shrewsbury), noted that 'natural science ... is practically excluded from the education of the higher classes in England. Education with us is, in this respect, narrower than it was three centuries ago.'

It would be wrong to suggest that there were no influential advocates for science in the second half of the 19th century. John Stuart Mill, and especially Matthew Arnold, argued for a concept of a liberal education that placed humanities and science on an equal footing. A volume of Essays on a *Liberal Education*, published in 1867 under the editorship of Dean Farrar, then assistant master at Harrow, also reflected the widespread dissatisfaction with the conventional curriculum. Among the contributors, Professor Henry Sidgwick and Canon J M Wilson (a master at Rugby) stressed the importance of science.

Nor were all industrialists opposed to technical education. Heinrich Simon, a German immigrant who settled in Manchester and built up the Simon-Carves engineering company, pressed for the modernisation of education along German lines. Many British industrialists were wedded to similar ideas and their names were perpetuated in colleges such as Owens College in Manchester and Firth College in Sheffield – places that were the pinnacle of technical education in major industrial towns in the second half of the 19th century. But they struggled against a tide of contrary opinion.

The Taunton Commission, 1868, recommended the establishment of a national system of secondary education based on the accepted class divisions in English society at the time. It envisaged three grades of secondary education in separate schools:

- *First-grade schools*, with a leaving age of 18 or 19, would provide Newman's 'liberal education' – including Latin and Greek – to prepare upper- and upper-middle-class boys for the universities and the older professions.

- *Second-grade schools*, with a leaving age of 16 or 17, would teach two modern languages besides Latin to prepare middle-class boys for the army, the newer professions and departments of the Civil Service.

- *Third-grade schools*, with a leaving age of 14 or 15, would teach the elements of French and Latin to lower-middle-class boys, who would be expected to become 'small tenant farmers, small tradesmen, and superior artisans'.

Science in schools was associated with vulgar industry, while the study of Latin and Greek was a mark of social class. Talking about the upper-middle classes, the Taunton Commission noted:

> They would no doubt ... be glad to secure something more than classics and mathematics. But they value these highly ... for the value at present assigned to them in English society. They have nothing to look to but education to keep their sons on a high social level. And they would not wish to have what might be more readily converted into money, if in any degree it tended to let their children sink in the social scale.

In the ancient universities, Greek remained compulsory for scientists at Cambridge up to 1919 and at Oxford until 1920. Indeed Rothblatt (1981) claims that Cambridge dons in the Victorian era felt that almost no subject that could be 'turned to the benefit of business' deserved university recognition. The influence of Oxford and Cambridge universities was great because between 1209 (the foundation of Cambridge) and 1829 (the foundation of University College London) no new universities were created in England. For over 600 years there were only these two.

It was undeniable that an increasing proportion of goods were being made in Germany or the USA. There was a particular concern about the manufacture of dyestuffs, an industry that had been started in Britain but was dominated by Germany after 1913 because of their superiority in organic chemistry. But right up to the Second World War and beyond, a high proportion of MPs and civil servants, who had by and large been to public schools, clung to the idea that the best form of education was the study of theology, Latin and Greek. This, after all, is what they had learnt at school and university. Public schools and Oxbridge became the model for the rest.

Martin Wiener, in his book *English culture and the decline of the industrial spirit, 1850-1980* (1981), describes the way in which English society reacted against the Industrial Revolution. The Romantic poets wrote about the spiritual superiority of the countryside. In architecture, the Gothic revival looked back to the Middle Ages, as did the leading designer of the late Victorian period, William Morris, and the Arts and Crafts movement, which Morris helped to create. Much the same was true of painting with the Pre-Raphaelites. All felt that England had been diverted from its true nature by the Industrial Revolution. There was strong streak of anti-urbanism, something that came to be reflected in the work of Ebenezer Howard and his Garden City movement.

In England, the top of the social hierarchy was the rural aristocracy. Once industrialists had made money, they or their children were often keen to build grand houses in the countryside and escape the lowering effect of manufacture. Industrialists found their way into the upper reaches of society by modelling themselves on men of landed leisure. The English were never psychologically attracted by industry and economic growth, and the image of England as the workshop of the world was ultimately displaced by that of the green and pleasant land, a preference for the rural over the urban.

By 1900, education for those who had left school was largely a 'night school' affair – evening classes provided by recently established local school boards. They offered catch-up courses for those lacking basic literacy or numeracy as well as more advanced classes in science, art and technical subjects. There was little contact with employers – the students were volunteers who came in after a day's work. There was no national plan so everything depended on local initiatives.

Over time, the administrative arrangements necessary to see improvements in post-school education evolved. The Local Government Act 1888 set up county and borough councils with the power to raise taxes for technical education, and in 1900 a new national Board of Education was created, the first national education authority for England and Wales.

In many ways, British education improved between 1890 and the 1920s. Technical colleges were started in provincial cities, often financed by local industrialists. Many were to develop into universities and had strong science and technology departments. There were new polytechnics and good vocational qualifications devised by the City and Guilds of London Institute. From the 1920s, the Board of Education worked with professional bodies to develop national qualifications in such areas as building, chemistry and engineering.

Yet there was complacency. Britain had the greatest empire the world had seen, and after victory in the First World War it was easy to see why there was an unwillingness to follow the example of Germany, despite the fact that the superiority of its technical education was well known.

All would have been different had employers shown enthusiasm for vocational education, but most did not. The Board of Education reported in 1906 that employers were mainly interested in moral qualities such as 'ready obedience, self-help and pride in good work for its own sake' (Simon, 1965). Employers were indifferent to calls for improved technical training.

In all areas of life, progress was held back by the disruption and material cost of the First World War and the prolonged depression of the 1920s and 1930s. During much of this period, the Board of Education and local education authorities were more concerned with cost control than development of adult education.

At the outbreak of the Second World War, there was still no consensus in government or amongst employers that vocational education was a necessary part of the country's needs. Most technical and commercial education was still undertaken on a voluntary basis by young men after work, usually in very second-rate premises. The law permitted local authorities to provide further and technical education but did not require that they did so, so provision was inevitably patchy. In places like Leeds and Sheffield, there were still no FE colleges so students went to evening classes in the classrooms of local schools.

The 1944 Education Act

The moment when all could have changed was the 1944 Education Act, as the government began to plan for the post-war era.

The Act was influenced by the 1938 Spens Report. Whereas in the late 19th century the school system had been openly based on social class, Spens recommended a new system based on intelligence and aptitude, arguing there should be three types of secondary school:

- Grammar schools for the academically able
- Technical schools for those with a practical bent
- New 'modern' secondary schools for the rest

The influence of the public schools was still there. R A Butler, President of the Board of Education and the minister responsible for the 1944 Act, handed over curriculum issues to the Secondary Schools Examination Council chaired by Cyril Norwood, former headmaster of Harrow.

The Norwood Report of 1943 (Norwood, 1943), concluded:

> We believe that education cannot stop short of recognising the ideals of truth and beauty and goodness as final and binding for all times and in all places, as ultimate values; we do not believe that these ideals are of temporary convenience only, as devices for holding together society till they can be dispensed with as knowledge grows and organisation becomes more scientific. Further, we hold that the recognition of such values implies, for most people at least, a religious interpretation of life which for us must mean the Christian interpretation of life. We have no sympathy, therefore, with a theory of education which presupposes that its aim can be dictated by the provisional findings of special sciences, whether biological, psychological or sociological, that the function of education is to fit pupils to determine their outlook and conduct according to the changing needs and the changing standards of the

day. We agree wholeheartedly that scientific method and scientific planning can do much to help in the realisation of the 'good life', and education which does not avail itself of such aid denies itself one means to the realisation of its ends. But our belief is that education from its own nature must be ultimately concerned with values which are independent of time or particular environment.

As for classics:

We are not led by mere conservatism to wish to preserve for the future the study of the Classics because their study is traditional in the Grammar Schools of the past; rather we would say that it is traditional, not from accidental reasons, but from a sincere conviction, however variously expressed, that, unless a culture attains to and preserves self-knowledge, its continuity is not assured; failure in self-knowledge is a symptom of threatening decay.

The committee even considered classics more useful than modern foreign languages:

A convention has grown up that Latin should be the second foreign language undertaken by a pupil. We would suggest that it should become a more frequent practice for pupils who show promise of linguistic and literary ability to take Latin as their first foreign language – a measure which is approved by some teachers of French, as well as a larger number of teachers of English.

Local Education Authorities were required to submit proposals to the new Department of Education for reorganising secondary schooling in their areas. Most went for the three types of school – grammar for the academic, technical schools for those who were good with their hands and secondary moderns for the rest – the structure recommended by Spens.

But whereas the grammar schools and secondary moderns went ahead, few technical schools were ever built: at their peak, only 3-4% of children attended one. The maximum number was 324 technical schools in 1946 but this had fallen back to 184 by 1964. In the post-war period there was no money available to develop such schemes, technical schools were expensive, and the government's priority was the new NHS, housing and social security. All available resources for education went to repairing war-damaged schools and providing accommodation for the growing number of school-age children – a consequence of the raising of the school leaving age (the 1944 Act raised it from 14 to 15) and then the post-war baby boom.

Because the technical schools were designed for those who could not get into grammar schools, they had lower status. The prestige of the grammar schools lent status to their form of curriculum and especially pure science. Applied science, the thing that was supposed to be taught in secondary moderns and technical colleges, was regarded as second-rate.

Another problem was the fact that many students failed to complete courses they had started at technical college. Many enrolled in courses for which they were poorly equipped, given their bad experience at school. The provision for girls was especially poor; the Crowther Committee (1959) noted that 'the country has hardly as yet made a beginning with the continuing education of girls after they leave school'.

Furthermore, most secondary modern schools moved into craft and technical teaching, so it was unclear why technical schools were needed at all. In 1955 the Conservative Minister for Education, David Eccles, took the decision not to sanction any more technical schools on the basis that technical ability could not be determined at age 11. Arguably it was this failure to establish technical schools that lies at the heart of England's relative weakness in technical education today.

As far as post-school education was concerned, the 1944 Bill made no specific reference to vocational education, simply laying a duty on local authorities to submit to the Ministry of Education development schemes for 'further education', including county colleges for young people. The Board of Education itself was lukewarm about a proposal to introduce county colleges offering full-time courses because it was felt that any encouragement to young people to attend courses in the day would make them unlikely to attend evening classes – and this in turn would allow them too much leisure time. In fact, in the 1940s and 1950s, FE seems to have been regarded by the Board as merely filling a space for boys waiting to do national service (compulsory up to 1963) and for girls a period before they got married.

1944 was a moment when firm action by central government could have caused the education system in England to change direction, but there was a general resistance to a centrally planned education system of the sort they had in France, which after 1794 saw the creation of the *École Polytechnique* for the production of engineers, or Prussia after 1826 when *Realschulen* were founded in every German town specialising in science and modern studies. What is more, the Local Government Act 1888 had handed control of schools to over 400 local authorities and the wartime government had to negotiate with all of them to gain control of the system – an impossible task.

Another abiding problem was the reluctance of the Government to manage education and training within one department. The Victorian idea of a liberal education had implanted in the minds of ministers and civil servants the firm belief that education and 'training for a job' were quite different things. In the run-up to the 1944 Education Act, the Board of Education was responsible for the school-level curriculum, the Ministry of Labour for training. The inability of these departments to work together helped keep technical education out of the Act, a problem that continued in subsequent years. Even in the 2010-15 Coalition government, further education and 'skills', as well as universities, came under the Department for Business, Innovation and Skills. These responsibilities were only transferred to the Department for Education in 2016.

School leaving age

1880	10
1918	14
1947	15
1972	16
2015	still 16 but all must be 'engaged in education or training up to age 18'

The post-war period

The post-war period was marked by economic decline, continued awareness of the weakness of technical education and a seeming inability to do much about it.

Schools

The wealthiest 7% of children went to private schools. In the immediate post-war period they continued their traditional emphasis on classics but after 1970 things started to change. Science teaching grew in importance, so that by 2000 a disproportionate number of those going to university to read sciences came from private schools. The same was true of modern languages.

Before the reforms of the 1970s, grammar schools were the preserve of the middle classes. Despite the mythology that grammar schools were the road for social mobility of the working class, this was never true. Few poorer pupils went to grammar schools and of those that did, many did badly.

Secondary modern and technical schools were for the working classes. For this reason, the vocational education they offered had an implied lower status – a further blow to those who wished to see technical education thrive.

The 1944 Act had established the principle of sorting children by aptitude into different types of school, but over time the assumptions that lay behind this started to crumble. Psychologists concluded that specific technical ability could not be detected at the age of 10/11, the age at which entry to secondary technical schools had been set. Many able pupils failed the 11+ exam but found that they were subsequently unable to take academic qualifications in the secondary moderns or technical schools. The course of their lives had been fixed by their performance in an exam aged 11.

So from the early 1950s, both professional and public opinion began to back the view that it was best to abolish selection at the age of 11 altogether. After 1965, the country moved towards comprehensive schools and the surviving secondary technical schools were absorbed into them. The proportion of pupils at comprehensive schools increased from 7% in 1964 to 90% in 1982 and has remained at a high level since. The 1964 Industrial Training Act placed the emphasis on workplace training and to some extent this absolved schools of the need to become involved in vocational courses.

These changes in school type were reflected in the qualifications pupils took at the end of compulsory schooling. It seems extraordinary now that before 1965 only the top 20% of the ability range (those in grammar schools and independent schools) took any exams (O levels). The rest (80%) left school at 15 without qualifications, although many moved into apprenticeships with day-release to study at a technical college.

In 1965 the more vocational Certificate of Secondary Education was introduced; if the O level was for the top 20% of ability, CSEs were for the next 40%. The remaining 40%, it was thought, should not take any nationally recognised leaving exams. So the population was clearly divided into three: academic, technical and the rest.

With the advent of all-ability comprehensive schools in the 1970s, it became clear that a system that required schools to divide the population in this way was unsatisfactory. 40% of those taking O levels failed and many of those taking CSEs could in fact have managed O levels – so both groups were misclassified. In 1986, O levels and CSEs were merged to create the GCSE – the General Certificate of Secondary Education. In many ways, this was a good thing, but it had some consequences for those pupils who had benefited from vocational CSEs. There was less hands-on learning and courses most relevant to work were lost. The importance of oral skills gave way almost completely to assessment by writing.

During the latter half of the 20th century, Britain's population received less education than its competitors. The minimum legal age became the default leaving age for the vast majority of young people. In 1960, the average number of school years completed in the UK was just 6.7, well below the US (10.6), West Germany (9.6), the Netherlands (8.1) and Sweden (9.0). For all countries, the number of school years has increased gradually, but the UK has remained behind the US and much of the G7 for the past 50 years (Aubrey and Reed, 2016).

Further education

In the 1950s and 1960s, new FE colleges were built, some called county colleges, and the numbers attending rose. During the 1951-64 period, FE expenditure rose by 1200%, twice the rate of that for secondary education (Richardson, 2007). A small proportion of the new colleges were national and funded directly by central government – art, navigation, mining, aeronautics, and several new sea training schools. But most were local authority FE colleges that in the early post-war period were technical and commercial colleges or colleges of art and design. Most importantly, many more employers became willing to release apprentices and young trainees during the day ('day-release') and this accounted for the big increase in the number of students. There were 51,000 day-release students in 1938, 644,000 in 1968. The number of full-time students rose from 20,000 to 244,000 over the same period (Aldrich, 2002).

Another important trend in the 1950s and 1960s was the growth in the proportion of students studying full-time to take academic qualifications at FE colleges – the Schools Certificate before 1951; O levels, CSEs and A levels later on. Some were retaking, others taking courses for the first time. Many FE colleges offered popular social science subjects not offered by local schools.

As well as helping students obtain qualifications that could lead to higher education, it was also possible for the colleges themselves to offer degree courses, often using University of London external degrees.

Concerns about the growing superiority of technology in the USA and USSR led to the establishment of ten Colleges of Advanced Technology after 1956 to teach more ambitious courses. For a while, these were an alternative to universities and polytechnics, but following the recommendation of the 1963 Robbins Committee all went on to become universities.

In 1956, the Ministry of Education identified four tiers of colleges – Colleges of Advanced Technology; Regional Colleges (which went on to become polytechnics in the 1960s); Area Colleges, which had some but limited numbers of advanced courses; and Local Colleges, which had large numbers of low-level courses, many part-time. But because the colleges had been established by separate local authorities, this was far from a neat classification and to the outside observer the system seemed quite confused.

Art schools flourished during this period, contributing to the influence of England on pop art, graphic design and youth fashion in the 1960s (Richardson, 2007). John Lennon attended the Liverpool College of Art.

Apprenticeships remained important, but trades unions – powerful up to the 1980s – were often accused of using them to preserve demarcations between crafts rather than upgrading skills. Indeed, apprenticeships were used by unions to limit entry to their trade because only those who had served an apprenticeship were permitted to do more skilled jobs.

The Crowther Report, 1959

In March 1956, the Minister of Education, David Eccles, asked the Central Advisory Council for Education (England) 'to consider, in relation to the changing social and industrial needs of our society, and the needs of its individual citizens, the education of boys and girls between 15 and 18'.

The Council was chaired by Sir Geoffrey Crowther (1907-1972), editor of *The Economist* from 1938 to 1956. He was concerned about the fact that 60% of 15- to 17-year-olds at that time were receiving no day-time education or training.

Crowther (1959) said that the education of young workers should be woven of four strands:

- Finding a way about the world as workers, consumers and citizens
- Forming standards and values
- Developing physical and aesthetic skills
- Continuing basic education, including with a vocational bias where appropriate

The report explained:

There seem to us, then, to be four main strands out of which the curriculum of the county college should be woven. There is, first, the task of helping young workers, many of them of limited intelligence, to find their way successfully about the adult world – to spend their money sensibly, to understand the many ways in which the welfare state touches their lives and can assist them, to see how its services are paid for, and to play their part as useful citizens.

Secondly, there is the more difficult job of helping them to define, in a form which makes sense to them, a standard of moral values by which they can live after they have left the sheltered world of school and find themselves in novel situations where they desperately need guidance.

There is, thirdly, the easier, and infinitely rewarding, task of helping them to carry over into their working life the pursuits and activities, physical and aesthetic, which they practised at school and too often abandon.

Finally, there is, as we have seen, a strictly educational task in the narrower sense. Many, perhaps most, of the county college students will have grave deficiencies in their formal school education which – now that they are out in the world and can see the handicap they have imposed on themselves – they will often be willing and anxious to put right. These, then, are the four strands.

In the present day the focus of education is on employability, the national economy and social mobility. It is instructive to note other strands were important in 1959, including moral values:

There can be no doubt of the disaster. On 1956 figures, one girl in fifty might expect to give birth to a child conceived before she was 17. It is important to disentangle the two strands – the rise in unsupervised association between teenage boys and girls; and the virtual disappearance of many of the old rules of right and wrong which were formerly accepted even when they were not obeyed. These two changes have happened at the same time, but they are not necessary consequences of one another.

There were, in other words, several aims apart from vocational training, including (according to the London County Council at the time) satisfying use of leisure time, training for citizenship and preparation for marriage.

1964 Industrial Training Act

Throughout the whole of post-war English history runs the question of whether employers could or should be left to arrange training for their employees. The 1958 Carr Report recommended that the state leave industrial training to industry. But by 1962, the government had become increasingly concerned about the weak economic performance of the UK compared to its competitors. With one eye on Germany as usual, they were unhappy about the volume and the quality of training going on. Many firms were not training at all, 'poaching' seemed rampant, and the apprenticeship system did not seem to be delivering the skills required by industry.

The 1964 Act gave the Minister of Labour statutory powers to set up industrial training boards (ITBs) containing representatives of employers and workers. Each board was responsible for overseeing training in its industry, setting standards and providing advice to firms. Most importantly, the ITBs paid allowances to trainees, financed by a compulsory levy on firms in its industry. They were able to determine the duration of training, the content of training, send people to college and reimburse firms' expenses.

But the ITBs were always rather weak. The various governments of this time were anxious to avoid conflict with unions and bosses, so progress was limited – although the volume of day-release by firms increased. The ITBs started to be wound up after 1981.

The Industrial Training Act had hoped to revivify apprenticeships but in fact damaged them. The number of apprenticeships fell from 240,000 in 1964 to 140,000 in 1974. Further decline continued in the 1980s under Margaret Thatcher, suspicious of apprenticeships as an instrument of trade union power in the workplace.

After 1975

Between 1945 and 1975, further education was a local affair, run by local authorities to reflect local needs. After 1975, the concerns that had led to the creation of the ITBs intensified – high youth unemployment and general economic weakness – and FE was progressively expanded. In the process it became the dominant form of post-compulsory education in England.

Between 1945 and 1975, FE was mostly small scale, locally controlled, most of the students were male, most courses were part-time and most were linked to a specific occupation. Over time, FE became large scale, centrally controlled, focused more on general skills development as opposed to training for particular jobs, there were many more places for women and more full-time courses. By 2005, 53% of the entire 16-year-old cohort were engaged in the FE sector. There were also many adults – by 2005, four-fifths of FE students were aged 19+. The local technical college became the FE college, although even today people refer to the college as the 'tech'.

In response to demand, in the 1970s colleges widened their remit and started to offer full-time courses to school leavers who were not able or ready to secure jobs and expanded programmes for young people with special educational needs. The introduction of the GCSE in 1986 as a common school leaving exam stimulated post-16 participation – more pupils had some academic success and felt able to continue in education, albeit in a college. Growing youth unemployment and the addition of liberal arts courses to the traditional diet of technical courses swelled numbers. Full-time college became a good alternative to staying at school: it felt more grown up.

As the economy continued to deteriorate and youth unemployment rose, the Department of Employment established the Manpower Services Commission (1973-88) to drive training for young people, making funding directly available to local authorities to fund college-based day-release courses. In 1990, 82 local Training and Enterprise Councils (TECs) were set up in England and Wales, handing control of training to local, employer-led management. The TECs identified local training needs and managed training for young people, the unemployed and adults wanting retraining, often sub-contracting to colleges as well as private providers.

In the 1980s and 1990s, general colleges of FE started offering access courses for mature students wishing to go to the rapidly expanding universities and polytechnics, as well as academic and vocational courses for school-leavers wishing to continue their education full-time. 1992-3 was the first year in which there were more students in England in their first post-compulsory school year studying full-time in colleges than in schools. Many more young women now started to go to college and the colleges employed many more female teachers.

In 1993, the then 464 colleges were 'incorporated' – transferred from local authority to central government funding. This was partly a response to the poll tax crisis and the need to reduce local authority spending, but there were also growing concerns about mass youth unemployment and an Audit Commission report suggesting that there was widespread inefficiently and waste (Audit Commission, 1993). Ken Clarke, the minister responsible, also hoped that freeing colleges from the burden of regulation imposed on them by local authorities would allow them to innovate and grow more rapidly.

Incorporation meant a transfer of power over property, staffing and courses from local government to college governing bodies and college leaders, giving them wide scope to make decisions. But the legislation also put new powers of oversight and intervention in the hands of central government. The funding of colleges was controlled by a new body, the Further Education Funding Council (FEFC).

In 1993, the Audit Commission and Ofsted published a seminal report, *Unfinished Business*, which concluded that 30-40% of 16- to 19-year-olds who started a course did not succeed – an enormous waste of both time and money. What is more, different colleges had wide variations in the cost per student – from £1000 to £7000 for those following the same course. The Further Education Funding Council responded to these revelations by tightening up the efficiency of colleges, part of the funding of a student being conditional on completion of the course.

Numbers of students in FE in England and Wales continued to grow – from 3.1 million in 1970 to 4.4 million by 2000, the majority of whom were part-timers. But over time, several FE colleges merged, leaving just 386 by 2006. As ever, there were several different types of college: a large group of 'general' colleges, sixth form colleges offering A levels, tertiary colleges, and specialist colleges offering agriculture and horticulture, art and design, and performing arts. In addition there were, in 2006, about 3000 independent colleges offering courses in areas such as English language, secretarial, and ICT.

After the 2005 Foster Review, the Labour government saw the FE sector as primarily an engine for economic growth. This led to the marginalisation of the wider role colleges play in their communities and created a system of further education characterised by repeated top-down reform, ministerial target-setting and state micromanagement. But there were still concerns that FE colleges were failing to meet the needs of employers or tackle the growing number of young people who were in neither employment nor training.

City Technology Colleges, 1988

In the early 1980s, research from the National Institute for Economic and Social Research showed once again how Germany appeared to have a superior technical education system to England. In 1986, the Conservative government announced that new city technology colleges (CTCs) would be built; the first opened in 1988 and was followed by 14 more over the next four years, all funded by central government. They had close links with businesses and industry (mainly through their sponsors), and often their governors were directors of businesses that supported the colleges. They were permitted to select pupils and so ran contrary to the prevailing comprehensive orthodoxy.

In practice, the CTCs did not specialise in technology. They were modern schools, with good facilities (especially IT), and often focused on business and economic awareness rather than technology.

Almost all CTCs have now converted to become academies.

Universities and polytechnics

In the 1950s and 1960s, there was an attempt to focus investment on a limited number of colleges with the more advanced courses. In 1956, several leading technical colleges were designated Colleges of Advanced Technology, and in 1965 they were elevated to university status, including Aston, Bath, Brunel and Loughborough.

In 1966 another group of leading technical colleges were designated as polytechnics – 27 at first, soon to be 30. The polytechnics were originally designed to lead technical education as a response to the progress being made in Germany, France and the USA, but after 1970 there was a marked decline in the proportion of students studying maths and sciences in school sixth forms and a swing towards arts and social sciences. So the polytechnics, which were supposed to promote vocational courses, found themselves offering increasing numbers of places in humanities and social science courses. By the 1980s, the number of graduate engineers that the UK was turning out was a third of that produced by France and just a quarter of that produced by Japan.

This is a key lesson for the future: the supply of courses is demand-led. If students do not wish to apply for technical or science-based courses, even if the economy needs these skills, such courses will not flourish.

Under the Further and Higher Education Act 1992, the polytechnics were allowed to become fully fledged universities; 33 new universities – all ex-polytechnics – were established in England during the 1990s and, in their attempt to become 'proper' universities, the focus on academic courses accelerated. The last degree-awarding institution to hold on to the name 'polytechnic' after 1992 was Anglia Polytechnic University until it became Anglia Ruskin University in 2005.

Why did the government allow polytechnics to become universities? Because it felt that the second-class status of polytechnics was unfair and that changing the name would raise their status.

Why did the polytechnics want to become universities? Because by doing so they gained better funding, greater prestige, more autonomy and they were better able to attract valuable overseas students.

Over time, a growing proportion of other institutions that had offered vocational courses turned into universities. This included Higher Education Colleges such as Cirencester Agricultural College (now Cirencester University), several teacher-training colleges and others with specialist training functions. Between 2000 and 2016, 36 extra universities were created in England.

Other countries, like Germany, France, the USA, Canada and the Netherlands, have specialist colleges offering level 4 and 5 technical qualifications. No new universities have started in the Netherlands since 1976 because they have chosen to focus on vocational education. In England, we have sanctioned the development of a binary system – universities offering level 6 courses and FE colleges offering mainly level 1-3 courses. Partly because of this, the level 4-5 courses in the middle have shrunk away.

Financing training: two blunders

Individual Learning Accounts, 2000-2001.
In 2000 the Blair government introduced Individual Learning Accounts. Keen to expand vocational training, they hit on the idea that, instead of paying FE colleges to run courses or finding ways of encouraging employees to train their staff, they would fund trainees directly by giving them their own 'learning account'. The trainee would put in small sum, the government would then put in a much larger sum, and the individual account holders would spend the cash in ways they thought were most useful to them. It was all part of New Labour's drive to 'empower' people by giving them the means to help themselves.

In the March 1999 budget, Gordon Brown announced that in 2000 every adult in Britain would be entitled to open an individual learning account. Only one company bid for the contract to administer the scheme: Capita. In order to make the scheme as simple and unbureaucratic as possible, anyone aged 19 or above could apply to Capita to open an account. The providers of the courses on which the money was to be spent simply had to register with Capita, with no checks into their past experience of providing training. The provider of the course simply had to send the names of the eligible students to Capita once a course had begun and Capita would send them the payment.

By the autumn of 2011, an improbable 2.5 million account holders had registered with the scheme, as had nearly 9000 training providers. It soon became apparent that fraudsters had invented thousands of phantom learners and many of the training courses were a fiction. The National Audit Office estimated that £67 million of the £196 million spent had been lost to fraud. Individual learning accounts were scrapped in 2001 (King and Crewe, 2013).

Train to Gain, 2006-10
Under Gordon Brown, 'Train to Gain' was set up to deal with the perceived skills shortages in the country. Funding was directed to employers providing skills training for staff, a shift towards a demand-led system.

Train to Gain comprised:

- a skills brokerage service to advise employers on identifying training needs and sourcing training
- flexible training, often delivered in the workplace and at a convenient time
- full public funding of training for employees taking specified courses and qualifications, and contributions to some other training part paid for by employers.

The main government funding agency at the time (the Learning and Skills Council) was, in the final years of New Labour, directed both to increase the number of contractors used, and to encourage the emergence of new awarding organisations offering brand-new qualifications to compete with existing ones, based on the belief that having large numbers of providers and awarding bodies would stimulate competition and drive up quality.

There is little evidence it achieved this. One of the lessons of the past 20 years is that allowing a free market of qualifications leads to complexity, and complexity is in itself a problem.

A National Audit Office report in 2009 found that Train to Gain was very expensive relative to outcomes: 'A half of employers whose employees received training would have arranged similar training without public subsidy'.

Train to Gain was scrapped by the incoming coalition government after 2010.

The jungle of qualifications

Academic qualifications are straightforward. At school we had O levels and CSEs, now replaced by GCSEs, and we have A levels, the most enduring of all qualifications. They were, and to some extent still are, run by university-linked exam boards, who have merged over time so we have just three left in England.

Vocational qualifications are much more complex because they reflect the needs of a diverse labour market. Hundreds of job types have spawned thousands of qualifications.

The existing system of vocational qualifications can be traced back to the 19th century. To help address concerns that the UK might be outpaced by Germany, the Royal Society for the Encouragement of the Arts, Manufacture and Commerce (RSA) began, in 1856, to offer a system of vocational exams for working-class students. In 1878 the City of London, together with the ancient craft guilds, set up the City and Guilds of London Institute, now known as City & Guilds, providing technical schools and exams in technological subjects. For much of the next century these two provided the bulk of vocational courses, the RSA in business and commerce, City & Guilds in technical subjects. In addition, professional qualifications in law, accountancy and banking evolved, their standards controlled by professional associations.

In the 1970s Ted Heath introduced a new set of national qualifications as good tertiary-level alternatives to A levels and university degrees – the Ordinary National Certificates and Diplomas (ONCs and ONDs) and Higher National Certificates and Diplomas (HNCs and HNDs). At first they successfully provided the sort of technical pathway that is common in other European countries, 'Higher Nationals' being offered in polytechnics with the possibility of proceeding to a full degree. However, from the mid-80s onwards this clearly understood pathway was obscured by a succession of other government reforms and these qualifications shrank.

National Vocational Qualifications, 1986-2007

In 1986 the Conservative government, concerned about the years of economic decline linked to poor skills training, established the National Council for Vocational Qualifications (NCVQ). The NCVQ reported to the Department of Employment and was told to develop a framework of national vocational qualifications (NVQs) into which all vocational qualifications would be incorporated. As with the 2017-2020 vocational reforms, the idea was that the qualifications would be based on 'standards' defined by employers – which tended to mean representatives of bigger companies. Students would have to demonstrate 'competences' – which meant they could perform activities within an occupation to the standards expected by employers. The competences would be assessed by observing the student doing an activity that replicated what they would do in a job. The Manpower Services Commission (civil servants) gathered together employers to write these standards – a huge operation costing millions. Alison Wolf (2002) estimates it cost £100,000-£300,000 for each new set of standards.

The theory sounded fine and by 1995 95% of occupations were covered by the standards. Here is one of the standards for level 2 hairdressing:

Learning outcomes	Assessment criteria	Evidence type	Portfolio reference	Date
1. Be able to use safe and effective methods of working when colouring and lightening hair	1.1 protect the client's clothing, skin and hair effectively throughout the service 1.2 position the client to meet the needs of the service without causing discomfort 1.3 keep the work area clean and tidy throughout the service 1.4 remove waste immediately at the end of the service 1.5 use working methods that · minimise the wastage of products · minimise the risk of cross-infection · make effective use of the working time · ensure the use of clean resources · minimise the risk of harm or injury to themselves and others 1.6 maintain personal standards of health and hygiene which minimise the risk of cross-infection, infestation and offence to clients and colleagues 1.7 use products and equipment identified as a result of consultation with the client			

But in the event, of the 800 or so NVQs that were developed, most were unpopular – half had no takers and many of the rest had only a few candidates. They failed in part because traditional qualifications remained popular with students and employers: NVQs were supposed to replace all existing vocational qualifications, but by 1996 they only accounted for 25% of vocational awards being made. They failed in part because students rightly believed that job-training schemes set up by the government had less value than academic qualifications. Wolf (2002) explains that the same thing happened in Germany and the Netherlands: vocational courses for young people became perceived as a rubbish bin for those who had failed academically.

At the same time, academic qualifications were becoming more popular. A levels had been designed for the 3% of the population entering universities in the 1950s, but by 1995 they were being taken by 36% of the population.

NVQs also failed because post-GCSE students rightly baulked at the idea of embarking on courses that only led to one very specific type of job. They preferred to keep their options open by doing a more general and often more prestigious course, such as a BTEC.

Another issue with the NVQs was their complexity. Each involved many dozens of criteria and the administrative burden on those assessing the students was unmanageable. In any case the standards written by representatives of the large companies often didn't suit the places where most people work – smaller businesses.

Many students started but failed to complete an NVQ. One common reason for this was that the nature of their job changed before they had finished the NVQ. Firms were in a continuous process of change and the rigid but complex NVQ standards could not keep up. Courses designed to equip students to do jobs that exist today do not necessarily prepare them for jobs of the future.

Faced with the unpopularity of the very job-specific NVQs, in 1991 the government attempted to salvage the situation by creating wider-ranging General National Vocational Qualifications (GNVQs) that could be awarded in both schools and colleges. The GNVQs had titles such as 'Leisure and Tourism' and 'Manufacturing'. GNVQs were attractive to students who wanted to stay at school but whose GCSE grades were too weak for them to embark on A levels. The aim was 'parity of esteem' with A levels – something that was never going to happen because they were taken by weaker students. In the end, the GNVQs failed because they, too, adopted the complex competency-based assessment model – teachers and students spent an average of two days a week just meeting assessment requirements and the bureaucracy was immense. GNVQs underwent further iterations when Advanced Vocational Certificates of Education (AVCEs) were introduced in 2000 and ran alongside GNVQs. Both were eventually phased out between 2005 and 2007.

Qualifications and Credit Framework, 2008-2015

The Qualifications and Credit Framework (QCF) was launched in 2008 as a framework for adult vocational qualifications. It established a building-brick approach to learning, qualifications, and credit transfer. It included a detailed set of rules, including how qualifications should be designed and structured.

All qualifications were to be broken down into units. Every unit in the framework had a credit value where one credit represented ten hours of learning time. Units combined into three different sizes of qualification:

- Awards (1 to 12 credits)
- Certificates (13 to 36 credits)
- Diplomas (37 credits or more)

The idea behind the QCF system was that it would allow students to gain a credit in one place and add to it with credits gained in another place or with a different awarder – it would provide flexibility. To make this possible there was a 'unit bank' where your credits were stored.

This new system also failed. There was little evidence that the units system resulted in students transferring between awarding organisations or different courses. The units format produced atomised qualifications and a tick box approach to the curriculum. It discouraged assessment that could confirm that a good standard had been reached across the whole course – just piling up a series of credits does not tell an employer what you can do. The QCF rules imposed a one-size-fits-all approach to the design of qualifications that was counterproductive. Few people ever understood the meaning of the 'awards', 'certificates' and 'diplomas'. The Whitehead Review in 2013 found that 'the complex, over-prescribed system is a barrier to many employers and does not, even with the help of significant levels of public funding, generate vocational qualifications that are valued widely or seen as a signal of marketable skills'.

In 2015 the QCF rules were removed by the exams regulator, Ofqual.

Core skills

From time to time, employers have urged the government to compel students to learn what are normally called 'core skills' or 'key skills'. This reflects the view of the Confederation of British Industries (CBI), representing large employers, that young people lack the skills they need – not just good written English, basic numeracy and ICT but also the ability to work in a team, to communicate well orally, to be organised, to be good at problem-solving and critical thinking. Particularly influential was the CBI's 1989 report *Towards a Skills Revolution*. These core skills were included in the specifications for the new General National Vocational Qualifications (GNVQs) after 1991.

The Dearing Review of 16-19 education (1996) found that 'employers would in particular wish to see the development of inter-personal skills in team working, presentation skills (including skills of oracy and personal presentation), and wider personal skills such as problem-solving and self-management of learning programmes'.

All of which seemed sensible enough.

In 1999 the Qualifications and Curriculum Authority (QCA) published assessment specifications for six 'key skills' at four levels. It also introduced new qualifications for three of the 'main key skills': communication, application of number and IT. These qualifications were classified by the government as having equivalent value to school qualifications, but in practice few people believed that – after all, they were for those who had failed to achieve decent GCSE grades. After 2010 the 'key skills' qualifications were replaced by 'functional skills' in maths, English and ICT.

An example of key skills

City & Guilds level 2 Key Skills – 'working with others' questions:

1. What have you learnt about planning work with others?

2. What have you learnt about working cooperatively towards achieving objectives you have identified?

3. What have you learnt about reviewing your contributions and agreeing ways of improving your work with others?

The Royal Society of Arts has developed a new secondary curriculum for the 21st century called Opening Minds, which concludes that there are five essential skills that should be the basis of the school curriculum:

- Citizenship
- Learning
- Managing information
- Relating to people
- Managing situations

The RSA explains:

These competences are broad areas of capability, developed in classrooms through a mixture of instruction and practical experience: children plan their work, organise their own time and explore their own ways of learning. Subject boundaries are less defined than in traditional curriculum teaching, with schools often integrating the teaching of several subjects together into modules or topics, where competences can be developed through the exploration of common themes. (RSA website)

In the schools which have adopted this approach the focus of the curriculum is projects, not subjects.

It is easy enough to agree that key skills/core skills are valuable. The difficulty with skills such as 'working with others' is **knowing whether they can be taught, whether such teaching works, and how they can be assessed**. Skills like 'planning work with others' cannot be assessed by means of an exam and the alternative tends to be a teacher ticking boxes. If teaching 'skills' is so problematic it may well be more valuable to spend the limited time available focusing on those things that clearly can be taught, such as maths and English.

As many people have argued (such as Christodoulou, 2014), the most reliable basis for 21st century skills is possession of wide-ranging knowledge across many traditional subjects. Time spent on teaching thinking skills or competencies rather than normal subjects carries a high opportunity cost – the pupils are not doing something completely useless, but nor are they using the time as well as they could. Time spent on activities supposed to promote 'transferable skills' is time not spent learning knowledge that really would build transferable skills.

Vocational GCSEs and the Diploma: 2001-2010

In 2001 David Blunkett announced the introduction of vocational GCSEs. Once again the objective was to bridge the divide between academic and vocational qualifications and, by making the vocational more attractive, to develop a more skilled workforce and a stronger economy. To enhance the attractiveness of vocational GCSEs they were each worth the equivalent of two normal GCSEs. The DFES booklet for teachers explained: 'GCSEs in vocational subjects provide the same standards and rigour as other GCSEs. As such they represent a positive choice for all students.' Subjects included Leisure and Tourism, Health and Social Care, Manufacturing, and Engineering.

But no one was fooled: the vocational GCSEs were aimed at those who struggled with academic subjects and were thus condemned to low status, whatever the branding.

Ed Balls's 14-19 Diplomas were another recent attempt at reform. Launched in 2008, the Diplomas were an attempt to integrate academic and vocational courses for 14- to 19-year olds. Under the qualifications, students specialised in one subject but also studied core subjects such as English and maths as well as completing a university-style dissertation. The Labour government claimed they would bridge the 'old-fashioned divide' between academic and vocational qualifications.

Initially, they were introduced in 14 practical subjects, including health, media, hair and beauty, hospitality, engineering and construction. But they were complex and unpopular, with only 15,000 students taking them in the first three years. As has happened so often, the Diploma was introduced with too tight a timescale. There was no piloting and very little consultation with the colleges.

Clearing the decks: 2010-2016

In 2010 the new Coalition government appointed Michael Gove as Secretary of State for Education. Gove and Schools Minister Nick Gibb believed:

- that the vocational GCSEs were far too easy and were certainly not worth the equivalent of two academic GCSEs. Schools were putting children in for these qualifications simply to raise their performance table position. Children from lower income homes were being put in for vocational GCSEs which limited their ability to take A levels and go to university. Vocational GCSEs were holding back social mobility.

- that many vocational courses for children up to the age of 16 failed to properly prepare them for further education or the world of work.

- that all children are capable of following an academic curriculum up to the age of 16.

The Wolf Report (Wolf, 2011) criticised the large number of vocational courses taken in schools that did not increase the students' prospects of getting a job or higher pay. It also emphasised the importance of improving standards of maths and English. The report led directly to the following reforms:

- The number of vocational alternatives to GCSEs which were permitted to 'count' in the DfE performance tables was cut; these courses vanished immediately.

- The DfE removed incentives to enter lower-achieving students onto courses and qualifications that weren't recognised by employers.

- The 14-19 Diploma, which – still in its infancy – was scrapped. Millions of pounds had been wasted.

- All pupils with a 3/D grade in English or maths GCSEs were required to receive tuition and resit these GCSEs.

- All pupils with a 2/E grade or worse in English or maths GCSEs were required to receive extra tuition and take functional skills exams in English and maths.

- The government established a common academic curriculum for all pupils up to the age of 16 – the EBacc.

In addition, steps were taken to toughen up the 11-18 academic curriculum:

- A new, more rigorous national curriculum was introduced for 11- to 16-year-olds.

- Modular GCSEs (courses divided into units which could be examined at points throughout the course) were scrapped. These courses, which had been accessible to the less academic, were replaced by tougher linear exams (all the exams at the end of the course).

- Modular A levels were also replaced by linear exams.
- Partly because modules were scrapped, opportunities to resit exams were reduced.
- The amount of coursework in GCSEs and A levels was reduced.
- After 2016, secondary schools were judged in the DfE performance tables by the progress made by pupils in their best eight GCSEs, of which one must be English, one maths, and three chosen from the sciences, computing, history, geography or a foreign language. This left three slots that could include subjects like art, music and design technology.

These changes, which have many benefits for the top 50%, made life harder for the less academic pupil. Not only does England lack a large vocational school sector of the sort found in other European countries, but all the focus in the past few years has been on strengthening the academic component of 11-18 education. The reforms were welcomed by many, including me, but they did less for those least academic children who had been helped by the modular examination structure in the period up to 2010.

What happened to design and technology?

Design and Technology is an important and worthwhile school subject that ought to inspire pupils to continue with vocational subjects. In terms of status, design and technology has come and gone over the past 30 years. Numbers taking the DT GCSE in the UK have slumped:

2000 – 424,000

2010 – 288,000

2017 – 166,000

There is an annual shortage of 69,000 trained engineers and only 6% of the UK's engineering workforce is female. DT, attractively taught, would be one way to tackle this.

This decline has been caused by competition from other subjects, like Photography and Dance, the pressure of the EBacc and Progress 8 performance measures which have prioritised traditional academic subjects, the higher cost of DT in a time of tight budgets and the severe shortage of DT teachers.

A summary of recent trends

1. The proportion of children taking and passing exams at school has greatly increased over time with the raising of the school leaving age, the introduction of GCSEs in 1986 and the decline in employment opportunities for young people. The proportion going on to A levels and university has also shot up. Before 1986, 40% of the population took no qualifications at school; now all do. In 1986, 16% of people went into higher education at some point; today it is 50%.

   In the 1950s and 1960s most young people left school at 15 or 16 and went into a job. Half of young men went into apprenticeships. This system collapsed because of the steep decline in jobs for 16- to 18-year-olds and the dismantling of apprenticeships in the 1980s.

2. As far as vocational training is concerned, employer-funded job-specific training, which was the norm in the 1950s, was to some extent replaced by state-funded general transferable skills.

3. Central government came to micromanage the education and training system with the introduction of a national curriculum in 1988, the growth of inspections and accountability frameworks in the 1990s, the incorporation of FE colleges in 1993, and schools rebranded as academies in recent years, funded from the centre rather than by local authorities.

4. Despite concerns about the poor standard of vocational education in England throughout the whole of the 20th century, attempts to improve the situation have struggled. Priority was given to schools and universities rather than FE because that is what voters appeared to care about most. Funding was in any case limited by the cost of two world wars and a long period of economic depression between them. There was a failure to establish a national strategy for further education. Many employers have been unwilling to support the training and education of their workforce.

   England in 2018 has a serious shortage of people with technical skills and this is holding back the development of both manufacturing and services. The problem stems in part from the fact that the government did not create high-quality technical courses for young people after the Second World War, and particularly the failure to establish the 'technical route' as a good alternative to A levels for 16- to 18-year-olds. Academic courses and universities have swept all before them.

Since the 1960s, there has been uncertainty about the ideal type of institutional structure for students studying beyond school leaving age (Richardson, 2007), which is why FE provision seems so varied and fragmented.

5. Historically most government officials have been ignorant about what goes on in FE colleges. Ministers are generally in post for a short time and the FE landscape is too complex for them to get to grips with it. Few people in power or in the press had personal experience of vocational education. They didn't 'get' FE.

6. FE colleges have been forced to become entrepreneurial, responding to local demand. They evolved into multi-purpose community institutions offering basic English and maths courses to those who did badly at school, technical and vocational courses, courses for those with special needs, adult education, English for recent immigrants, qualifications which can lead to higher education, and courses for the local community.

7. Academic qualifications have tended to have a high status; vocational qualifications, low status, with exceptions like medicine, law and accountancy. This is why technical and vocational courses have tended to be taken by those who have done less well at school. Attempts to achieve parity of esteem have always failed.

8. There has been continued uncertainty about whether vocational skills should be taught in school/college or in the workplace.

9. The perceptions of employers and students determine which qualifications are valued. Attempts by governments to create new qualifications and 'frameworks' have often failed. Governments have tried to improve vocational education by reforming the qualifications on offer. But other aspects of vocational education matter just as much as the details of qualifications, such as the funding of the colleges offering these qualifications, the supply of teachers and the attitude of employers to new qualifications.

Chapter 6

The skills deficit

In England we have lower levels of reading and maths amongst the bottom 60% of young people than many of our competitors. Even those who pass GCSEs often have weak literacy and numeracy, as do some of those going to university.

We also have much lower levels of technical training post-16 than most of our competitors. We have a particularly small number of people taking courses at level 4 and 5. Level 3 is A level, level 6 is degree-level, so levels 4 and 5 are what can be called 'sub-degree level'. In the UK we have far more people taking degree-level courses at universities than most developed countries, far more aged 16-18 taking level 1 and 2 courses, but few in the middle.

The adult skills budget has been the subject of particularly big cuts since 2010 and adult training (that is, people over the age of 18) has declined rapidly.

We have low levels of productivity per person and a high proportion of the population in low-skill jobs and on low pay. There are also massive disparities between the south-east of England and other regions in terms of qualifications, productivity and pay.

The skills shortage is worsening because the 1960s baby boom means that a large part of the skilled workforce will be retiring in the next few years. For example, EngineeringUK (2016) estimates that the UK will need 182,000 new engineers a year between 2012 and 2022, mainly to replace those retiring. At present we produce 113,000 a year.

Skills – including those required in the high-tech industries such as aerospace component parts, pharmaceuticals and green technologies – will be a crucial driver of future productivity growth and competitiveness. But according to the Government's 2017 industrial strategy, only 10% of the population holds a technical qualification as their highest qualification, placing the country 16th out of 20 OECD countries on this measure.

Businesses are consistently reporting that young people are leaving the education system unprepared for the world of work. In its 2016 Education and Skills Survey, the Confederation of British Industry found that the proportion of businesses who are not confident that there will be enough people available in the future with the skills necessary to fill high-skilled jobs has reached a new high of 69% (CBI, 2016a).

The changing context

In order to understand what skills we need we must look briefly at the changing social make-up and jobs structure of the UK.

Life expectancy in 1965 was 68 for men and 75 for women, but by 2015 had increased to just below 80 for men and 83 for women. The Office for National Statistics projects that the number of people aged 75 and over will rise 89% from 2014 to 2039, by which time 1 in 12 of the population will be aged over 80. The ratio of dependents to productive workers will worsen; there were 310 pensioners per 1000 people of working age in 2014, set to rise to 367 per 1000 by 2039.

The population of the UK continues to grow – from 60 million in 2004 to a projected 69 million by 2024. The labour force, which was 30 million in 2004, will be 34 million by 2024 (UKCES, 2016a).

The population has been greatly changed by immigration. The 2011 census showed that 14% of the population belonged to a minority ethnic group. About 80.5%% of the UK population was white British, 2.2% is mixed, 7.5% is Asian and 3.3% is black. Of the 6.7 million pupils aged 5-16 in England, 27% were from ethnic minorities; the figure was 82% in inner London.

Figure 6.1: Long-term international migration, UK, 2007 to 2017

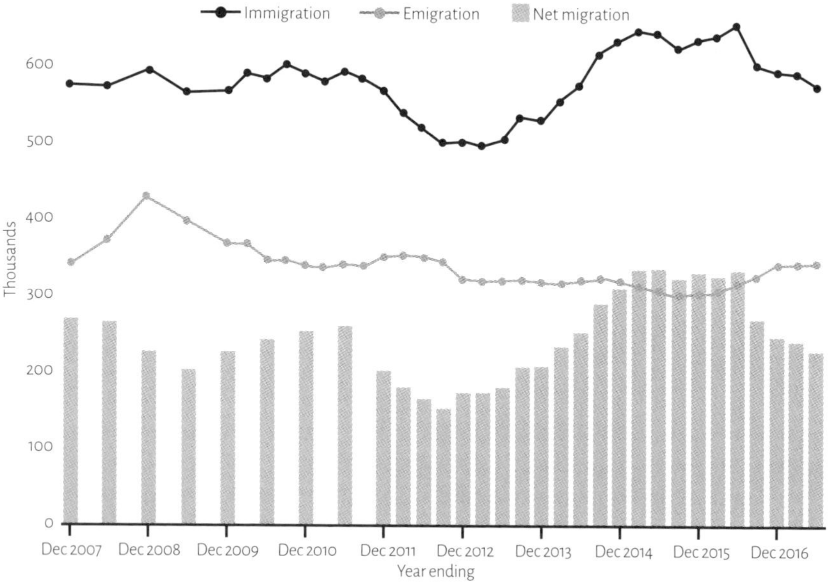

Source: ONS (2017f)

Migrant labour is substituting for lack of home-grown skills. The number of foreign-born people of working age has more than doubled since 1993. Six million of the UK population are foreign citizens – nearly 10% – including, in 2017, 916,000 Poles, 362,000 Indians and 233,000 Romanians. Many are graduates working in non-graduate jobs. International migration is particularly important to the wholesale and retail, hospitality, public administration and health sectors, which employ around 1.5 million non-UK nationals (ONS, 2017b).

In 1971, 45% of the male workforce was in the working classes, 10% in the highest socioeconomic group (professional and managerial – class 1 out of 8); the class structure was pyramid-shaped. Forty years later we have a more even distribution. Today 30% of men are working class and 18% are in class 1, reflecting the decline of the manufacturing industry and the expansion of the service and finance industries.

In 1971 just over half of women worked, rising to two-thirds today. More women than men now go to university and women outnumber men in some high-status occupations such as medicine and law. Women are expected to comprise 56% of the net increase in jobs between 2010 and 2020 (Sutton Trust, 2017). More middle-class mothers are returning to work, and better educational attainment for women is opening up more highly skilled roles.

People stay in education much longer today than they used to. In 1965 around 20% of 16- to 17-year-olds stayed on at school. Today, 94% of 16- to 17-year-olds are in full-time education or training. The expansion of tertiary education since the 1990s has had a profound effect on average educational attainment and means that, as time marches on, the probability of any child having highly educated parents is increasing.

Sectoral and occupational change

When looking at the changing structure of employment one looks at two types of data – sectoral change and occupational change. Sectoral change means growth or decline of the different sectors of the economy measured by output. Occupational change means the changing number of jobs in each sector. The two are clearly very closely related but government data classifies them differently.

Analysis of employment change by sector of the economy

The simple graph on the next page shows the changing structure of UK employment, 1841-2011, if the economy is split into just three types of activity:

Figure 6.2: The changing structure of UK employment

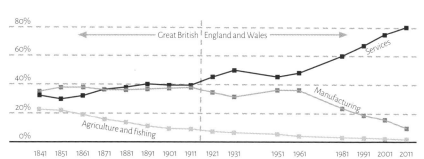

Source: ONS (2013)

The table below gives a more detailed account of the employment structure:

	Employment 2015
UK	**27,755,000**
Agriculture	402,500
Manufacturing	2,371,400
Electricity, Gas and Water	294,200
Construction	1,192,800
Wholesale and Retail	4,493,600
Hotels and Restaurants	1,961,400
Transport and Communications	2,231,000
Financial Services	1,005,000
Business Services	4,786,300
Public Administration	1,356,400
Education	2,607,900
Health and Social Work	3,791,000
Arts and Other Services	1,261,800

Source: Vivian et al (2016)

The graph opposite shows 2014 to 2024 forecasts made by the UK Commission for Employment and Skills. The graph has three elements: percentage change in the number of jobs, percentage change in the gross value added (the output of the sector), and the bubble size which shows the proportion of the nation's jobs in each sector.

The primary sector (agriculture, fisheries, forestry, mining) is declining as a result of import substitution and, as far as employment is concerned, improved efficiencies. Coal, oil and gas supplies are running out.

Figure 6.3: Performance of broad sectors of the economy by forecast output and employment change, 2014-2024

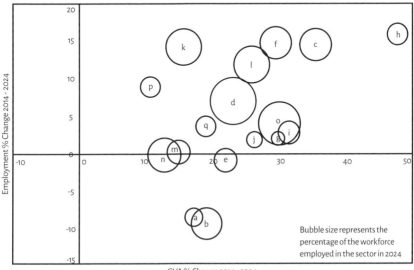

a. Primary sector and utilities
b. Manufacturing
c. Construction
d. Wholesale and retail trade
e. Transport and storage
f. Accommodation and food

g. Media
h. Information technology
i. Finance and insurance
j. Real estate
k. Professional services
l. Support services

m. Public administration and defence
n. Education
o. Health and social work
p. Arts and entertainment
q. Other services

GVA = gross value added, a measure of output

Source: UKCES (2016a)

Manufacturing employment will decline as a result of overseas competition and greater efficiencies.

Construction jobs will grow fast as the country's population continues to rise, the housing stock ages, there is more public and private investment in new housing, and because of large new infrastructure projects such as Crossrail and HS2.

Retail, accommodation and food jobs will all grow.

Business and other services will continue to grow, not least the large finance and insurance sectors, as will IT jobs.

Public administration, education, health and social work will continue to grow in response to rising demand but constrained by limits to government expenditure. According to the City & Guilds report *Great Expectations*, the ageing population means that the human health and social work sector will experience the most growth over the coming years: 23% of all new jobs created between 2015 and 2022.

Changing employment by gender

The impact on men and women of these trends will differ because of the gender imbalance within different occupations:

Figure 6.4: The distribution of women and men within each occupation

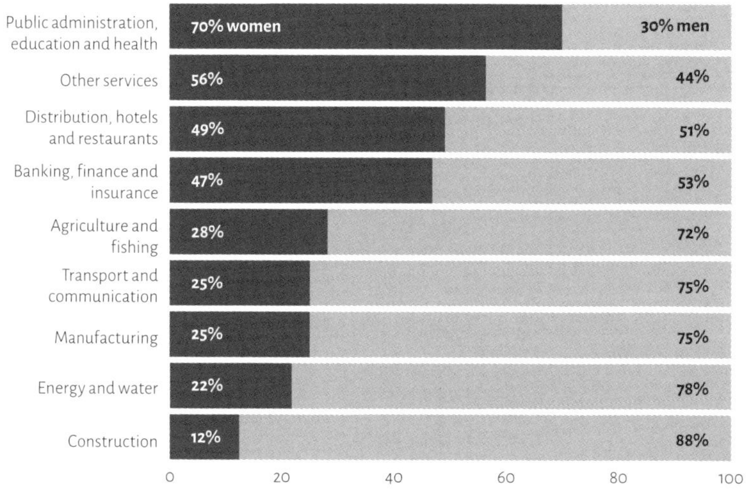

Occupation	Women	Men
Public administration, education and health	70% women	30% men
Other services	56%	44%
Distribution, hotels and restaurants	49%	51%
Banking, finance and insurance	47%	53%
Agriculture and fishing	28%	72%
Transport and communication	25%	75%
Manufacturing	25%	75%
Energy and water	22%	78%
Construction	12%	88%

Source: ONS (2013)

The tables across the page look at the trends by gender. At the top end, both men and women show strong growth in the top three occupational categories. The decline in administrative and secretarial jobs affects mainly women; the decline in skilled trades affects men rather more.

Many of the growing social (care) and personal service occupations have a mostly female workforce. For example, at least three-quarters of receptionists, hairdressers/barbers, nurses, care assistants, primary teachers, sales assistants and waiters/waitresses are female.

The fall in 'elementary' jobs for women (-430,00) compares to a rise in such jobs for men of +726,000. In 1994 there were many more women than men doing such low-level jobs. In 2004 the numbers were similar but by 2014 there were significantly more men than women doing elementary jobs.

UK females, occupational categories

Employment levels (thousands)	1994	2004	2014	2019	2024
Managers, directors and senior officials	502	822	1139	1303	1421
Professional occupations	1863	2526	3318	3658	3926
Associate professional and technical	1090	1559	1972	2183	2338
Administrative and secretarial	3269	3130	2740	2484	2342
Skilled trades occupations	556	435	402	405	409
Caring, leisure and other service	1462	2045	2596	2764	2911
Sales and customer service	1589	1734	1677	1633	1612
Process, plant and machine operatives	531	335	261	231	214
Elementary occupations	2038	1916	1659	1620	1608
Total	12,900	14,502	15,765	16,281	16,780

UK males, occupational categories

Employment levels (thousands)	1994	2004	2014	2019	2024
Managers, directors and senior officials	1546	1862	2165	2308	2381
Professional occupations	2133	2721	3278	3456	3545
Associate professional and technical	2114	2436	2665	2782	2838
Administrative and secretarial	747	796	825	831	833
Skilled trades occupations	3357	3370	3210	3171	3105
Caring, leisure and other service	249	398	538	596	632
Sales and customer service	582	755	923	972	991
Process, plant and machine operatives	1864	1869	1806	1760	1722
Elementary occupations	1437	1887	1993	2102	2163
Total	14,031	16,094	17,402	17,978	18,212

Source: UKCES (2016a)

Analysis of employment change by skill level

Analysis of trends shows that there is a growth in higher-skills jobs, continued demand for low-skills jobs such as the care and hospitality sectors, but shrinkage of what might be called the skilled middle such as clerical or blue-collar jobs. This produces an egg-timer shape to the labour market.

Figure 6.5: The future shape of the labour market

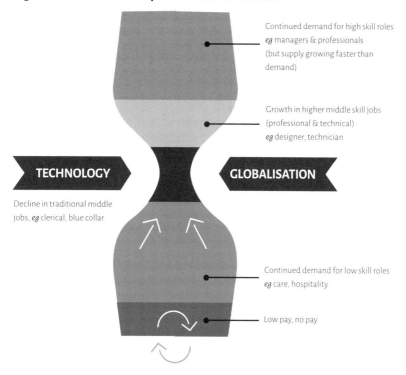

Source: UKCES (2014b)

The egg-timer shows the population being divided into sheep and goats – the sheep getting degrees and higher-level jobs, the goats getting level 1 or 2 qualifications and low-level jobs. The occupational polarisation of the UK labour market and the relatively low proportion of people with intermediate level skills makes it harder for those in the bottom 50% to make progress in their lives by moving up the ladder from low-level to intermediate-level skills and jobs.

If a country operates on the basis that there is limited supply of people with intermediate skills, you have what is called a low skills equilibrium: firms cannot get skilled labour so they compete on the basis of costs rather than quality.

If we look at employment trends for both men and women together, the picture is as follows:

UK employment – major groups

Employment levels (thousands)	1994	2004	2014	2019	2024
1. Managers, directors and senior officials	2049	2684	3304	3612	3802
2. Professional occupations	3996	5247	6596	7115	7471
3. Associate professional and technical	3205	3995	4638	4964	5176
4. Administrative and secretarial	4016	3926	3565	3315	3176
5. Skilled trades occupations	3913	3805	3611	3576	3514
6. Caring, leisure and other service	1711	2443	3134	3359	3543
7. Sales and customer service	2172	2489	2600	2605	2603
8. Process, plant and machine operatives	2395	2204	2067	1991	1936
9. Elementary occupations	3475	3803	3652	3722	3771
Total	26,931	30,596	33,167	34,259	34,992

Source: UKCES (2016a)

These SOC groups are in order of skill level 1-9. It can be seen that the number of high-skill (1, 2, 3) and lower-skill (6, 7, 9) jobs increases while the number of middle-skill jobs (4, 5, 8) is declining.

So the fastest growing sectors in the UK are managers, directors and senior officials (+1.75 million between 1994 and 2024), professional occupations (+3.47 million), associate professional and technical (+1.97 million), and care, leisure and other services (+1.8 million).

The greatest losers are skilled trade occupations (-399,000 jobs between 1994 and 2024), and administrative/secretarial jobs (-840,000).

Very similar changes are found in other developed countries, including the USA. Holmes (2014) found that throughout Europe between 1996 and 2008, intermediate level jobs were disappearing; but for every ten middle-skilled jobs that disappeared in the UK about four of the replacement jobs were high-skilled and five were low-skilled. In Ireland, the ratio was eight high-skilled to two low-skilled, while in France and Germany it was about seven to three. So the UK is doing significantly worse than other EU countries.

McIntosh (2013) observes that, with the growth of low-skill jobs, wages would rise if there were an inadequate supply of labour. But wages have not risen because there is labour supply coming from immigration, displaced middle-skill workers and former benefit recipients pushed into work by benefit eligibility changes.

The main reason for the decline in intermediate-level jobs is that these are the jobs most vulnerable to replacement by technology, especially ICT. They are routine tasks that are easily programmed, such as secretarial or factory production jobs. The jobs that cannot easily be replaced by computers are non-routine jobs both at the top (managerial and professional jobs) and at the bottom (care workers, labourers, shop assistants).

A second but related reason for the relative decline in intermediate jobs is that many of these are in manufacturing, where the country has faced a huge increase in overseas competition, especially from China. In order to compete, UK companies have had to reduce labour costs by investing in replacement technology.

Autor *et al* (2012) looked at local labour markets in the US. They found that imports from China had reduced employment in several occupation groups but most in the middle ground. Technological change associated with growth in employment in the highest-rank occupations has had no impact on the lowest-ranked occupations, but has significantly reduced employment in the middle-ranked occupations of routine production, clerical and sales jobs.

Although the number of intermediate jobs is declining over time, not least as a proportion of the total, the number remains quite large – by 2024 there will still be nearly 7 million administrative/secretarial and skilled trade jobs in the economy. As workers retire or leave, these posts will have to be filled. Even in the declining middle, we will need over a million new administrative workers between 2014 and 2024, for example. So it would be wrong to conclude that intermediate-level education is not needed – far from it. And there are many intermediate-level jobs for which training is essential, such as radiologists, paramedics, mechanics and builders.

The missing middle in qualifications

In England there is a big gap between those with university degrees and everyone else. Other countries put many more young people through courses that are between those offered at school (like A levels) and university degrees.

Musset and Field (2013) for the OECD found that many professional and technical jobs require a one- or two-year course beyond school, and in some countries as much as one-quarter of the adult workforce have this type of qualification. Nearly two-thirds of overall employment growth in the European

Union is forecast to be in the 'technicians and associate professionals' category – the category most closely linked to this sector. Many jobs will require some post-secondary qualification but less than a university degree.

In England the numbers taking mid-level vocational qualifications is low:

Figure 6.6: Percentage of adults aged 20-45 who have short post-secondary vocational education and training as their highest qualification

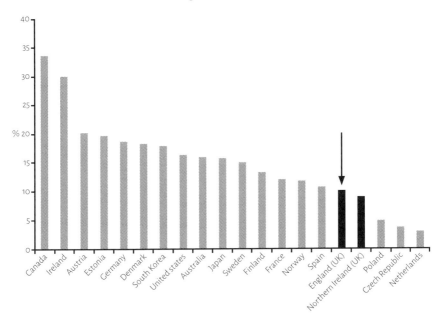

Source: Musset and Field (2013)

The graphs on the following pages show recent OECD data. Skills attainment is classified according to three levels: low, intermediate and high.

Figures 6.7-6.9: Distribution of the 25- to 64-year-old population by highest level of education attained, 2016

Low Skills (Below Upper Secondary) % Qualified

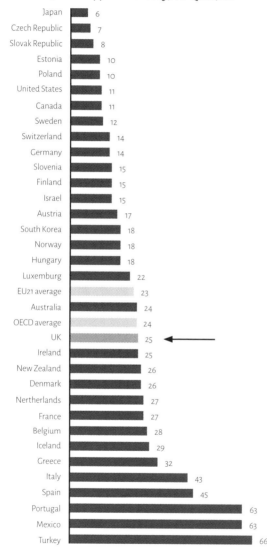

Intermediate Skills (Upper Secondary) % Qualified

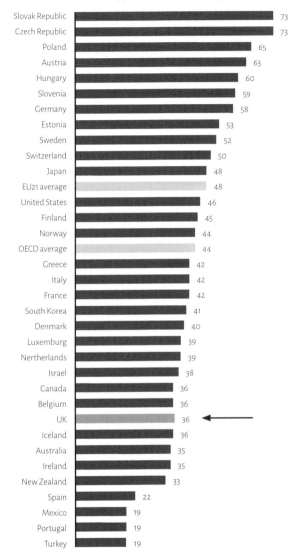

Slovak Republic	73
Czech Republic	73
Poland	65
Austria	63
Hungary	60
Slovenia	59
Germany	58
Estonia	53
Sweden	52
Switzerland	50
Japan	48
EU21 average	48
United States	46
Finland	45
Norway	44
OECD average	44
Greece	42
Italy	42
France	42
South Korea	41
Denmark	40
Luxemburg	39
Nertherlands	39
Israel	38
Canada	36
Belgium	36
UK	36 ←
Iceland	36
Australia	35
Ireland	35
New Zealand	33
Spain	22
Mexico	19
Portugal	19
Turkey	19

High Skills (Tertiary) % Qualified

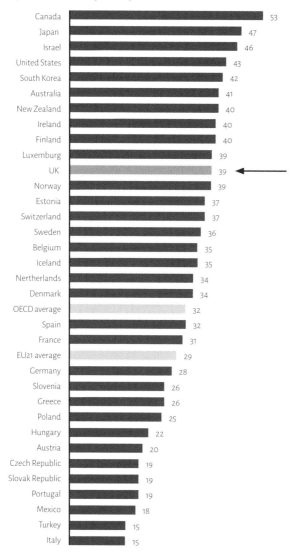

Canada	53
Japan	47
Israel	46
United States	43
South Korea	42
Australia	41
New Zealand	40
Ireland	40
Finland	40
Luxemburg	39
UK	39
Norway	39
Estonia	37
Switzerland	37
Sweden	36
Belgium	35
Iceland	35
Nertherlands	34
Denmark	34
OECD average	32
Spain	32
France	31
EU21 average	29
Germany	28
Slovenia	26
Greece	26
Poland	25
Hungary	22
Austria	20
Czech Republic	19
Slovak Republic	19
Portugal	19
Mexico	18
Turkey	15
Italy	15

Source: OECD Education Database and Labour Force Survey, ONS.

For low skills the UK is ranked 20th (*ie* there are 19 out of 32 other countries with smaller proportions qualified at this level). 25% of the adult population are qualified at this level.

36% of the UK's adult population are currently qualified at intermediate level, giving a ranking of 25th out of 32 OECD nations.

In terms of the proportion with high skills, the UK was 11th.

So we do well in terms of the proportion educated at a high level, less well in terms of the relatively big proportion with only low qualifications and badly in terms of the proportion with intermediate qualifications. What is needed, it seems, is for more to move out of the low-skills group into the intermediate-skills group.

The situation is improving

UKCES research found that, driven by the expansion of universities, over the period 2003-2013 the UK saw a shift towards attainment at the higher qualification levels (level 4 and above) and away from those without formal qualifications or qualifications at the lowest levels (less than level 2). The proportion of the adult population qualified at a high level increased from 26.8% to 37.5%, whilst the proportion with no qualifications or low-level qualifications as their highest qualification fell from more than a third to less than a quarter (UKCES, 2015a). The projected distribution is as follows:

Projected distribution of qualifications in the UK (19- to 64-year-olds)

	2013		2020		2013-2020 change	
	%	Number ('000s)	%	Number ('000s)	%	Number ('000s)
Level 7-8	8.4	3260	10.5	4148	2.1	888
Level 4-6	29.0	11.207	36.3	14,321	7.3	3115
Level 4+	37.5	14,467	46.9	18,470	9.4	4003
Level 3	19.9	7681	18.2	7188	-1.7	-493
Level 2	19.3	7437	18.0	7075	-1.3	-362
Level <2	23.4	9019	16.9	6674	-6.4	-2346
Level 1	14.4	5570	11.5	4540	-2.9	-1029
No qualifications	8.9	3450	5.4	2133	-3.5	-1316
All qualifications	100	38,604	100	39,406	0	80 2

Source: UKCES (2015a)

So efforts to reduce the UK's 'tail' of poorly qualified individuals are meeting with some success.

There is a significant gender difference in terms of qualifications. Women have pulled ahead of men in terms of achieving higher (level 4 and above) qualifications and this trend is set to continue. At present, men and women have similar proportions at level 2 or below but the position of women is predicted to improve faster than that of men.

Literacy and numeracy

A Programme for International Student Assessment (PISA) survey in 2013 found that in almost every country in the developed world younger adults performed better than older people. However

> In England and Northern Ireland, the differences in proficiency between younger and older generations are negligible. Although young people in these countries are entering a much more demanding labour market, they are not much better equipped with literacy and numeracy skills than those who are retiring.

> In fact, England is the only country where the oldest age group has higher proficiency in both literacy and numeracy than the youngest. (OECD, 2013a)

Looking at 55- to 65-year-olds alone, England was ranked 3rd out of 24 in the developed world for literacy, behind only Japan and Slovakia, and 11th for numeracy.

But amongst 16- to 19-year-olds, England was bottom for literacy and nearly bottom for numeracy. In England one-third of those aged 16-19 have low basic skills – weak numeracy and, to a lesser extent, literacy. Many more young people continue to further and higher education than their parents but they do so with weak basic skills. What is more, many of those who have passed GCSE maths and English still have low levels of numeracy and literacy compared to those obtaining parallel qualifications in other OECD countries.

Many students fail to achieve a pass in English and/or maths GCSEs at age 16. Such students are required to continue with these subjects but in 2016 only 27% of the 128,201 students aged 17 and above who resat English GCSE passed. And of the 173,628 from the same age group who resat GCSE maths, only 29% passed. So the policy of requiring students to resit is doing badly.

Figure 6.10: Percentage of adult with low skills (literacy and/or numeracy below level 2) in different age groups

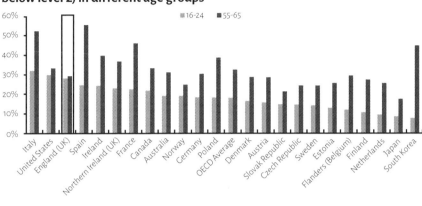

Source: OECD (2013)

In this analysis, 'below level 2' or 'low skills' in literacy means an inability to read and understand the instructions one might see on a bottle of aspirin, unable to write anything other than a short letter, note, or form. And for numeracy it means struggling with simple quantitative information, such as a petrol gauge in a car, identifying departure times and working out durations or time remaining, or interpreting relatively simple data and statistics in texts, tables and graphs.

Figure 6.11: Percentage of 16- to 19-year-olds with low literacy and numeracy (below level 2)

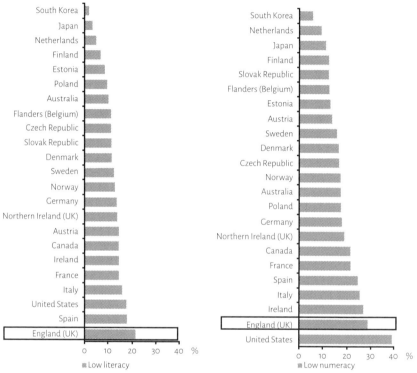

Source: Kuczera et al (2016)

The Trends in Mathematics and Science Study is conducted by the International Association for the Evaluation of Educational Achievement. It takes place every four years and attempts to measure the knowledge and skills relative to an internationally-determined mathematics and science curriculum for pupils in both Year 5 and Year 9.

In 2015 England came 10th out of 56 countries or jurisdictions for Year 5. But England has a long tail of low-performing pupils in mathematics. The variation in TIMSS scores in England is significantly higher than that of many other countries and significantly lower than that of only two developed OECD jurisdictions – New Zealand and Turkey (Jerrim *et al*, 2017).

The main reason for the bad performance of England is schooling. Although the best pupils do well, the tail of low achievers is longer than in other countries and indeed the standard reached by the large group in the middle is not high enough.

In England, the weak basic skills of young adults compared with other countries can be traced back to a lower standard of performance at the end of initial education. The priority of priorities is therefore to improve the standard of basic schooling in England, improving both average and minimum standards (which are especially weak in England).

Even for those with GCSEs that include maths and English, the basic skills outcomes are weaker than for many upper secondary qualifications obtained in other OECD countries. England should set more demanding basic skills standards linked to upper secondary completion. This means developing appropriate goals to encourage all young people to continue to develop their maths and English skills beyond the age of 16. (Kuczera *et al*, 2016)

For some pupils it would have been more appropriate to sit a level 1 qualification at age 16 rather than jump to level 2 and fail. FE colleges have 24 weeks to make up for 11 years of failure at school – an impossible task. What is more, very little information is passed on to colleges by schools. For example, colleges never see the Year 11 GCSE scripts of their students, which, if they did, would allow them to identify the areas of weakness that need to be addressed. Funding for literacy and numeracy courses often goes to students who were 'narrow failures' when they first took their GCSEs, rather than those who failed badly.

Our education system has been dumbed down so that even people with qualifications lack basic numeracy and literacy:

Among those with upper secondary qualifications (particularly those other than A levels) low-skills are more common than among the comparably qualified in other countries. So within every level of qualification – below upper secondary, at upper secondary, and at postsecondary level young people in England very often lack the basic skills of their similarly qualified counterparts in other countries ... This means that despite the rapid expansion of educational opportunities, and a relatively well qualified cohort of young adults, the basic skills of this cohort have remained stubbornly weak. (Kuczera *et al*, 2016)

The OECD found that in England basic skills (literacy and numeracy) are strongly associated with socioeconomic background measured by parents' education, and this effect is much stronger among young people.

Within every qualification level, a higher proportion of young adults in England have low basic skills compared to other OECD countries (see page 123 for a definition of low basic skills):

Figure 6.12: Share of young adults with low basic skills within each qualification level

16- to 34-year-olds, by highest qualification

Qualification level	Average of OECD Survey participants	England
Below UK level 2	29.8%	48.0%
UK level 2 and 3	15.0%	20.7%
Post-secondary non-university (UK level 4 and 5)	10.2%	21.4%
University (UK level 6 and above and some level 5)	3.6%	6.9%

Source: Kuczera et al (2016)

An explanation for the fact that we have such a long tail within each qualification level is that pupils in England make slower progress after the age of 15 than is the case in many other countries, partly because the education system in England is organised so that there is a break at the age of 16. Many students scrape a GCSE in English or maths at age 16 and then give up these subjects. A second reason is that GCSEs taken at age 16 are (or were, before recent reforms) less demanding than equivalents in other countries.

PISA is the Programme for International Student Assessment, a worldwide study by the Organisation for Economic Co-operation and Development (OECD). PIAAC is the Programme for the International Assessment of Adult Competencies, often called the Survey of Adult Skills, also run by the OECD. The graph opposite shows how 15-year-old students scored in PISA in literacy measures compared to other countries and how the same people scored as young adults a few years later for literacy in the PIAAC Survey of Adult Skills. So England scored 497 on PISA for literacy and 281 on PIAAC. Japan scored 500 on PISA (not much better than England) but 300 on PIAAC (much better than England).

Figure 6.13: Comparison of 15-year-olds in 2006 on PISA assessment with that of 20- to 22-year-olds in 2012 on PIAAC assessment, literacy scores

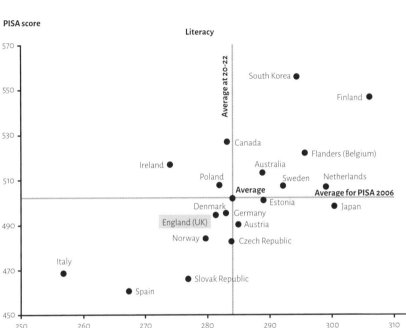

Source: Kuczera et al (2016)

What are the consequences of poor numeracy and literacy?

Obviously, if you leave school without a pass in GCSE maths or English you are much less likely to get a good job and more likely to be unemployed.

Also, if you do badly at school, you find it much harder to improve your numeracy or literacy once you leave. Adults who have done poorly at school are less likely to believe they need to improve their maths or English. They are hard to motivate, especially in a classroom in an FE college or sixth form college. They will probably be in a poor quality job where their employer is less likely to want to help them develop missing skills. What is more, labour market returns from a small improvement in their skills seem negligible – they need to improve significantly if this is going to produce an improved career trajectory.

So once a child leaves school it is an uphill battle to improve their literacy and numeracy from a low level.

So it comes as no surprise that there are 9 million working aged adults in England (more than a quarter of those aged 16-65) with low literacy or numeracy skills or both:

Figure 6.14: How many people have low basic skills?

Percentage of all adults aged 16-65

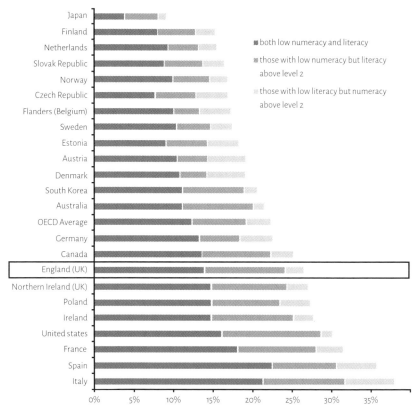

Source: Kuczera et al (2016)

Skills shortages

The 2015 Employer Skills Survey, run by the UK Commission for Employment and Skills (UKCES), found that:

> Overall, vacancies and skill-shortage vacancies have increased significantly over the last two years, with some sectors in particular facing heightened difficulties in recruiting staff, such as in Construction and Finance. Manufacturing remains one of the sectors most likely to report that their vacancies are hard to fill for skill related reasons, despite declining employment levels, and this has been persistent over the Employer Skills Survey series throughout the 21st century. (Vivian *et al*, 2016)

The skills lacking among applicants span both people and personal skills as well as technical and practical related skills. The main people and personal skills lacking commonly related to time-management and customer-handling. Skills relating to operational aspects of the role, as well as complex analytical skills, were the main technical and practical skills lacking.

Figure 6.15: People and personal skills lacking among applicants:

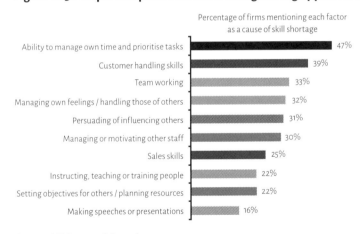

Source: Vivian et al *(2016)*

Figure 6.16: Technical and practical skills lacking among applicants

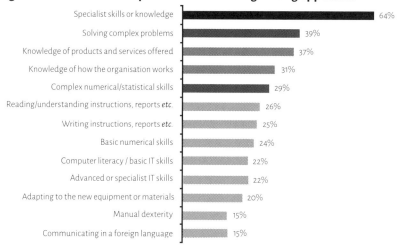

Source: Vivian et al *(2016)*

The survey found that almost a quarter of vacancies in the country are now in areas of skills shortages, representing over 200,000 jobs. These skill shortages will not be met by reliance on the country's universities. The highest density of skill-shortage vacancies was recorded in respect of skilled trades posts:

Figure 6.17: Percentage of UK job vacancies that were proving difficult to fill due to skill shortage, 2015

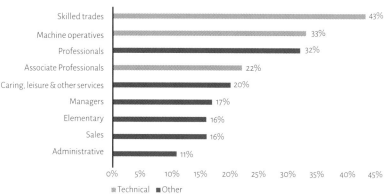

Machine operatives are increasingly in short supply, as are skilled trade roles such as chefs, metal working production, maintenance fitters, vehicle technicians, mechanics and electricians. The top four sectors with the highest proportion of vacancies affected by skill shortages were electricity, gas and water; construction; transport and communications; and manufacturing. Plugging the gap for technical skills would particularly help UK manufacturers since they are disproportionately affected by the lack of technical skills. A higher-skilled workforce is central to improving our weak productivity and competitiveness.

As a country we are good at high-tech production, but this still comprises a small proportion of the GDP. We need low- and medium-tech skills, not least to supply firms with components through integrated supply chains. Our supply chains are weak. In car manufacture, for example, just 40% of parts for UK-based manufacturers come from domestic suppliers, compared to over 60% in Germany and France.

According to the Government's 2016 Post-16 Skills Plan, areas of particular skills shortage include:

- House-building, where incentives for subcontractors to invest in training and modernise delivery are weak, and there are recruitment difficulties in London and the south east.

- Nuclear – the workforce will need to grow significantly as a result of the UK's programme, which includes building five new civil nuclear plants by 2030. As things stand, by 2025 70% of the highly skilled workers in the nuclear industry are due to have retired.

- High-speed rail, where big new projects are underway.

- Digital – there are many degrees on offer, but few are aimed at the technician level where employers report vacancies.

- Across science, technology, engineering and maths (STEM) occupations, where many more technicians and professional scientists, engineers and technologists are needed.

STEM (science, technology, engineering and maths)

High-skill science and technology jobs are a driver behind much of the UK's recent economic growth. They are an area where the UK is world-class, but where growth is limited by a shortage of skilled labour. Around 2.8 million UK jobs can be described as STEM occupations. According to UKCES, in 2013 43% of vacancies for professionals working in science, research, engineering and technology were hard to fill due to skills shortages – twice the average for all occupations. Engineering and IT professionals seem to be in particularly short supply. An increasing proportion of STEM jobs are found outside manufacturing, in professional service sectors, communications and information sectors.

The reasons for the low take-up of STEM courses are as follows:

- The fact that we allow pupils to drop maths and science when they are 16. Arguably the weakness of the English system is that we narrow our curriculum so much at age 16 – typically down to three or fewer subjects. Decisions that are taken in other countries at the age of 20 are taken by English pupils at age 16, when they know little about the employment consequences of the decisions they are taking.

  One response to this criticism is to scrap the current A levels system (and possibly GCSEs too) and move to a position where we teach a broad sixth form curriculum, postponing specialisation to age 18. This would mean that students going to university would know less in some subjects than they do now and universities might have to add a year to the length of a degree.

  Another response is to do what they do in America, where universities having a general first year with students choosing their 'major' only after they have tasted a number of options.

- 86% of GCSE physics students do not continue the subject to A level and 72% of maths students drop the subject after GCSE. But if young people drop maths and science at age 16 it becomes impossible for them to move to a quantitative or science-based course later on.

- A level sciences ARE difficult compared to many other subjects. The Centre for Evaluation and Monitoring at the University of Durham has been publishing materials about this for many years. For example, if you look at the average GCSE grade of pupils getting an A grade in an A level, you find it is lower for some subjects than others. The 'hard' subjects include Latin, maths, further maths, physics, chemistry, modern foreign languages. So pupils taking these subjects get lower grades at A level than they would have done had they taken the 'easier' subjects. There is no requirement for exam boards to align subjects by degree of difficulty (partly because 'degree of difficulty' is so hard to define).

  So, for example, candidates who get a grade B in English literature at GCSE tend to get a B or C in English literature A level while those who get a B in physics GCSE get a D in physics A level (this is called 'comparative progression analysis'). Of those who get an A*/A grade in English literature GCSE, over two-thirds get a C or better in the A level, while with physics fewer than half do (Ofqual, 2017).

- Schools are judged by their success in GCSEs and A levels regardless of the subjects taken. So they are incentivised to push pupils towards 'easier' subjects.

- FE colleges are financed by successful completion of courses. This militates against the growth of qualifications and programmes with a significant maths and science 'loading' because they are more difficult.

- Engineering is wrongly perceived as a low-status manual job (Royal Academy of Engineering, 2016).

- The exclusion of design technology as a subject from the EBacc performance measure has contributed, along with falling school budgets, to declining numbers. DT teachers are hard to recruit. But DT is an important route into engineering and design careers.

- Girls regard maths and science as 'male' subjects. In England, female students remain in the minority in A level computing (9.8% of entries, 2017), physics (21.6%) and further mathematics (27.5%) especially.

In 2015/16, only 50% of girls with GCSE A grades in maths continued to AS/A level maths compared to 70% of boys. Only 25% of girls with an A*/8-9 in GCSE physics take the A level, so the UK has had the lowest rate of female employment in engineering in Europe. Currently, 96% of those with engineering apprenticeships are male (Sutton Trust, 2015).

In the USA, Wang *et al* (2013) found an explanation. They did a national study of over 1000 high school students and established that:

◊ 70% more girls than boys had both strong maths *and* verbal skills;

◊ Boys were more than twice as likely as girls to have strong maths skills but *not* strong verbal skills;

◊ People (regardless of whether they were male or female) who had *only* strong maths skills as students were more likely to be working in STEM fields at age 33 than were other students;

◊ People (regardless of whether they were male or female) with strong maths *and* verbal skills as students were less likely to be working in STEM fields at age 33 than were those with only strong maths skills.

Here are their conclusions:

Results revealed that mathematically capable individuals who also had high verbal skills were less likely to pursue STEM careers than were individuals who had high math skills but moderate verbal skills. One notable finding was that the group with high math and high verbal ability included more females than males.

Our study provides evidence that it is not lack of ability that causes females to pursue non-STEM careers, but rather the greater likelihood that **females with high math ability also have high verbal ability and thus can consider a wider range of occupations than their male peers with high math ability, who are more likely to have moderate verbal ability.** (Wang *et al*, 2013)

Recent changes to university funding may have a negative impact on STEM subjects in universities. Before 2012, universities received much more grant money from the government for expensive STEM subjects than for the cheaper subjects like history and English. Since 2012, universities have received more similar amounts of money per student for all types of course.

In the table below, Group A courses include clinical stages of medicine and dentistry, Groups B and C include STEM subjects with laboratory or fieldwork elements (Group C is split into two bands, C1 and C2, with C1 considered marginally more expensive) and Group D includes all other subjects. The funding for Group D courses grew by 47% from 2012 to 2016, much faster than that for STEM courses (Belfield *et al*, 2017b). Universities are incentivised to expand the cheap category D courses because they make a handsome profit on them.

University funding per student per year (2017 prices)

	Course price group				
	A	B	C1	C2	D
Share of students	2%	20%	18%	28%	33%
Funding under 2011-12 system					
HEFCE funding	14,543	5337	3736	3736	2536
Fees	3681	3681	3681	3681	3681
Total	**18,224**	**9018**	**7417**	**7417**	**6217**
Funding in 2016-17 under new system					
HEFCE funding	10,180	1527	255	0	0
Fees	9162	9162	9162	9162	9162
Total	**19,342**	**10,689**	**9417**	**9162**	**9162**
Change in funding	+6%	+19%	+27%	+24%	+47%

Source: Belfield et al *(2017)*

Yet there are good reasons for young people to study STEM subjects. Graduates that study STEM subjects have, on average, higher employment rates, lower unemployment rates and higher median salaries than the graduate population as a whole.

Engineering jobs

There are 700,000 pupils in a year group in English schools. Of these only 28,000 (4%) opt for A level physics and maths, the two subjects you need in order to read engineering at university. Of these, 14,000 read engineering, but many go into non-engineering jobs like finance. That leaves 9000 graduate engineers a year – far too few.

According to projections by the University of Warwick's Institute for Employment Research there will be demand in engineering enterprises for 265,000 skilled entrants annually through to 2024, of which around 186,000 will be needed in engineering occupations to meet both replacement and expansion demand. The total size of employment for those with level 3 skills will shrink, although significant replacement demand of around 57,000 entrants per year at this level will remain. At level 4 and higher, the annual requirement for engineering occupations is expected to be just over 101,000 annually (EngineeringUK, 2017).

EngineeringUK's model for the supply of entrants into engineering roles with level 4+ skills, through higher education and higher-level apprenticeships, projects that there will be around 41,000 entrants of UK nationality annually. Their estimates of the supply from EU and other international graduates project the potential addition of up to a further 40,000 graduates, comprising a total of just over 81,000. This assumes that similar numbers of international students will continue to study in the UK and continue to be eligible to work in engineering in the UK post-Brexit. Based on these estimates and assumptions, projected supply will fall short of demand by at least 20,000 per year.

At postgraduate level only 25% of taught postgraduates in engineering are of UK origin, 15% from EU nations and 60% outside the EU. Engineering is highly vulnerable to Brexit and visa regulations (EngineeringUK, 2017).

Digital sector jobs

The digital technology sector grew 32% faster than the rest of the economy between 2010 and 2014 and created 1.56 million new jobs, a rate 2.8 times faster than the rest of the economy (All-Party Parliamentary Group for Education, 2017). In 2017 a survey by the British Chambers of Commerce found that 76% of businesses had a shortage of digital skills in their workforce.

In 2015, a report from the UK Commission for Employment and Skills (UKCES, 2015b) stated that the digital and creative sector, employing 2.1 million people in 2012, was worth around £134 billion gross value added in 2014. The report emphasised the importance of digital skills to the economy and recognised that, although digital technology was pervasive across all aspects of life, there was a significant digital skills shortage.

By 2030 90% of jobs will require some digital proficiency, yet 23% of adults lack basic digital skills (House of Commons Science and Technology Committee, 2016). A recent OECD survey found that half of the adult population in England are categorised as level 1 or below in ICT proficiency – they have 'no ICT skills at all or can only carry out the simplest of tasks such as writing an email or browsing the web' (OECD, 2016b). There is an urgent need to increase the budget for adult skills training.

The National Curriculum for schools has a good syllabus for computing, including coding, but half of schools do not offer computing GCSE, mainly because of a shortage of teachers.

The impact of technology on jobs

Advances in artificial intelligence mean that technology has the potential to replace a far wider range of tasks than ever before. Research by Michael Osborne and Carl Frey on behalf of Deloitte (2014) found that 35% of UK jobs are at high risk of computerisation in the next 10 to 20 years. These are mainly routine administrative jobs or routine manual tasks.

Technological disruption could negatively impact women more than men. Far more women than men are in the occupations most at risk of automation: 41% of women are in administrative and secretarial, sales and customer service and elementary occupations compared to 25% of men (Frey and Osborne, 2013). Women are also underrepresented in the managerial, professional and associate professional occupations least at risk of automation (40% of women versus 47% of men).

However, in their follow-up report Frey and Osborne (2015) estimated that while 800,000 lower-skill jobs had been lost in the previous 15 years as a result of technology, 3.5 million higher-skill jobs had been created by the same process. What is more, these new jobs pay on average £10,000 a year more than those that were lost. Every region of the country has benefited from the new jobs which have, in terms of extra wages, added £140 billion (2001 to 2015) to the national economy.

Technological innovation has resulted in fewer humans being deployed as sources of muscle power and more doing jobs such as nursing and care of others. Just 1.1% of the workforce was employed in the caring professions during the 1871 census; by 2011, these professions employed almost a quarter of the workforce in England.

Fastest growing occupations since 1992

Occupations	Employment in		Change since 1992
	1992	2014	
Total employment	24,746,881	30,537,415	23%
Nursing auxiliaries and assistants	29,743	300,201	909%
Teaching and educational support assistants	72,320	491,669	580%
Management consultants and business analysts	40,458	188,081	365%
Information technology managers and above	110,946	327,272	195%
Welfare, housing, youth and community workers	82,921	234,,462	183%
Care workers and home carers	296,029	792,003	168%
Actors, dancers, entertainment presenters, producers and directors	47,764	122,229	156%
Financial managers and directors	88,877	205,857	132%

Fastest shrinking occupations since 1992

Occupations	Employment in		Change since 1992
	1992	2014	
Total employment	24,746,881	30,537,415	23%
Footwear and leather working trades	40,715	7528	-82%
Weavers and knitters	24,009	4961	-79%
Metal making and treating process operatives	39,950	12,098	-70%
Typists and related keyboard occupations	123,048	52,580	-57%
Company secretaries	90,476	43,181	-52%
Energy plant operatives	19,823	9652	-51%
Farm workers	135,817	68,164	-50%
Metal machining setters and setter-operators	89,713	49,861	-44%

Source: Stewart et al (2015)

Technology destroys jobs that can be automated, such as agriculture and washing clothes, but it creates jobs at a faster rate in countries with the skill levels required. It creates jobs in areas that benefit most from new technology, such as medicine. It drives down the cost of many consumer goods, leaving people with more disposable income and that generates new jobs in leisure and personal services.

The gig economy is one sector that has thrived as a result of technology – people using apps to sell their labour. The best-known examples are Uber and Deliveroo and there are a growing number of platforms facilitating working in this way.

Automation is not a new phenomenon. The inventions of the seed drill in 1701 and the flying shuttle in 1733 both had a profound effect on agricultural labour and the textiles industry respectively, although, as with the current technological advances, these were not felt immediately due to financial, political and cultural factors that inhibited change (Wright, 2017).

But the new revolution may be different because it involves not the substitution of human *physical* labour by machines but the substitution of human *mental* labour by artificial intelligence. It is hard to know whether artificial intelligence will overall have a positive or negative impact on employment.

The 2017 Pearson Nesta report on skills for the future (Bakhshi *et al*, 2017) looks at the impact of automation on different job sectors in the USA and UK up to 2030. Bakhshi predicts that around one-tenth of the workforce are in occupations that are likely to grow as a percentage of the workforce, around one-fifth are in occupations that will likely shrink – a figure much lower than other recent studies of automation have suggested.

Jobs like teaching, hairdressing or care work will be little affected by automation, while jobs like low-level accountancy will be wiped out.

Main categories of jobs in the UK most likely to expand up to 2030:

Title	Current Employment
Food preparation and hospitality trades	479,645
Teaching and educational professionals	1,569,250
Sports and fitness occupations	170,183
Natural and social science professionals	227,020
Managers and proprietors in hospitality and leisure services	299,143
Health and social services managers and directors	88,651
Artistic, literary and media occupations	397,323
Public services and other associate professionals	524,068
Other elementary services occupations	1,066,177
Therapy professionals	123,632
Engineering professionals	475,217
Media professionals	164,649
Welfare professionals	177,879
Electrical and electronic trades	468,429
Health professionals	545,874

Source: Bakhshi et al (2017)

The table above shows jobs most likely to expand up to 2030. What do these expanding jobs have in common? They include health and education-related and other service occupations that people need. The list includes activities that are not subject to the influence of international trade: food preparation, elementary services, hospitality and leisure services and sports and fitness. The list includes lower-skill occupations (food preparation and hospitality trades and other elementary service occupations) that consumers value. Creative, digital, design and engineering occupations generally have a bright outlook. Quite a few expanding jobs require knowledge of science or scientific methods.

Main categories of jobs in the UK least likely to expand to 2030:

Title	Current Employment
Mobile machine drivers and operatives	150,233
Elementary administration occupations	197,537
Elementary sales occupations	151,411
Elementary storage occupations	399,420
Customer service occupations	469,574
Customer service managers and supervisors	150,753
Assemblers and routine operatives	243,409
Elementary agricultural occupations	92,209
Other administrative occupations	823,137
Printing trades	66,981
Process operatives	280,931
Metal forming, welding and relating trades	113,545
Sales assistants and retail cashiers	1,489,794
Animal care and control services	109,668
Plant and machine operatives	144,883
Housekeeping and related services	100,279
Administrative occupations: finance	753,388
Other skilled trades	111,153
Administrative occupations: records	396,852
Secretarial and related occupations	673,395
Construction and building trades	837,300
Elementary security occupations	280,115
Elementary process plant occupations	251,160
Managers and proprietors in other services	589,787
Road transport drivers	951,011
Textiles and garments trades	55,975
Vehicle trades	289,312
Elementary cleaning occupations	691,623
Other drivers and transport operatives	83,150

Metal machining, fitting and instrument-making trades	299,920
Sales-related occupations	166,780
Leisure and travel services	193,102
Building finishing trades	212,316
Agricultural and related trades	373,080
Business, finance and related associate professionals	688,927
Caring personal services	1,327,903

Source: Bakhshi et al *(2017)*

What about jobs in decline? Many of the jobs in this list are those adversely affected by technological advances and global competition.

In England there has been a lively debate over the past 20 years about the issue of whether schools should teach subject knowledge or general skills. The Bakhshi analysis helpfully answers this question by showing that both are needed for the future workforce. Broad-based knowledge areas such as English language, history and philosophy are all associated strongly with occupations projected to see a rise in workforce share. Foreign languages and STEM subjects are also especially valuable. But at the same time they highlight the importance of certain skills, such as the ability to make good judgements, the ability to come up with lots of ideas, originality, the ability to get along well with people.

The top five skills and knowledge attributes associated with the UK jobs that will grow fastest up to 2030 were found to be:

- Good judgement and decision-making
- The ability to come up with ideas
- Originality
- Science
- The ability to analyse needs and product requirements in order to create a design

They make the point that in the same way that certain sorts of knowledge are needed by specific occupations (a doctor needs to know science) so certain skills are linked to specific occupations (a doctor needs quick judgement and good social skills, but not originality). In planning for the future, we need to help young people develop both the knowledge *and* skills needed for future work because both are needed. A helpful conclusion.

Soft skills

Soft skills include attitudinal characteristics such as confidence, motivation, and self-awareness; life skills such as social skills and time-keeping; and transferable skills like problem-solving and teamwork. The decline of stable career paths and the rise of automation of routine work are likely to place a greater premium on these skills in the future. The Sutton Trust has shown that social or non-cognitive skills such as aspiration, confidence and personality can have an important effect on income (De Vries and Rentfrow, 2016).

In 2016, the Institute of Directors conducted a survey that showed that 38% of their members were suffering from an inability to find the right person to fill a vacancy, and the skills that these employers most often reported as lacking in young people fall under the broad umbrella of soft skills, with 33% worried specifically about communications skills, 35% about team working and 36% about resourcefulness (Institute of Directors, 2016, cited in All-Party Parliamentary Group for Education, 2017).

A recent CBI skills survey found that by far the most important factor employers weigh up when recruiting school and college leavers is their attitude to work (89%) followed by their aptitude for work (66%); these rank well ahead of formal qualifications (23%). School and college is not equipping all young people with what they need to succeed: around half of businesses are not satisfied with school leavers' work experience (56%), their skills in communication (50%), skills of analysis (50%) and self-management (48%). Many also reported room for improvement in essential capabilities such as business and customer awareness (69%), literacy and use of English (32%), basic numeracy (29%), and teamworking (26%) (CBI, 2016a).

As far as graduates are concerned, the survey found that businesses look first and foremost for graduates with the right attitudes and aptitudes to enable them to be effective in the workplace – nearly nine in ten employers (87%) rank these in their top considerations, far above factors such as the university attended (13%).

The OECD *Skills Outlook 2017 – Skills and Global Value Chains* report (OECD, 2017a) found that, powered by information technology, a growing proportion of the economy of developed countries is based on *global value chains* – the design, production, marketing and sale of a product depends on input from a range of different countries. This, of course, is a form of globalisation, but one that generates wealth. Companies able to work with several other countries to make and sell a product need employees with certain skills, including soft skills such as communication, self-organisation and readiness to learn.

Figure 6.18: Skills indicators based on the Survey of Adult Skills

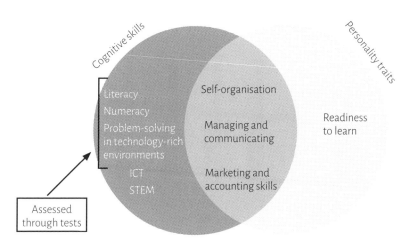

Source: OECD (2017a)

Can soft skills be taught? The research evidence suggests that a high proportion of such personal characteristics are genetic or learnt at home. They cannot be readily taught in a formal way, but they can be taught in the context of another activity such as work experience, cadet forces, community service and team sports (Gutman and Schoon, 2013; Didau, 2017). Good FE colleges like Abingdon and Witney College (page 161) regard training in soft skills as an essential part of their mission.

Consequences of the skills deficit

1 Per capita productivity is low

Low productivity (how much is produced for an hour's work) is the Achilles' heel of the UK economy. It has a big effect on living standards: if we cannot improve productivity we cannot improve real pay. On average, workers in France, Germany and the United States produce around as much in four days as UK workers do in five (ONS, 2016a). Our ability to improve standards of living over time is almost entirely dependent on productivity growth. What is more, low productivity is not new: by 1911 both the USA and Germany had overtaken the UK.

Figure 6.19: Productivity of US, UK and German industry, 1871-1990 (index of GPD per person engaged; UK = 100)

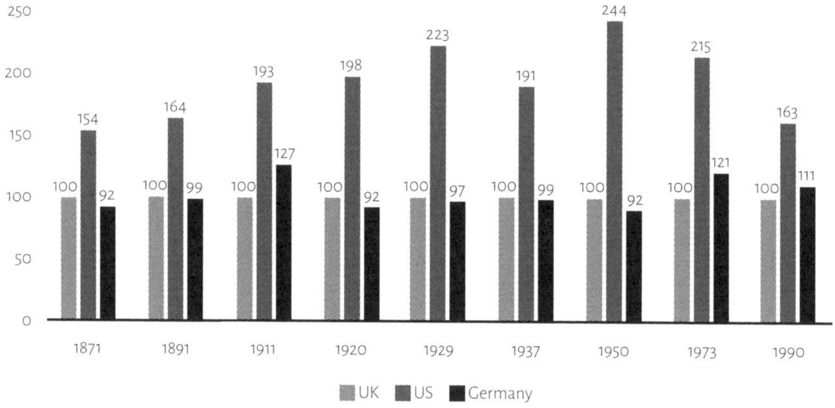

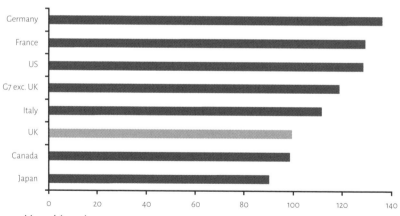

Source: Broadberry and Mahony (2004)

Figure 6.20: GDP per hour worked, 2015, where UK = 100

Source: Harari (2017)

Productivity is also crucial in determining long-term growth rates of an economy. Stronger productivity growth leads to stronger GDP growth, which in turn increases tax revenues.

Productivity grew at 2% *pa* before the 2008 recession. It was inevitable that productivity would fall slightly during that recession; what is remarkable is the fact that productivity has not improved since then – it has flatlined.

Poor productivity is not just about a lack of skills. 80% of UK employment is in services, compared to 10% in manufacturing and 10% in construction, agriculture and energy. Historically, manufacturing industry delivers much stronger increases in productivity than services, largely because factories are better able to invest in labour-saving technology. Many service sector activities rely on personal interaction with an individual or a group of people, such as retailing, restaurants, health and education, and this limits scope for productivity growth. The US economist William Baumol pointed out that an orchestra could never achieve the same productivity growth as a factory – a phenomenon now known as 'Baumol's cost disease'.

But beyond that, we know that our productivity is held back by lack of investment and by the appalling amount of time it takes for the UK to develop transport and infrastructure projects. The Heathrow runway consultation started in 2000; the current plan is to have this runway open in 2026. There is also too much emphasis in the UK on short-term returns to shareholders and not enough investment in technology for long-term productivity gains.

So there is more to economic growth and productivity than skills. But in a review of the relationship between 'basic skills' (numeracy and literacy) and economic success, the OECD concluded that 'growth is directly and significantly related to the skills of the population ... a population's knowledge capital, or collective cognitive skills, is by far the most important determinant of a country's economic growth' (Hanushek and Woessmann, 2015). They believe that the economic benefits of increasing the skills of the UK workforce are potentially huge: if all young people in the UK acquired basic numeracy and literacy by 2030, by 2095 the economy would be 13% larger than would be expected otherwise.

Supporting this thesis, Hayward *et al* (2014) did research for the Department for Education which estimated the **lifetime productivity gains** (value of output) to those who had passed GCSEs, A levels and apprenticeships. Individuals achieving five or more good GCSEs (including English and maths) as their highest qualification are estimated to have lifetime productivity gains worth around £100,000 on average, compared to those with worse qualifications. Men with two or more A levels as their highest qualification have lifetime productivity returns of around £90,000 compared to those with 5-7 good GCSEs; for women the figure is around £76,000.

Men with level 2 apprenticeships as their highest qualification have a lifetime productivity gain of around £139,000 compared to those qualified at lower levels; the premium for women is around £67,000. This figure is even higher for those who acquire level 3 apprenticeships as their highest qualification, with lifetime returns for men of £175,000 compared to those who have level 2 qualifications; and £78,000 for women. The figures for women are lower because they go into lower-paid types of jobs.

2 Low pay

Clarke and D'Arcy define low pay as hourly earnings below two-thirds of the median rate. Low pay grew sharply in the 1980s and has since remained relatively stable at more than one in five working people, or over five million (Clarke and D'Arcy, 2016). Younger workers, the self-employed, low-skilled and part-time employees are most likely to be affected. Over half the country's employees had no real pay increase between 2008 and 2017.

Low wages are bad for the people receiving them and bad for the Exchequer in terms of income tax receipts and a high welfare bill. Most people who receive welfare cheques are not unemployed but suffer 'in-work poverty' – they are people with jobs who receive benefits. Low pay for large numbers produces social inequality, disillusionment and a loss of social cohesion. Low pay depresses the whole economy because it leads to lack of demand for goods and services.

The number of low-skill jobs has increased to about 35% of all employment – many in retail, cleaning, hospitality, social care, routine clerical jobs, and call centres. This has happened for several reasons: unions and wage councils are weaker; more mothers are taking part-time jobs; since 1999 the system of tax credits had the effect of supplementing wages and helped keep wages down; since 2004 many East Europeans have been willing to take jobs on low pay in the UK. At the same time, the better-paid middle-level jobs in factories have disappeared because of automation and the decline of the industrial base in the UK.

In England there is a vicious cycle of low training, low skills, low pay, low capital investment and low productivity.

3 Trade deficit

Because we are not good at making things, we have a huge trade deficit with other countries. The balance of payments deficit in 2015 was £100 billion, the highest in the G7 countries (ONS, 2016b).

4 Regional inequality

There is a huge and growing inequality between the rich London and the south-east and the rest of the country. Many areas suffer from structural unemployment caused by the collapse of big employers, such as mining, steel and shipbuilding in the north-east and textiles in Lancashire.

In 1961 manufacturing accounted for a third of jobs in England; today it is 1 in 11 (ONS, 2015). The number of manufacturing jobs has fallen from 8.9 million in 1961 to 2.9 million today, on top of a further 500,000 jobs lost from coal mining (Beatty and Fothergill, 2016). The deindustrialisation of Britain has gone further than almost any country in the world and this effect is obviously felt most strongly in those areas which relied most on manufacturing – the central valley of Scotland, south Wales, the industrial north-east and north-west, Yorkshire and Humberside, the West Midlands. The effect has been felt least in the south-east which has a much more diversified economy and a greater concentration of high-earning service jobs.

Figure 6.21: UK jobs in manufacturing

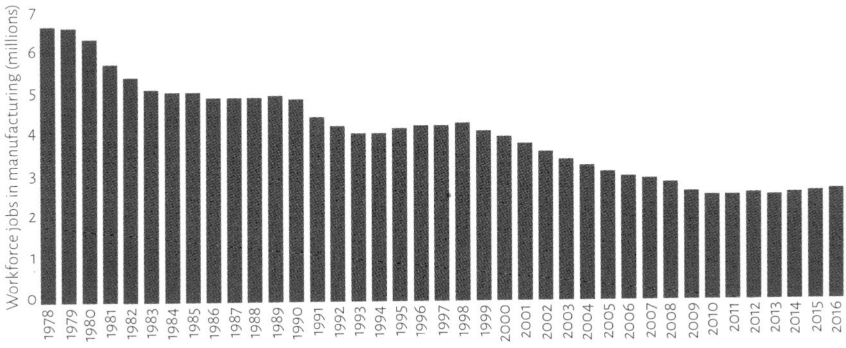

Source: Beatty and Fothergill (2016)

The London area has continued to attract people with better qualifications, more firms in the expanding sectors such as finance, more jobs offering higher pay. The 2017 apprenticeship levy will stimulate apprenticeship creation most in the areas which need it least, because London and the south-east have more of the larger firms who pay the levy. According to the ONS (2016), since 1997 London has moved from being 59% higher than the UK average gross value added per person (a measure of economic performance) to 72% above, while most other regions have fallen further behind the national average.

Regional disparities are wider in the UK than in other western European nations. In the UK, 61% of people live in areas with incomes 10% below the national average compared to only 50% in Germany, and just 40% in Italy (ONS, 2016c).

5 Unemployment

Unemployment in the UK has been relatively low in recent years. But the development of technology in the next 15 years means that a third of jobs may be at risk of some automation (Frey *et al*, 2016); this includes advanced robotics, artificial intelligence and autonomous vehicles. Globalisation means more multi-national companies may choose to locate jobs overseas.

Are we over-stating the problem?

However, some commentators have rightly said that we should be careful not to over-react to the egg-timer qualifications and jobs structure.

On the demand side we should remember that some countries have many more technical jobs than we do because they just have a differently structured economy.

> The UK's strength lies in the size of its pool of high skilled labour. In contrast, countries like Germany have based a successful economic strategy on a skills base that is weighted towards intermediate skills, with a relatively small proportion qualified at a higher level, but also only a small proportion of the population holding no qualifications or low level qualifications. (UKCES, 2015a)

If we simply increase skills with no change in the demand side, we will end up with more over-qualified people. ONS data suggests that many recent graduates are employed in non-graduate jobs (page 217).

A report by UKCES (2016a) shows that the workforce is becoming better qualified over time, but there is little evidence that this is caused by an increase in demand by employers for better qualifications. It simply reflects the fact that more people are taking and passing exams.

UKCES data suggests that firms are not even using the skills they have at their disposal. This is why 16% of the workforce (4.3 million workers) have skills and qualifications above those required by their current roles.

As has been pointed out, we still need plenty of people to do low-skill jobs – cleaners, shop assistants, security staff and so on. And we may well need an increase in the number of some lower-skill jobs, notably in the hospitality and in the care sector.

On a final note of optimism, we are doing well in terms of higher-level education. That matters because, according to the OECD (2015), more than half of the GDP growth in OECD countries over the past decade was related to earnings growth among individuals educated to a tertiary level.

How important is education anyway?

Not everyone needs a paper qualification. For the bottom 20%, getting a vocational qualification will not improve their employment or their promotion prospects or their pay a jot. They do mundane jobs that do not require a qualification, and saying that a qualification will help them is misleading. They will be trained on the job and receive the limited promotion possible on the basis of performance.

Nor should we think that getting more students onto vocational courses is sufficient in itself to improve the situation England finds itself in. We need to have an industrial strategy that drives demand for skills across the bulk of the economy. We need systems of work organisation, job design and employee relations that stress the importance of using and developing skills in the workplace. Improving vocational training will not in itself increase the number of higher-paid jobs.

Governments have tended to justify spending on education in terms of the economic return such expenditure will bring, but the evidence for this is thin. Of course richer countries have a more educated population, but that's because they have more money to spend on schooling. South Korea is an oft-quoted example – excellent education, very high GDP. But all such countries started their economic ascendency before they had the money to advance education. This is very obviously true of China: educational investment post-1980 followed economic growth; it did not precede it.

The most successful country in the world economically since the Second World War has been the USA, but the PISA tables place the USA low on the international rankings of school effectiveness. Educational standards in the USA are weak, yet economic growth has been prodigious.

In the UK we have encouraged rapid growth in expenditure on education. Total (central government and local authority) expenditure on education in 2015-16 was some £83.4 billion, 12.5% of total government spending. The compulsory education participation age has now risen to 18, while at the younger end huge sums are being spent to encourage children to go to nursery schools. School class sizes have been cut, especially at primary level.

Figure 6.22: Government education spending – United Kingdom from 1950 to 2017

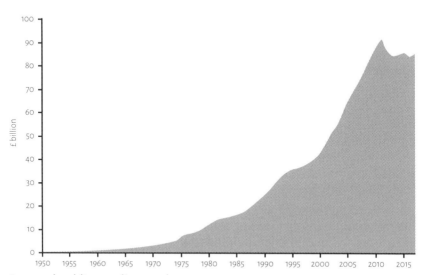

Source: ukpublicspending.co.uk

Post-18 education has exploded, especially at university level. In 2016 there were 2.3 million students of all types in UK universities (HESA). This is going to cost the taxpayer a huge amount because over 70% of graduates will never repay all their loan (Belfield *et al*, 2017b).

1.3 million people work in schools in England – over 1 in 12 of all working women and including 450,000 full-time-equivalent teachers. 410,000 staff work in UK higher education, about half teaching and half not (HESA). Education is expensive because it depends on huge numbers of people: technology has not increased productivity.

Because the burden of such cost increases is so great, teacher salaries have to be held down. So it becomes harder to recruit good teachers, the one thing which really matters in terms of pupil outcomes. At university level the student-teacher ratio has steadily worsened, meaning that the quality of the experience is much less good.

There is a danger of spending more and more money on education when the evidence suggests that the returns from education for the less able are limited. In recent years there has been a tremendous emphasis on using education as a 'tool for social mobility'. 'Equality of opportunity' is often regarded as of greater importance than the quality of education itself. This is right up to a point. All pupils should have the opportunity to go to a good school and all should be taught well enough so that a high proportion gain decent GCSEs. The emphasis on getting most pupils up to a good level in English and maths is right. But whether it is sensible to extend this thinking to university degrees is another matter.

Much of the focus on education and training over the past 100 years has been based on the assumption that the UK is in decline compared to the obvious competitors, especially the USA, Japan and Germany. The Cambridge historian Robert Tombs has questioned this thesis (Tombs, 2017). He analyses the syndrome of 'declinism', the worry we had about British decline, which started in the 1880s when German competition for manufactured goods was first felt, and again in the 1960s and 1970s as a result of decolonisation.

Tombs notes that Britain's growth in per capita GDP has kept pace with that of the USA since 1945, whether inside or outside the EU. In the 1950s and 1960s the growth rates of countries like France and Germany were higher than that of the UK because their economies had been destroyed and they were able to shift workers from their large but unproductive agricultural sectors into manufacturing. But in fact throughout the post-war era the UK has had one of the strongest economies in the world – despite having rather weak vocational training.

Throughout much of the post-war era there was a strong feeling that the reason the British economy was doing so much worse than the USA, Japan, Germany and France was that we had a weak system of education and technical training. In his detailed analysis of British industry, Geoffrey Owen (2000) concludes that this was not the case:

> The training and education system was flawed in some respects, and these flaws affected the performance of British firms in certain industries, principally those which relied heavily on craft skills. But it was not a central source of weakness in manufacturing as a whole.

Conclusion

The first problem we face is globalisation. We cannot compete across the world on the basis of cheap labour so we have to compete on the basis of skill. We need to move up the value chain by investing in both people and technology. We have succeeded in doing this with motor vehicle manufacturing, not least thanks to Japanese investment, and this needs to be replicated in other sectors such as construction and retailing.

The second big issue is lengthening working lives. If people are going to work until they are 70, many will need retraining at some point. Adult education needs to improve. At present, the limited public funding is heavily targeted at young people and those with very low-level qualifications. An estimated one million people aged over 50 in the UK are involuntarily out of work.

The third issue is the need to improve basic literacy and numeracy, where our tail of underachievement is much too long. We need to be much more ambitious in this respect than we have been.

Chapter 7

Technical and vocational education today

Under 16s

Anyone over 60 remembers that all schools used to teach vocational courses, such as cookery for girls and woodwork for boys, and that before the 1970s there were schools in every town whose function was to train less-academic children for the work they would start when they were 15 or 16.

Before 2010 governments of all types tried to promote vocational courses alongside GCSEs, but since then there has been a drive to ensure that all children have 'equal access' to an academic GCSE curriculum – maths, English, science, computing, a modern language, history or geography. There was a good reason for this: pupils from disadvantaged backgrounds had previously been pushed into less-demanding vocational courses from the age of 14, which had the effect of shutting off academic routes to university. All pupils, the 2010 Coalition government reasoned, could not only manage but had a right to access an academic curriculum up to the age of 16.

16- to 18-year-olds
Destinations after GCSEs, England

Destinations	Destination year					
	2010/11	2011/12	2012/13	2013/14	2014/15	2015/16
Number of pupils	568,410	557,365	551,585	561,115	548,280	543,290
Overall going to a sustained education or employment/training destination	89%	89%	91%	92%	94%	94%
Apprenticeships	15%	5%	5%	5%	6%	6%
Sustained education destination	86%	86%	88%	90%	91%	90%
Further education college	37%	37%	37%	38%	38%	38%
School sixth form – state funded	37%	37%	38%	39%	39%	39%
Sixth form college	12%	12%	12%	13%	13%	13%
Other education destinations	–	1%	1%	1%	1%	1%
Sustained employment and/or training destination	3%	3%	2%	2%	3%	3%
Destinations not sustained	9%	9%	8%	7%	5%	5%
No activity captured in data	2%	2%	2%	1%	1%	1%

Source: Department for Education (2017i)

The main providers of full-time education for 16- to 18-year-olds in England are schools, sixth form colleges and FE colleges. But there are big geographic differences: 55% of pupils in London go on to school sixth forms compared to a quarter in the north-west. The other northern regions and the West Midlands also have fewer pupils continuing to school sixth forms than the national average. London has by far the smallest proportion of pupils continuing to further education colleges at 25%, compared to 38% nationally. Pupils are most likely to progress to further education colleges in the north-east (47%) and south-west (45%). This reflects difference in post-16 provision available in these areas of the country (Department for Education, 2017j).

Pupils from low-income homes are less likely to attend school sixth forms and more likely to attend FE colleges than other pupils.

Around 50% of young people choose A level courses at age 16, a figure which has stayed remarkably constant in recent years. What has not stayed constant is where they study these A levels because, with the increased autonomy given to schools since 2010, many more have opened new sixth forms, driving down the numbers taking A levels in FE colleges. In many areas a sharp split has emerged, with academic courses in schools and vocational in colleges.

Many 16-year-olds used to find work when they had taken GCSEs but the government stepped in to stop that. From September 2013, young people had to stay in full-time education or training for a full academic year after Year 11 (their GCSE year) and from 2015 they had to continue learning until their 18th birthday. So the proportion of young people aged 16-18 staying on in full-time education has grown hugely, from under 50% in the mid-1980s to about 80% now.

Data published in August 2017 showed that 18.4% of 16- to 18-year-olds in England were in neither education nor training – young people whom the rules state should be in education or training but who are not. No action is being taken to enforce the 2015 ruling.

Adults (19+)

There were 2 million adults (19 and over) participating in government-funded further education in 2016. Many have a job or family commitments and travel to their local college. Participation in further education amongst those aged 19+ has been declining over time. Most of the reduction has been in workplace learning and level 2 and level 3 classroom-based learning. However, there has been a significant increase in the number of apprenticeships undertaken by those aged 19+ – rising from around 160,000 starts in 2009/10 to 374,000 starts in 2014/15. About 700,000 adults in England were engaged in an apprenticeship in 2017.

The relative failure of the UK to develop a strong system of technical education explains much of why the UK has a higher share of adults with low levels of education. OECD data show that a fifth (19.3%) of those aged 25-64 have as their highest level of education something below upper secondary level – more than twice the level of the US. Germany has lower levels of university graduates but far higher levels of workers with intermediate skills, a fact that is sometimes used to explain its substantial lead over the UK in labour productivity:

The highest level of education completed by the 25- to 64-year-old population

	UK	USA	Germany
Below upper secondary	19.3%	9.9%	13.5%
Upper secondary	34.8%	44.5%	58.2%
Tertiary	45.9%	5.7%	28.3%

Source: OECD (2016a)

Where are the vocational courses taught?

There are four main types of technical and vocational qualification providers: FE and tertiary colleges, sixth form colleges, private training providers and 'other publicly funded providers' (mainly local authorities).

FE providers in England in 2014

Provider type	Number of publicly funded subjects	Total number of learners (market share)	Median number of learners	Composition by age	Proportion that are full-time	Share of apprenticeships
General and tertiary FE colleges	247	2,214,669 (54%)	6749	Age 16-18: 36% Age 19-24: 19% Age 25+: 45%	36%	12%
Sixth form colleges	94	192,903 (5%)	1926	Age 16-18: 89% Age 19-24: 3% Age 25+: 7%	90%	1%
Private training providers	546	840,162	527	Age 16-18: 37% Age 19-24: 29% Age 25+: 32%	12%	59%
Other publicly funded providers	281	829,852 (205)	1517	Age 16-18: 20% Age 19-24: 28% Age 25+: 50%	28%	11%

Source: Hupkau and Ventura (2017)

Figure 7.1: Colleges in England

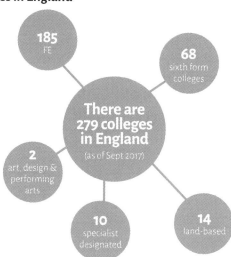

Source: AoC website

Sixth form colleges

The sixth form colleges teach academic courses – A levels and level 3 BTECs – as well as some level 1 and 2 vocational courses and functional skills. They are large – on average 2000 students, compared to school sixth forms with 200 students – but not as large as FE colleges.

Further education colleges

Further education is little understood but of the greatest importance and rarely talked about in the media. Yet it has been at the heart of vocational training for many years. It is an alternative route to success for young people who are not (usually) going to university. It gives many who struggled at school a second chance. It provides opportunities for those caught in the cycle of low skilled jobs and unemployment who want to better themselves. FE is important for refugees and members of immigrant groups needing to acquire English language skills. FE colleges are important for individual lives, for the economy and for social cohesion. In recent years there has been a perception that there is a growing gulf between those who have and those who have not; FE improves the lot of those who need education most, including those with special needs and disabilities. FE colleges are at the heart of many communities.

'Further Education' (FE) means most teaching and courses after the age of 16, with the exception of schools, sixth form colleges and universities (the latter being called 'higher education'). FE encompasses a huge range of students in terms of age, ability, subjects of study and purposes of study. FE colleges offer a mix of academic and vocational qualifications, including apprenticeships, BTECs, A levels, English for speakers of other languages, English and maths for those who have not passed the GCSE, university access courses and vocational training, often related to the local economy. Since 2013 some FE colleges have been funded to enrol 14- to 16-year-olds in order to complete their secondary schooling. Adult education includes activities not necessarily connected to work, such as history or pilates. So they are unlike the specialist technical colleges found in other parts of Europe.

In England the FE sector receives public funding of £7 billion a year to educate and train four million students. More than half of these are in 185 general FE colleges, the rest being in 700 charitable and commercial providers. There are also some specialist colleges like art and design and the land-based colleges which serve the rural economy by providing training in agriculture, animal sciences and fishery.

There are 18 or so tertiary colleges which combine the functions of a further education college and a sixth form college, teaching a wide range of courses, both vocational and academic, primarily to the 16-19 age group. In a pure tertiary model, schools within a given area do not operate sixth forms but instead young people progress to a single local institution that provides both their 16-19 education and adult learning for the wider community.

The majority of enrolments at FE colleges are adults, but because they tend to be part-timers the bulk of the college workload is often with 16- to 18-year-olds.

The people in FE colleges

Diversity

- **23%** of 16- to 18-year-olds and 30% of adults in colleges are from an ethnic minority background.
- **106,000** college students are aged 60 or over.
- Colleges provide higher education for local people from nontraditional backgrounds – the average distance between home postcode and learning location for undergraduate students attending a college is **17 miles** compared to **52 miles** for those at a university.
- **17%** of students on further education and skills provision have a learning difficulty and/or disability.
- **17%** of 16- to 18-year-olds in colleges were eligible for, and claiming, free school meals at age 15, compared with **9%** in maintained school and academy sixth forms in 2014/15.

Source: Association of Colleges (2016)

FE colleges have certain advantages. They tend to serve a local population and are therefore suitable for people who cannot travel far – mothers with children, for example, adults with a job nearby, disabled people, those studying part-time. They also have better links with local employers than many universities.

FE colleges have suffered budget cuts. After 2010 the education budget for pupils aged 5-16 was protected but the funding for post-16 education was cut. In an environment where cuts had to be made, it was felt more important to protect younger pupils than older. Secondary schools were also affected by budget cuts to their 16-19 group but they were shielded from the impact of this by using some of their 11-16 budget to fund the older students. FE colleges are unable to do this because they do not usually have younger students.

Since 2007, Ofsted has been responsible for inspecting FE colleges. In 2017 Ofsted reported that more than a third of FE colleges inspected in the previous year were 'less than good' (Ofsted, 2017). In many, teaching was not demanding enough and attendance at lessons was low. However, Ofsted operates a risk-based approach to inspection in FE which skews inspections in any particular year towards lower-performing colleges.

In his final speech as Chief Inspector of Schools, Sir Michael Wilshaw was critical. Referring to the skills shortage in the UK and the poor quality of some FE colleges, he said: 'For half a century, the FE sector has been the Cinderella arm of the education service ... We can no longer afford to accept mediocrity on such a grand scale' (Wilshaw, 2016).

Criticisms made by Ofsted (2016) were:

> We found a number of common weaknesses in the provision of study programmes, which are not confined to general FE colleges but are disproportionately evident there. In providers that required improvement or were inadequate, inspectors found:
>
> - a failure to equip many students, particularly those studying vocational subjects at level 3 and those studying below level 3, with the necessary knowledge, skills and attributes to achieve and progress to their full potential.
>
> - in almost all, teaching that was not demanding enough, resulting in slower progress and lower standards.
>
> - too few students improved their grade when retaking GCSE English or mathematics.
>
> - variable quality of information, advice and guidance was provided

to meet the full range of students' needs, such as those who were not intending to make applications for higher qualifications.

- too few students undertook challenging and well-planned work-related and extra-curricular activities.

- attendance at lessons was low, or an ongoing issue, on most of the study programmes at these providers.

Wilshaw was being pessimistic: Ofsted's own data shows that there are many good FE colleges. In the 2017 Ofsted Annual Report the proportion of general FE colleges judged to be good or outstanding was 69%. The report noted the negative impact of underfunding and the fact that relentless policy change makes it harder for college leaders to improve matters.

In 2016-17 the government organised 'Area Reviews' of all further education (FE) and sixth form colleges in England to 'enable a transition towards fewer, larger, more resilient and efficient providers, and more effective collaboration across institution types'. The options include greater specialisation, mergers or closures of institutions. This process has been rushed in some areas and has not included schools – so the duplication of A level provision between FE and schools (many with uneconomic sixth forms) continues. Mergers between FE colleges and low-tariff universities are planned, including London South Bank University with Lambeth College and Southampton Solent University with City College Southampton.

FE colleges are in competition with schools and universities for the more academic students but are less well resourced than either. They do not generally have the power to award their own qualifications, unlike universities – so when they offer degrees they do so in collaboration with a partner university. Universities have the capacity to offer the sort of courses found in FE colleges, but some universities may be reluctant to: their Teaching Excellence Framework has a focus on retention rates and expansion into the FE market would be a risk in this respect.

FE colleges pick up quite large numbers of students who have embarked on A level courses at schools or sixth form colleges but found them too difficult or unmotivating. This is especially the case in London and the south-east of England where GCSE results are so strong – to some extent these pupils have overachieved at 16 and struggle with more advanced academic courses. London has many schools with sixth forms and they have financial reasons for persuading students to stay on and do A levels – even when that is not in their interests.

FE colleges have much to be proud of. They have millions of students, a breadth of activity including employment skills, basic skills, second chance and higher education and they produce good results for many from disadvantaged backgrounds. According to the DfE 2015 dataset, 55% of those who had been at FE colleges for Key Stage 5 (*ie* aged 16-18) taking level 3 qualifications continued in education, 30% went into sustained employment and only 12% went into destinations which were 'not sustained' (did not last 6 months). The UK FE team at the international World Skills competition do very well compared to most other countries.

So the main issues facing FE colleges seem to be:

1. Uncertainty about what they are because they have so many different functions – as the examples below will illustrate. Some see the huge variety of courses on offer as a strength, but there is a danger that this reflects a lack of clarity about key purposes and a dilution of focus.

2. The complexity and ever-changing nature of the funding arrangements, which has created a high level of uncertainty. Confronted by cuts, some colleges have opted to retreat to the low-risk areas of 16-19 provision and apprenticeships. Funding cuts have particularly hit adult education.

3. Too many government initiatives that fail to address the overall system. Isolated initiatives involving new qualifications or institutions but little else are unlikely to have lasting impact.

4. The contradiction between central government controlling all the policy and strategy levers while expecting colleges to be responsive to local needs.

5. Their relationship with universities.

Who controls FE?

Since 1993 the control of further education has shifted from local to central government but with a significant amount of power transferring to colleges themselves. Colleges were given charitable status. Governing bodies became the employers of staff, setting terms and conditions rather than taking national instructions. They took control of budgets and land. This is significantly more independence than academies have but within an increasingly tough national system of control.

There have been three main policy levers that government has used to regulate FE: formula-based funding (chapter 9); regular inspections (now by Ofsted); and the publication of statistical performance data such as student success rates, destination data and learner and employer satisfaction scores.

These policy levers have been made possible by the evolution of information technology. The application of a complex national funding formula to over 1000 providers in various forms of ownership would have been impossible without ICT. Technology also allows government to compare course-by-course success rates against a variety of national benchmarks. The development of the Individual Learner Record (ILR) has been important: it is now possible to match the ILRs to the employment status and the earnings of former students as a means of judging the effectiveness of colleges.

Example: Abingdon and Witney College, Oxfordshire

This excellent college has 15,000 students including around 2000 students aged 16-19. All follow vocational pathways and around half are studying at level 3; the remaining 16- to 19-year-olds are evenly split between levels 1 and 2.

Around a third of adults take courses leading to qualifications including in English, mathematics, English for speakers of other languages, access to higher education and a range of vocational subjects. Others follow degree programmes and professional and technical qualification. The rest attend community-learning provision.

The college has a land-based specialism covering equine studies, horticulture, agriculture and animal care.

So the courses on offer include:

1. Basic skills – English and maths, English for speakers of other languages.

2. Gateway courses for students who have disengaged with school or who are NEET (not in education, employment or training).

3. Level 1 courses for school leavers who left school without GCSEs who choose from vocational pathways including Public Service and Active Sport, Health and Social Care, Creative (Art, Media, Design), Service Industries (Hair, Beauty, Retail, Hospitality, Fitness, Travel and Tourism), and Enterprise (IT, Retail Business, Hospitality, Hair, Beauty).

4. Courses for students with special needs.

5. Vocational courses at all levels in a range of areas such as accounting, beauty therapy, construction, engineering, health care, motor vehicle engineering, music technology and sport. The college makes a big effort to make students undertake 'live briefs' – projects suggested to them by local firms, like designing an app for a particular purpose.

At level 3, these courses lead to university, employment or an apprenticeship.

6. Apprenticeships. The college has around 450 apprentices studying such things as business administration, health and social care, horticulture, motor vehicle, accounting, engineering and manufacturing.

7. Advanced courses such as Foundation Degrees and HNCs, as well as Access to Higher Education and professional qualifications. They have strong links with Oxford Brookes University.

All courses are to some degree about preparation for work, so all include an element of transferable skills such as working in a multidisciplinary team, punctuality and appropriate dress.

Private providers

Ever since the vocational reforms of the early 1980s, a great deal of adult government-funded training has been carried out by private companies. There are over 10,000 of them, mostly for-profit but including some charities, and they obtain annual contracts to provide training courses and placements. They include a vast number of relatively small organisations providing training in a very specific sector. Almost no one knows much about the private providers but in England they receive around a third of central government adult (19+) skills funds.

Why do independent providers manage so much of the vocational education in England, including apprenticeships? They were established by the Manpower Services Commission in the 1980s in a drive to get market forces to improve the scope and quality of vocational courses, to 'let a thousand flowers bloom'. Private providers are successful because they are more agile than FE colleges. They have better contact with employers and they respond more quickly to their needs. Colleges have to spend their time worrying about things like funding allocation, the area reviews and the subsequent mergers. Private providers are businesses and it should come as no surprise that they are often more business-like.

Private providers are less regulated than colleges and don't (for example) have to make decisions in public, respond to Freedom of Information requests or abide by public procurement rules. They also don't have any statutory obligations to enrol young people with learning difficulties.

There has been continued concern about the monitoring of standards of private companies subcontracted to deliver government-funded training courses. In 2017 there were 472 lead providers who subcontracted to 1200 other companies who were spending £693 million of government funds. Ofsted is inevitably struggling to inspect such a large number of companies.

Some private providers are weak but others, like Rolls Royce, are world-class. According to the Education and Skills Funding Agency's 2017 employer satisfaction survey, 88% of the more than 60,000 employers surveyed said they were satisfied with independent training providers in 2016/17, while 84.6% said the same of colleges. But there were 20 employer-providers inspected by Ofsted in 2016/17, and a disappointing 55% received a grade 3 or 4 – below the expected standard.

University Technical Colleges

There are about 50 UTCs in England, sponsored by universities and local employers. They are for pupils aged 14-18. A UTC curriculum includes one or two technical specialisms, linked to the skills gaps in its region. For example, Silverstone UTC, which opened in September 2013 at the Silverstone racetrack on the Northamptonshire/Buckinghamshire border, specialises in high performance engineering and event management.

As well as their core academic subjects, students study GCSEs, A levels and other relevant qualifications matched to these specialisms.

UTCs have struggled to attract pupils because, at the age of 14, few pupils wish to change schools and few schools encourage their pupils to leave. Many schools start their GCSE courses in Year 9 – it is therefore unlikely that pupils will want to leave at the end of that year, after the courses have begun. UTCs have reported a lack of interest from industries and businesses in working in partnership with them. Their specialist curriculum has meant they have sometimes found it difficult to recruit teachers with relevant and current technical expertise. In some areas local schools view UTCs as opportunities to pass on low-attaining or poorly behaved pupils (Ofsted, 2016).

The young people who attend UTCs are more likely to be from low-income backgrounds, to have made poor progress in primary school, and to have attended secondary schools rated poorly by Ofsted. They are children who have been failed by the school system.

Between 2013 and 2017, seven UTCs closed or announced closure, despite costing an average of £10 million each to establish. As of 2017, 60% of UTCs visited by Ofsted had been rated 'inadequate' or 'requires improvement'.

But UTCs are a good idea. In the future they may adapt to taking more pupils at age 13 or 16. From 2017, schools are required to give FE providers access to their pupils, including UTCs, so that they can have better information about the options available.

Studio schools

Studio schools are 14-19 vocational schools and are small – up to 300 pupils. They provide a work-related curriculum with pupils doing vocational and academic qualifications as well as work experience. They often teach through projects. They have year-round opening and a 9-5 working day in order to feel more like a workplace than a school. A good example is the Space Studio, Banbury, which focuses on science and maths.

Studio schools started in 2010, but by 2017, 16 had closed and 34 remained. They have suffered from the same issues as the UTCs – it is hard to recruit students at 14. The future of the studio school model is in doubt.

Specialist Academies

A number of free schools have set up or are setting up with a vocational slant. Schools for pupils up to age 16 have to follow a conventional curriculum but can have a specialism. Ian Livingstone, founder of Games Workshop, one of the world's biggest games companies, is sponsoring the Livingstone Academies in east London and Bournemouth with a curriculum rooted in science, technology, engineering, arts and maths (STEAM), especially computer coding and 'digital creativity'.

The film company Working Title is to open a 1000-place sixth form college in Islington with a concentration on film and digital media.

Inspection systems

Heads of colleges say that they are battered by a combination of Ofsted inspections, the FE Commissioners and the Education Funding Agency so that they often feel they are doing nothing other than prepare for the next bout of scrutiny.

Inspection of FE colleges by Ofsted faces a number of challenges. Many colleges are very large and offer a huge range of courses. It is probably a mistake to attempt to form judgements about a college as a whole when there may be a diversity of outcomes.

Since 2015 FE colleges have been inspected against the same measures as schools, using a common inspection framework. Ofsted likes data and inspections are understandably influenced by progress measures. The difficulty is that it is easier to measure progress in GCSEs than in vocational courses, which are often assessed as simply passes or fails. While it is easy to measure value-added at GCSE by comparing your students against the hundreds of thousands taking the same qualification, this is not possible with a pass/fail course like hairdressing.

As with schools, how well you do in terms of inspection results depends in large measure on the type of students you take. If you have a large number of very weak students taking level 1 courses, your results will be depressed.

Several college heads feel that pressure to have good course completion rates encourages colleges to put students in for easier qualifications. If a college offers more level 3 STEM courses, for example, they will have a higher failure rate.

Summary

1. For those UNDER 16 the great majority are at mainstream schools where they take mainly academic GCSEs. Vocational courses have been withdrawn since 2010. University Technical Colleges and Studio Schools have attempted to offer vocational training to pupils from age 14 but are struggling.

2. What happens to those AGED 16-18 depends on their GCSE results and the nature of school and college provision in their local area. Half stay on at school or go to a sixth form college, usually to take A levels or a level 3 BTEC. 38% go to FE college, many to repeat maths or English GCSEs and study a more vocational subject.

3. Those AGED OVER 18 either go to university (almost half in 2017) or to an FE college or they become an apprentice or they get a job.

What courses are on offer?

In recent years, governments have taken the view that it was their job to specify what should be taught in FE (in some detail) while allowing 'providers' to take responsibility for much of the actual teaching. This thinking stands behind various attempts to hand 'purchasing power' to individuals (through Individual Learning Accounts (page 94) or employers (as with the recent apprenticeship reforms).

There are several types of non-degree vocational courses in England:

1. **Applied general** qualifications are vocational courses that represent an alternative to A levels as a route to higher education as well as a path to a job or apprenticeship. They are regulated by Ofqual and include BTECs, Cambridge Technicals, Diplomas and level 3 Certificates. Applied General qualifications provide learning in a vocational area, for example applied science, business or sport. About a quarter of students going to university have BTECs.

The term 'applied general' is a dreadful one that should be dropped as soon as possible. It means nothing to most people.

2. **Functional skills** are Entry level, level 1 and 2 courses in English, maths and ICT for students who cannot achieve a good grade in the GCSE. They can be standalone as well as a part of technical qualifications and apprenticeships.

3. **Technical and vocational education** often comprises one- or two-year college courses. Some equip students with the specialist knowledge they need for a specific occupations, such as engineering, computing or hospitality. Others are more general – they provide wider employability skills.

4. Employment-based **apprenticeships** (a mixture of paid work and training).

In addition, FE colleges can offer GCSEs, A levels, university access courses, university-sponsored foundation and degree courses, English for speakers of other languages (ESOL) and Secure English Language Tests (SELT), job-specific training, cultural and recreational courses for adults, and courses for people with a variety of special needs.

Many of these courses can be part-time. Some are purchased by local employers for their staff. Some, like apprenticeships, involve learning both on the job and in college. Some colleges run commercial enterprises such as restaurants or hairdressers to create a realistic work environment for their students.

In terms of the balance between qualifications, in 2017 students took 4.9 million GCSEs and 1.9 million AS and A levels. They took 780,000 functional skills qualifications, 230,000 applied generals, 395,000 tech awards, 160,000 tech levels and 135,000 technical certificates and 425,000 ESOL/SELT qualifications. These leaves a massive 4.4 million 'other technical and vocational qualifications' and 620,000 'other general qualifications' which relate to occupational areas in **general**, rather than any specific job.

There are 500 AS/A level courses on the Ofqual register but there are well over 15,000 vocational courses – far too many for students or employers to comprehend. This is the problem that the reforms described in chapter 12 are trying to address.

The pic chart below shows what 16- to 17-year-olds as a whole are doing. Most take A levels; many level 3 applied generals; many are resitting GCSEs.

Figure 7.2: Participation of 16- and 17-year-olds, 2016

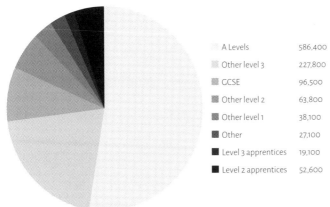

A Levels	586,400
Other level 3	227,800
GCSE	96,500
Other level 2	63,800
Other level 1	38,100
Other	27,100
Level 3 apprentices	19,100
Level 2 apprentices	52,600

Source: Fletcher (2017)

The tables on the next page summarise the numbers taking qualifications by age and by level in FE colleges as opposed to schools. Because those who go into FE have often struggled with GCSEs at school, large numbers are on level 1 and 2 courses. Very few people are taking 4+ courses outside universities – 39,200, compared to over a million on level 1 and below courses.

FE and skills participation 2013/14 in England by qualification level

	Below Level 2 (excluding English and Maths)	English and Maths	Level 2	Level 3	Level 4+	Total FE and Skills	%
Total Learners	1,007,500	1,354,900	1,600,600	1,011,300	39,300	3,913,500	100.0%
Age							
Under 19	247,600	403,100	469,500	523,200	2900	983,900	25.1%
19-24	170,500	292,700	358,800	224,500	10,300	748,400	19.1%
25-49	431,000	558,400	620,000	226,200	21,700	1,589,200	40.6%
50+	158,300	100,700	152,300	37,300	4300	588,400	15.0%
Unknown	100	<50	<50	<50	<50	3700	<0.5%
Gender							
Female	435,000	735,300	814,400	562,300	23,600	2,120,200	54.2%
Male	572,400	619,600	786,200	448,900	15,600	1,793,200	45.8%

Source: Department for Education and Education and Skills Funding Agency (2014)

A main function of GCSEs and A levels is to put students in rank order for the purposes of university or college entry and to enable employers to select on the basis of academic competence should they wish to. Grades are critical in terms of which course you might be able to do, which university will or not accept you. Those wishing to study medicine need AAA or better in science A levels – nothing else will do. Fairness and accuracy is critical, so the exams have to be subject to strict Ofqual rules and closely monitored. Teacher-assessed coursework is disliked by Ofqual because it is less reliable as a means of assessment than a written exam.

But the main function of vocational qualifications is not to put students in rank order. Their main aim is to create employability and to confirm whether students can, or cannot, perform a series of defined technical tasks – yes or no.

They have to be assessed by practical tests. Such tests must be fair and the desired standards have to be closely defined. But the rules of the game can be less rigid than would be normal with a GCSE/A level. We can be more relaxed about teacher assessment – and indeed, given that written exams are less central to the task, we have to be.

All qualifications are placed into one of nine levels so users understand their relative degree of difficulty, from Entry level then 1 to 8.

GCSEs grades 4-9 (*ie* a bare pass and better) are level 2, A levels are level 3, an honours degree is level 6, a doctorate level 8.

Examples	
Entry level, divided into three sublevels	Entry level 1 functional skills
Level 1	Level 1 functional skills, Level 1 NVQ
Level 2	GCSE grades 4-9; Level 2 NVQ
Level 3	A levels; 16-19 tech levels, Level 3 NVQ, City & Guilds craft awards
Level 4	Level 4 professional certificates, *eg* Higher National Certificate
Level 5	Level 5 professional certificates, *eg* Higher National Diploma
Level 6	BA degree
Level 7	MA degree
Level 8	Doctorate

Example: Croydon College

In 2017 the excellent Croydon College had 1400 full-time 16- to 18-year-olds, 55% doing level 1 and 2 courses, 45% at level 3. There were also 4000 adults, some at levels 1 and 2 but most at level 3. The college supported 600 apprentices. 1000 take GCSE English or maths each year, 1000 take functional skills.

The college also takes some Year 11 (16-year-old) students on contract with the local authority. Many are looked after children from outside the EU and the priority is to teach them English.

The courses on offer for students aged 16-18 are:

Level 1 or below – such as a one-year City & Guilds hair and beauty diploma for which the entry requirements are:

> *Evidence of a commitment to learn and the ability to study at this level shown at interview.*

English and maths at Entry level 2 or above.

Level 2 – such as a one-year City & Guilds hairdressing, entry requirement:

A minimum of 3 GCSEs at grade D, including English or a level 1 related qualification.

Mathematics at Entry level 3 or above.

Most level 2 students go on to a level 3 course or apprenticeship.

Level 3 – such as a one-year City & Guilds hairdressing diploma, entry requirement:

A minimum of 4 GCSEs grade C or higher, one being English or maths or a related level 2 vocational course at Merit or higher.

English and maths assessed at Level 1 or above.

Courses offered to adults (aged 19 and above) include the above and level 4 qualifications such as:

Level 4 Higher National Certificate – such as Construction and the Built Environment (Building Services Engineering), a part-time two-year course. This course is for people who have already worked in construction. Entry requirements are one or more of the following:

BTEC Diploma at level 3 or equivalent in an appropriate area.

An A level profile that demonstrates strong performance in a relevant subject area. This profile is likely to be supported by GCSE grades A* to C in maths and a science.

Other related level 3 qualifications.

An Access to Higher Education Certificate awarded by an approved further education institution.

Relevant work experience.

All students are taught general courses such as citizenship and digital skills.

The College includes a large arts department offering courses in art, design and fashion, performing arts and music, film and media – at different levels and validated by the University of the Arts, London.

The College has a university element offering full- and part-time degrees validated by the University of Sussex. 500 students a year take this route, mostly local women with an average age of 31.

Apprenticeships are offered by local employers and involve training on the job plus a day in the college each week. For example, a local school offers an advanced IT professional apprenticeship for someone with some existing IT skill.

Here is a summary of the courses on offer:

Level	Summary	Examples of qualifications
Pre-entry and entry level 1, 2 and 3	Entry level courses are one-year courses which develop English and mathematics skills for progression on to a vocational programme of study.	Skills for Life qualifications ESOL Certificate
Level 1	Level 1 courses are usually studied for one year and will introduce you to a vocational area and prepare you to progress on to the next level of study.	Foundation Learning BTEC level 1 diploma
Level 2	Level 2 courses are usually studied for one year and are designed to develop your range of skills and knowledge further so you are ready for an advanced level of study or employment.	BTEC level 2 diploma NVQ level 2 Intermediate apprenticeship
Level 3	Level 3 courses are usually studied for two years. They relate to broad occupational areas and combine practical and academic study. They are a route to university education or into employment.	BTEC level 3 diploma NVQ level 3 Advanced apprenticeship
Level 4-6	Level 4-6 courses are university degree level courses which will stretch and challenge your knowledge and thinking skills in order to prepare you for graduate level employment.	Higher national certificate (HNC) Foundation degree (FdA) Bachelor's degree (BA) Higher apprenticeship

We observed the level 2 Tech certificate course in plumbing. The striking fact was that, despite the use of an online assessment system, the teacher still had to sign 50 types of various forms – so box-ticking is alive and well. 16- to 17-year-olds also faced a barrier in terms of work experience because they could not be insured to weld in the workplace. This will be a problem with the new T levels, where there is an expectation of three months' work experience.

We observed a car maintenance course where the main problem was the fact that the course content lagged behind the development of new automative technology; and anyway the college could not afford to buy the latest types of car for students to work on.

We dropped in on a level 3 beauty therapy diploma course and saw how successful such a course could be. All the students worked part-time in local salons and all were guaranteed good jobs.

This college is absolutely essential to an area with a high level of disadvantaged students. Given the racial mix of Croydon, it also plays a role in social integration.

Applied Generals: the BTEC

BTEC stands for Business and Technology Education Council, the body that first governed the qualifications (it's now Pearson). BTECs are semi-vocational qualifications and include subjects such as business, agriculture, animal management, applied science, applied law, business, construction, engineering and sport – you can't study subjects like history or English as a BTEC. There was a threefold increase in the number of pupils taking a BTEC between 2006 and 2015.

Level 3 BTECs are mainly taken by students who are too weak academically to do A levels but do not wish to take a vocational programme which leads to a specific job. In some subjects, notably arts, ICT and sport, Applied Generals are preferred to A levels by some universities. A BTEC can be taken as a short course (so you might take three subjects at once) or a long course (so you might just do one course).

To give some idea of scale, in 2017 there were 1.9 million AS and A levels awarded compared to 230,000 Applied Generals. But the BTEC level 3 qualification is the route into university for a quarter of undergraduates – 40% at a university like Nottingham Trent.

In part this increase in popularity has been because of two unhappy developments.

Firstly, UCAS has drawn up a table of tariffs which are designed to permit universities to compare the value of different qualifications, but UCAS has over-valued the level 3 BTEC – it is easier to get a given number of UCAS points with the BTEC than with A levels. Tim Gill, a research officer at Cambridge Assessment, found that undergraduates who had taken A levels were much more likely to get a good degree than BTEC students with the same number of UCAS points. He concludes: 'Given that the UCAS tariff points are meant to be (broadly) equivalent for every qualification, some other method of calculating equivalent points scores might be advisable' (Gill, 2015).

The second issue with the BTEC is grade inflation, as the graph below shows. While other qualifications have brought grade inflation to a halt, BTEC grades are roaring ahead. In 2016 over 30% of BTEC awards were graded starred distinction. These are considered equivalent to A* at A level, yet under 10% of A levels were graded as such. This grade inflation happened at the same time as the GCSE results of those taking BTECs had actually fallen, something that was not true of those taking A levels.

Figure 7.3: Proportions of three-grade A level, three-grade BTEC and IB Diploma cohorts achieving the 'top grades'

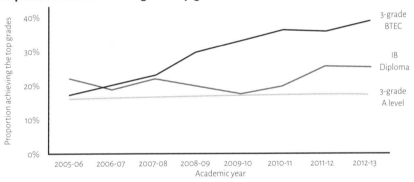

Source: HEFCE (2015a)

Up to 2017, level 3 Applied Generals were based on internal assessment by the teachers – a system which has clear advantages (it provides drive throughout the course) but is beset by concerns about teachers inflating marks. Following a decision by the DfE, from 2017 a minimum of 40% of the Applied General assessment must be externally examined if the results are going to 'count' for performance tables.

Whereas A levels all follow a set of Ofqual regulations – a common specification in each subject, common standards – that is not true of Applied Generals where there is a wide range of content, differing assessment arrangements and different awarding systems. There needs to be further change to establish common standards.

Notwithstanding these criticisms, Applied Generals are well worth having. Reforms over the period 2011-18 have maintained the 'gold standard' of A levels.

If A levels are demanding then it is a good thing to have a slightly less demanding qualification, with an interesting mix of different subjects, which can provide a path to university for less-academic students. Academic ability is a gentle slope from highly intelligent at one end down to very low ability at the other. It is a mistake to think we can divide the population into those who are academic and those who are not, with a cliff edge between the two. That is why we need BTECs – academic courses that keep options open but are less demanding than A levels. That is why we should not overdo the academic demands of BTECs.

And there is more to life than academic ability. There are practical, manual, social, visual, creative and artistic skills that aren't very easily assessed by A levels.

As T levels are introduced, the current government expects the majority of funding for 16- to 19-year-old students studying level 3 qualifications to be directed to T level and A level programmes. They are keen to ensure that the system is as simple as possible and are proposing to review the range of other qualifications, including Applied Generals. This important qualification is now under threat.

Apprenticeships

Apprenticeships were developed in the late Middle Ages by craft guilds as a way of establishing minimum standards but also to keep rivals out of the business – an apprenticeship was necessary to gain a license to practise in a regulated profession. Apprentices were beginners. After a few years they graduated to become *journeymen* and after that *masters* or *master craftsmen*. To become a master you would have to pay a sum of money and produce an excellent piece of work – a masterpiece – before you could actually join the guild.

England's long-standing apprenticeship system was almost destroyed outside a few sectors by industrial change and the increase in the number of degree-qualified people in the workforce. The number of apprentices reached a very low ebb in the early 1990s. The Government made efforts to recover the situation but there was a bad diversion in the mid-2000s when apprenticeships involved no employer, just a training scheme. Now we are in a period of reform.

No one is very sure whether it is right to describe an apprenticeship as a qualification. Probably not – it is a job with training, in a skilled occupation. So apprenticeships are offered by firms, not by colleges. An apprenticeship is a combination of work-based experience (80% of the time) and college learning (20%). Apprenticeships are of varying degrees of demand ranging from level 2 (the equivalent of five GCSE passes) to level 7 (the equivalent of a master's degree). They take from a year to four years to complete.

In addition to the employers and the colleges, in England a network of additional specialist 'training providers' has been created to manage apprenticeships.

In the 2015-16 academic year there were 509,400 apprenticeship starts. 57% were at level 2, 38% at level 3, 2% at level 4, 3% at level 5, and 0.2% at level 6. So the great majority are rather low-level. In 2015 a quarter of employers with recent apprentices were in the Health and Social Work sector, making this by far the largest group. There was limited provision in terms of levels 4-7 or STEM apprenticeships.

So apprenticeships in England tend to be at a lower level and shorter than in many countries (where three to four years is very common, for example in Austria, Australia, Canada and Germany). In Germany, around two-thirds of an age cohort undertakes an apprenticeship by the time they are 25 (though many are not able to find one immediately after leaving school). In Denmark around a third do so (Wolf, 2011). So several countries have a far more developed system than England. In England the majority of apprentices of all ages are *existing employees* rather than new entrants to the labour market.

Apprentices aged 16 to 18 are in the minority. They make up around a quarter of those who start and complete an apprenticeship and in fact only 7% of 16- to 18-year-olds were apprentices at the end of 2016. This is because of concerns over employing inexperienced young people, and because unfortunately adult apprenticeship starts can include people who are already employed and who are 'converted' into apprentices: they are accrediting existing skills. Also, young apprentices cannot drive and also cost more to insure in the workplace.

Figure 7.4: Apprenticeship Participation by Age, England, 2010/11 to 2015/16

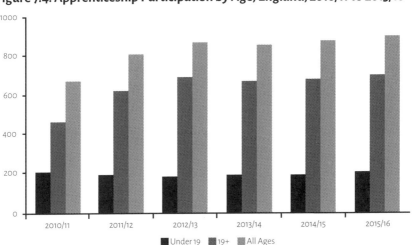

Apprentices are paid, but usually at a low rate. In 2017, apprentices under 19 could be paid as little as £3.50 an hour. They are supposed to be paid for their off-the-job training time but many are not. A recent survey found that one in five apprentices was paid below the legal minimum.

Peter Urwin's study of apprentices in 2017 showed that apprentices tend to be from significantly less-deprived backgrounds than students taking other qualifications in FE settings. The poorest students cannot obtain apprenticeships because their academic profile is too weak (Exley and Martin, 2017).

Broughton (2015) found that level 3 apprenticeships deliver high wage returns, providing a premium of 16% on hourly earnings compared to those having a level 2 qualification. But he could not find a statistically significant wage premium attached to undertaking a level 2 apprenticeship. However, although the labour market returns for completing level 2 apprenticeships are low, some use level 2 qualifications as the platform to access level 3 apprenticeships.

Following the 2012 Richard Review, reformed apprenticeships were launched in 2013. The review concluded that apprenticeships had become too bulky, with too many optional units and pathways leaving employers unclear over what skills an apprentice had actually gained. In particular, Richard felt that employers were too far removed from the development process. The reforms attempt to meet these criticisms.

Each reformed apprenticeship has three elements.

Firstly, an **apprenticeship standard** – a two-page document developed by employers that describes the knowledge, skills and behaviours required to undertake a specific occupation well. In 2013 the Coalition Government began the process of replacing the existing system of 'frameworks' with these standards, developed by self-selecting groups of employers called Trailblazers. In 2017 the Institute for Apprenticeships took over the process of standards approval. The standards have on the whole been written by large employers and there is a concern that they are less suitable for the small and middle-sized firms where most people work.

This is an example of a level 2 apprenticeship standard:

Beauty professional apprenticeship standard

Route 1 – beauty and make-up consultancy	The apprentice will be able to competently:	The apprentice will know and understand:
Instruct the use and application of skin care products and make-up	Consult, prepare, plan and deliver skin care and make-up instruction, and evaluate the success of skin care and make-up instruction with customers.	Methods of demonstrating skin care and make-up application techniques and use of tools and equipment, how to tailor your skin care and make-up instruction to meet individual needs and occasions.
Advise customers on eye and brow products	Advise and recommend methods and products to enhance the appearance of the eyebrows and lashes with customers.	Eyebrow hair removal, different types of products used for eyebrow artistry and their effects, colour eyelashes, and how to attach, maintain and remove semi-permanent and temporary eyelashes.
Advise customers on facial products	Advise and recommend the use of facial products and equipment to improve and maintain skin condition with customers.	The anatomy and physiology of the face, the range and uses of products and equipment, specialist skin products, and the structure and function of the skin.
Advise customers on nail products	Advise and recommend methods and products for enhancing the appearance of the nails and hands with customers.	The types of techniques, products, tools and equipment, and the anatomy and physiology of the hands and feet.
Promotional activities	Plan, prepare, implement and evaluation promotional activities	Venue and legal requirements, promotion planning, selling skills, and budgeting
Stock control	Effectively implement stock control methods	Stock reviews, batch control, stock rotation, purchase systems, trigger points, and vendor-managed inventory (VMI).
Making beauty recommendations to clients	Identify the targets for sales, inform and gain the customers' commitment to using additional services or products.	Service and product promotion techniques, how to make a sale, buying signals.. The principles of brand awareness, pricing structures, and product ranges.
Options		
Perfumery	Evaluate and establish customers' fragrance preferences and recommend an appropriate fragrance choice.	History, origins, types, brands, skin reaction, the principles of blending fragrances, the psychological effects of fragrances and relationship to olfactory and limbic systems.

There is nothing new about standards of this sort – they have always existed. Have a look at the standards for graduate doctors published by the General Medical Council (*Outcomes for graduates* and *Promoting excellence: standards for medical education and training*).

Employers and training providers can decide for themselves how they are going to teach apprentices these standards.

The second element is an **assessment plan**, also developed by employers, which covers what will be assessed and how, and includes additional elements such as functional skills in English and maths.

And the third is an **end-point assessment** – a holistic assessment at the end of the course, delivered by an approved **end-point assessment organisation (EPAO)**. This includes practical and written elements. The end point assessments also have to have **external quality assurance** chosen by the 'provider' from a number of independent bodies.

So there is a distinction between the role of the employer – defining the skills, knowledge and behaviours an apprentice must acquire and demonstrate – and the role of assessment professionals – designing the means by which this is evaluated at the end.

Ofqual is one of several external quality assurance options available – too many. It is inevitable that firms offering apprenticeships will seek out the 'softest' quality assurer on the market.

There were 2.4 million apprenticeship starts during the 2010-15 parliament and the aim is to have another 3 million starts in the period 2015-2020. Apprenticeship starts is one thing; apprenticeships completed would be better – only 67% of those that should have been completed in 2015/16 actually were completed

In order to fund apprenticeships and impel employers to invest in training, all employers with an annual payroll of more than £3 million pay an apprenticeship levy costing 0.5% of their annual pay bill. This involves less than 2% of all UK employers. The cost of the levy can be redeemed by employers to cover the cost of off-the-job training for apprentices but not other costs, such as in-house training and the apprentices' salaries.

The cost of training an apprentice is split between the employer and the government – what is called 'co-investment'. Large firms that pay the levy access this money to pay for apprentices along with a 10% top-up paid by the government. Smaller firms, who don't pay the levy, contribute 10% of the cost of each apprenticeship they create, while (in theory) the government funds the rest.

Critics argue that the apprenticeship levy is a very blunt tool in which contributions are unlikely to bear any relation to the skills needs of individual employers and their sector more generally. It is not sufficiently focused on those parts of the economy, and of the country, where training is most needed. 40% of levy-paying employers based in the southeast. The levy is encouraging businesses to use funding for management courses for existing employees instead of offering lower-level apprenticeships to young people and new employees. It is especially important to strengthen level 2 provision, where apprenticeships can make the biggest difference to the young and the disengaged.

The 20% off-the-job training rule for apprenticeships has been widely criticised. Different types of apprenticeships need different levels of off-the-job training: some more, some less. For many employers, the 20% level is too difficult to manage – it means doing without an employee for one day a week. Apprentices who are required by government rules to do extra maths and English require further study time on top of the 20%, meaning employers see those candidates as even less attractive. So apprenticeships are much harder to find for 16- to 18-year-olds who did badly at school, which includes many of those from disadvantaged backgrounds.

The number of apprenticeships has fallen since the introduction of the levy. The 10% financial contribution from non-levy-payers and the mandatory requirement for 20% off-the-job training are blamed. The organisations that are going to manage apprenticeships ('providers') have to bid for ESFA money, but in 2017 the management of this 'procurement process' was appalling.

Ofsted have spelt out some of the issues with apprenticeships:

> Our 'Getting ready for work' survey found that there were a number of financial, social, geographical and cultural barriers that limited the take-up of apprenticeships. 'Fear of missing out' on traditional routes such as sixth forms and universities is a major barrier. The quality of apprenticeships is also a factor: both students and parents were clear-sighted about the quality of apprenticeships. There was good awareness that the apprenticeships of some major national businesses, such as Rolls-Royce, were excellent destinations. Apprenticeships at post-18 were gaining wider acceptance and credibility among students at school sixth forms, particularly for career paths such as engineering or accountancy. However, the more widely available apprenticeships were perceived to be of variable quality, and both parents and students were concerned about the consequences of taking up a placement that was primarily about 'cheap labour' or where low quality might restrict rather than widen future options. (Ofsted, 2016)

In the 2016-17 academic year, 189 apprenticeships providers were judged by Ofsted on the delivery of their apprenticeships. 6% were found to be 'outstanding', 43% 'good', 40% were rated 'requires improvement' and 11% were 'inadequate'.

The reforms to apprenticeships have been criticised in other ways. There is no overall quality control and many providers are untested. The quality of apprenticeships is hard to police and some employers may continue to offer low-quality training and turn the apprenticeship into a tick-box exercise. It is true that employers set the standards, but arguably they should be benchmarked against German apprenticeship standards to confirm that we are not setting the bar too low. It is often said that about a third of standards used at the moment are good, a third are satisfactory and a third are poor.

The use of end-point assessments means that apprentices who fail leave the programme without anything tangible (such as unit accreditation). This system disadvantages those apprentices who need bite-sized step-by-step progress – often those who are most in need of an apprenticeship to make progress in their lives.

In a report for the Sutton Trust, Fuller *et al* (2017) looked at the progress of 565,000 16-year-olds over 12 years and found that:

- Just 7% of young men and 11% of young women who were eligible for free school meals took up an apprenticeship at level 3 (A level standard).
- There is a stark gender difference in earning prospects for young people entering apprenticeships – almost four times higher for men than for women.
- Only 17% of young people who took a level 2 (GCSE standard) apprenticeship progressed to a level 3, though this rose to 25% in later years.
- Two-thirds of current apprentices were previously existing employees and have been 'converted' into apprentices, making apprenticeship a largely adult programme. Employees may not be improving their skills if they are merely accredited for their existing competences.

Young people who do apprenticeships improve their prospects of getting a stable job because they have the work experience that is so highly valued by employers. But unfortunately, schools are quite bad at promoting apprenticeships to their leaving students.

Degree apprenticeships

From September 2015, places on the first degree apprenticeships became available in four industries: digital, automotive engineering, banking relationship management, and construction. Degree apprenticeships in many other jobs have since been announced, linked to specific universities and colleges. Degree apprenticeships are small in number – 2000 between 2015 and 2017. But they are growing rapidly. Most are local firms linking with local universities but there are exceptions such as the Dyson Institute at Malmesbury (accredited by the University of Warwick), which recruits nationally.

A degree apprentice is paid by and employed by a firm and the apprentice takes a relevant part-time degree at a university or college over three to six years. So the attractions of a degree apprenticeship are that the apprentices have a paid job and get a university degree with no fees. They are more-or-less guaranteed a job with a good firm when they graduate, but having the degree keeps options open.

For the employees, they are more likely to attract good applicants. Or they can offer degree apprenticeships to existing employees as a way of encouraging them to stay.

For the universities, they will attract good students and will forge links with local companies. Degree apprenticeships might be a way to win back the part-time students, especially the mature learners and those from lower socioeconomic groups who are traditionally debt averse,

There is a worry that degree apprenticeships are potentially so attractive that they will all be snapped up by middle-class students. On the other hand, if they become high status, as they might, they will help raise the status of apprenticeships generally. There is also a concern that degree apprenticeships are not really apprenticeships at all – there is limited interplay between the university course and the in-work experience; they look more like repackaged academic degrees than apprenticeships.

Nuclear scientist and engineer degree apprenticeship: part of the standards

Occupational Skills & Knowledge:

At the end of the apprenticeship the nuclear scientist and nuclear engineer will be able to:

1. Work competently in a technical nuclear environment, understand and promote personal responsibility for Health, Safety, Radiation

Protection, Environmental Protection, Quality, Security, Safeguards and principles of Risk Management.

2. Analyse engineering and scientific problems selecting and using mathematical, engineering and scientific tools to provide suitable solutions to nuclear applications, with considerations of the entire life cycle of a nuclear facility.

3. Develop and critically apply knowledge of the concepts, principles and theories of engineering science relevant to the interdisciplinary fields of nuclear technology.

4. Demonstrate an understanding of stakeholder requirements, commercial awareness, business improvement, project and business management techniques relevant to the nuclear industry.

5. Apply their science or engineering discipline knowledge to the development, operation, maintenance and progression of technologies used for Decommissioning (e.g. remote handling and robotics), Waste Management, Reprocessing, and Nuclear Power Generation.

6. Specify, plan, manage, conduct and report on nuclear projects

7. Synthesise information from a variety of sources and apply to the solution of a particular nuclear technology application.

8. Accurately observe, record and draw conclusions from data and experimental evidence, recognising inherent uncertainties and limitations.

9. Apply design processes including materials selection that meet nuclear industry standards.

10. Demonstrate an understanding of Regulatory requirements both national and international.

11. Develop technical reports that meet requirements of the prevailing verification process.

12. Demonstrate knowledge of the nuclear industry (past, present and future) and the business, political and community environment in which the company operates including personal role within the organisation, ethical practice and codes of conduct.

13. Demonstrate an understanding of root cause analysis and learning from experience (LFE) processes.

14. Demonstrate knowledge of the technology, safety, environmental and economics of nuclear fuels and the nuclear fuel cycle.

15. Apply the standards for nuclear professional practice as required by the industry and professional body institutions.

Contains public sector information licensed under the Open Government Licence v3.0

Traineeships

Introduced in 2013, traineeships are a training programme for low-skilled people aged 16-24 to help prepare them for an apprenticeship or job. They are designed for young people who are unemployed, have little work experience, and are qualified below level 3, but who can be prepared for employment or an apprenticeship within six months. The traineeship programme has three core elements:

- A work placement
- Work preparation training
- English and maths support if required

Traineeships are unpaid, but employers can cover travel and expenses and trainees can also receive Jobseekers Allowance.

Traineeships suffer from a lack of secure funding. Part of the funding is dependent on trainees progressing to an apprenticeship job or further study within 6 months of completing the traineeship, but a six-month traineeship cannot rectify what 11 years of schooling failed to provide.

Only 600 of 3400 completions for 19- to 24-year-old trainees in 2015/16 went on to start an apprenticeship. The figure was higher for under-19s – with 3200 of 7000 completions progressing to an apprenticeship. Overall progression to apprenticeships stood at only 37%, but many others find jobs as a result of having completed a traineeship.

Maths and English

Everyone seems to agree that a reasonable level of numeracy and literacy is the most helpful single requirement if a young person is going to develop useful technical and vocational skills. Without numeracy and literacy it is hard to make a success of vocational courses. But in FE colleges, a high proportion of new learners (more than half the students in around half the colleges) do not have at least a GCSE grade C in English, mathematics or both.

Things are improving. The proportion of young people eventually attaining level 2 qualifications in English and maths by age 18 has been increasing each year, from 46% in 2005 to 70% in 2015. This has predominantly been driven by increases in GCSE passes at age 16, but the proportion of those without level 2 English and maths at 16 but who attain both by age 18 has also risen.

In my interview with Alison Wolf, she commented:

> Students desperately need maths GCSE, the only qualification which is widely recognised by employers. So those who just fail maths GCSE should retake it. However, it is very dispiriting to have to resit an exam you failed at school. That is why they need to take a different GCSE, an adult GCSE (yes, we have had adult GCSEs in the past). This would place more emphasis on skills which adults actually need in their work, less on algebra and geometry perhaps.

Since 2015 all those with a D/3 grade in maths or English GCSE have been required to continue study of the GCSE alongside their FE courses. Those with lower GCSE grades study functional skills in English and/or maths.

Functional skills are offered at Entry level, level 1 and 2. The emphasis in terms of the syllabus is on everyday and work contexts. They are one of the highest-volume qualifications after GCSEs, with 830,000 certifications a year. Unfortunately standards are not uniform across the many different awarding organisations offering functional skills, something Ofqual is tackling. They are pass/fail only.

Functional skills qualifications are offered in English, maths and ICT. The level of functional skills taken will depend on the level the student is at. Quite a large number of recently arrived foreign students take Entry level Functional Skills English.

After 2015 the English language and maths GCSEs were made more demanding, worsening the problem for the weaker 50%. Arguably this large group are spending too much time on academic elements of these courses when in fact they need to concentrate wholeheartedly on functional skills – the foundation stones of reasonable literacy and numeracy. Functional skills need to be a bit demanding or they lose any value to employers; the students themselves need to know that employers welcome the qualification.

The high failure rate of those resitting GCSE maths or English a year after they have left school is not surprising. Steinberg *et al* (2009) show that 16- to 17-year-olds are mature cognitively (see graph opposite) but immature psychosocially – which means they are less good at planning for their future, more likely to take risks, less likely to persevere, less likely to defer gratification. Psychosocial maturity has to wait until they are in their 20s. This is an important finding for those trying to motivate 16- to 21-year-olds.

Cognitive maturity is high by age 16, psychosocial maturity is low until age 25, as this graph shows.

Figure 7.5: Proportion of individuals in each age group scoring at or above the mean for 26- to 30-year-olds on indices of cognitive capacity and psychosocial maturity

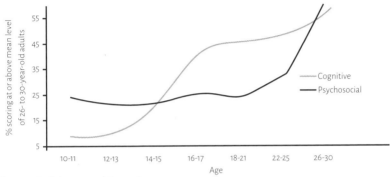

Source: Steinberg et al (2009)

The truth is that some of those who have actually passed GCSE maths and English still have very weak literacy and numeracy. The standards we set for a pass in this country are low. That is why all students doing vocational courses should continue with these subjects to some degree.

Technical qualifications

In 2017 students took 395,000 technical awards, 135,000 technical certificates and 160,000 tech levels.

Technical awards are level 1 and level 2 qualifications. At Key Stage 4, students sometimes take up to three technical awards alongside academic GCSEs. An example would be the City & Guilds level 2 Technical Award in Constructing and Maintaining the Built Environment.

Technical certificates are level 2 technical qualifications. They are for students aged 16+ who wish to specialise in a specific industry or prepare for a particular job. An example would be City & Guilds level 2 Diploma in Sound and Music Technology.

Level 3 Tech levels – for example, there is a City & Guilds level 3 Advanced Technical Certificate in Agriculture, or AQA level 3 Foundation Technical Level Business: Marketing Communications, or City & Guilds level 3 Advanced Technical Diploma in Hairdressing.

By 2022 T levels (page 274) will replace Tech levels.

Direct Claims Status (DCS) qualifications

Direct claims qualifications are those where the awarding organisation devolves responsibility for approving certification to the individual centres. For example, there might be a social care qualification run by a college. The awarding body will appoint an 'external quality assurer' who has to ensure that the college follows agreed processes and assesses students to the correct standard. Sometimes the qualification is a certificate that simply states that the candidates have 'completed the course'. The college will have an approved 'Internal Quality Assurer' whose job is to check that the agreed processes and standards have been adhered to. Usually the college will be visited by the awarding body every one to three years to check that standards are being maintained, often by looking at portfolios of work. But the key point is that the college (or private provider) is trusted to decide themselves whether a student has 'passed' and gets the certificate or not. There is no exam marked by an independent organisation in the way there is with GCSEs and A levels.

DCS can work well and it cuts down on bureaucracy and costs. It enables colleges to tell students if they have passed as soon as the course is completed. But of course the system can be corrupted. The awarding organisations make money from the DCS qualifications and may be tempted to turn a blind eye to maladministration. The only penalty the awarding bodies have at their disposal is to suspend a college's DCS status and that will cost them money. There are long gaps between the inspection visits when nothing is checked. It is easy for colleges to hide work they do not want seen. Tutors at the centres may be under pressure to pass all their students and be tempted to give undue levels of help.

Access courses

Access courses are not necessarily vocational, but as they constitute an important part of what FE colleges offer they are included here. They are designed to get students who have not done well at school to a sufficiently high level that they can go to university. The courses are negotiated with specific local universities who specify the levels of knowledge and skills they are looking for. In recent years there has been a big emphasis on widening participation – getting more black students or those from low-income homes, for example, into universities. Access courses have been a great success, measured by the large numbers of former Access students entering the professions. They are also evidence that FE colleges and universities are capable of working together for their mutual benefit.

Example: Capital City College Group

The Capital City College group comprises three colleges and one training centre in London with a massive 37,000 students and 1700 staff between them. The annual budget is £110 million, as big as many universities. Such a large group obviously achieves economies of scale; for example, resources to support areas within the four centres that need improving. Each college retains its identity and board.

The group serves the local economy of central London and beyond; their courses include:

- Levels 1 and 2 courses including traineeships and BTECs.

- Level 3 A levels, BTECs, vocational courses including Access to Higher Education Diplomas in Business, English and Media Studies, Health and Human Sciences, Hospitality, Leisure and Tourism, Law, Midwifery, Nursing, Pharmaceutical and Bio-Medical Sciences, Science and Engineering, Teacher Training. If a student finishes a degree the loan they took out for the Access course is written off.

- University of the Arts London diplomas in art, design and creative industries at different levels.

- English for speakers of other languages (ESOL), although the numbers have declined as people who need to learn English have been progressively priced out of London.

- Courses for students with learning difficulties or disabilities.

- Apprenticeships at several levels.

- Functional skills (maths, English and ICT).

- Alternative education courses for difficult pupils aged 14-16 who have been referred by their school or an agency.

- Level 4/5 Foundation degrees. A Foundation Degree is a level 4/5 qualification and the equivalent to the first two years of a full Honours Degree. It can be studied part-time. It is a qualification in its own right but can lead on to level 6 courses.

- Level 6 Honours degrees in Hospitality Management, Culinary Arts, Business Management or Tourism Management.

- Adult community courses such as cookery or pottery commissioned by Camden Council.

When I visited the group, I saw three classes that illustrate the diversity of the courses on offer:

1. Courses in cooking, catering and hospitality. Many students enter at the age of 16, starting on a level 1 course then working up year-by-year to level 2 and 3. They learn how to be chefs, working under expert supervision in excellent kitchens. The food they produce is served in a brasserie and restaurant to the general public. Some go off to do apprenticeships; all do work experience as part of the courses. 98% go straight into jobs.

   Why should they not go straight from school to be trained in a hotel or restaurant? The answer is that, in the eyes of the employers, many are simply not work-ready. They have to learn punctuality, communication skills, self-discipline as well as technical skills in the college. What is more, they will get a far wider range of experience at a college than they would working as a trainee for a restaurant, not least because they will do work experience in a range of different settings. Escoffier and the Ritz are patrons of the catering and hospitality departments.

2. A group of adult opticians taking a two-year, one-day-a-week course in contact lenses. Some were paying for themselves; some were sponsored by their employer.

3. A group of students in their 20s taking a one-year level 3 applied science Access course which will permit them to enter university to study for a degree in such things as pharmacy, ophthalmics, radiography or nursing.

The Capital City College group makes part of its income from sources other than taxpayer-funded grants or student loans. Some comes from the restaurants, some from letting space to outside users, but most comes from employers who pay colleges to run apprenticeship training and bespoke courses, such as the opticians course described above.

The CEO of the group stressed the point that the courses they offer are a response to demand. There has been a big recent increase in the number of 16- to 18-year-olds wanting courses in health and care, for example, so these have expanded accordingly. Knowing about local labour requirements matters hugely. People often tease FE for turning out too many hairdressers, but there is a big demand for trained hairdressers, while fewer want to be engineers or digital technologists.

The value of a course can go beyond its vocational value. A BTFC in performing arts may not lead to a job in acting but it will teach literacy, teamwork and other useful employment skills, and a student refused a place on a performing arts course may be lost entirely to further education that might enable them to succeed in alternative work.

The successes of FE

In many ways, FE colleges in England have been and are a great success. They have a critical role as a provider of education and training for both 16- to 18-year-olds and adults. Post-16 participation, retention and success rates have all risen. The results of international skills competitions have shown how brilliantly trained some FE students are. We have a system in England that is quite well regarded by other governments abroad. Our colleges have survived – and in some cases thrived – despite political meddling, media neglect and a society that values university education over everything else. Self-governing colleges have provided very capable at turning themselves around when they fall into difficulty and very flexible in absorbing and acting on new imperatives.

The 2011 Wolf Report suggested that: 'Among 16 to 19 year olds ... at least 350,000 get little to no benefit from the post-16 education system [each year]' based on statistical evidence that identified little or no return to a large amount of vocationally oriented learning at level 2 and below.

Bibby *et al* (2014) dispute this finding. FE engages with the most disadvantaged in society, who often have a very weak exams and employment record, and they get quite a good wage return from FE learning. They estimated the earnings, employment probability and probability of being on benefits for those who achieve their highest learning aim whilst studying at an English FE institution, relative to those who had the same highest learning aim, but did not achieve.

The three- to five-year average earnings premiums were: 2% for those achieving a highest qualification below level 2, 11% for full level 2 qualifications; 9% for full level 3 and 8% for level 4+. All qualifications from level 2 upwards also made it more likely that you would have a job and not be on benefits.

Gavan Conlon and Pietro Patrignani (2013) combined information from the Individual Learner Record between 2002/03 and 2005/06 on learner attainment, earnings information and employment information from HM Revenue and Customs, and benefit receipt and duration information. They found that the average hourly earnings associated with vocational attainment at level 1 and level 2 ranged between 2.5% and 5% compared to non-completers. In contrast, at level 3, although there was a relatively limited earnings return in the first two to three years post completion, the earnings premium increased relatively quickly in subsequent years.

A similar outcome was found with level 4 qualifications, with completers achieving an immediate 4% earnings premium compared to non-completers, which further increased to almost 12% seven years post-completion.

The subject studied matters greatly. The subjects appearing to offer the strongest returns at level 3 were Engineering and Manufacturing Technologies and Construction, Planning and the Built Environment, with level 3 completers achieving an 8.3% increase in annual earnings in the first year post-qualification relative to non-completers, which increased steadily to approximately 15% in the fourth year post-completion and beyond.

There is also plenty of evidence that most apprenticeships produce good results. The 2015 BIS employer survey results (Department for Education and Department for Business, Innovation & Skills, 2016) suggested that 86% of employers were happy with the quality of apprenticeship training and 87% happy with the quality of assessment. Employers said they experienced a wide range of benefits as a result of training apprentices. Improved productivity, product and service quality, staff morale, staff retention, as well as the generation of new ideas, were all cited by at least two-thirds of employers.

Baroness Sharp's report for the Independent Commission on Colleges in their Communities (Sharp, 2011) found that many colleges have very strong local brands and are 'active shapers in their communities', fostering aspiration and providing opportunities for individuals to advance their social, economic and personal ambitions.

But vocational training in England is not as strong as it could be

Frontier Economics (2017) concluded that the characteristics of good vocational qualifications are that they should be:

- *Recognisable.* A qualification is recognisable if all relevant stakeholders can quickly and easily identify learners' skill levels.

- *Rigorous.* A qualification is rigorous if all learners holding a particular qualification meet the required standard.

- *Responsive.* A qualification is responsive if its content remains relevant and responds positively to changing employer and learner demands.

- *Innovative.* Awarding organisations are able to innovate to find new and better ways of meeting current or anticipated demand.

There are a number of reasons why vocational qualifications, especially those for 16- to 19-year-olds, do not always have these characteristics. In assessing the strengths and weaknesses of vocational education in England we are helped by recent research reports including:

- The OECD *Skills Beyond Schools* (Musset and Field, 2013) and *Survey of Adult Skills* reports (OECD, 2013; OECD, 2016c)

- *Review of Vocational Education: The Wolf Report* (Wolf, 2011)

- The Sainsbury Report, *Report of the Independent Panel on Technical Education* (Sainsbury, 2016)

1 Failure by government to give vocational training priority

The Institute for Fiscal Studies released a report in 2017 tracing the spending patterns on education by governments over the past two decades. Back in 1990, spending per student in FE was 50% higher than in secondary schools, whereas now it is 10% lower.

The annual public investment for each apprentice aged 19 and over is 18% of that spent on each higher education student annually (University and College Union, 2016). The government in England spends about £1000 a year on adults taking FE qualifications, while in universities students take out income-contingent loans of up to £9250 a year to pay for tuition, with additional funding from the government for lab-based subjects. Universities, unlike FE colleges, also have a huge additional income stream from overseas students. The university sector expanded from one in six to 50% of young people in 30 years.

Figure 7.6: FE college and university income changes 2009/10 to 2015/16

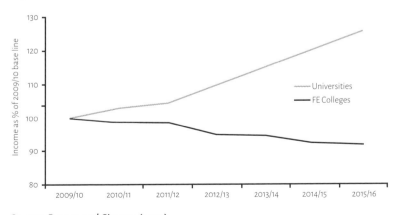

Source: Porter and Simons (2015)

Funding for adult skill training has been cut:

Figure 7.7: Adults skills budget in England

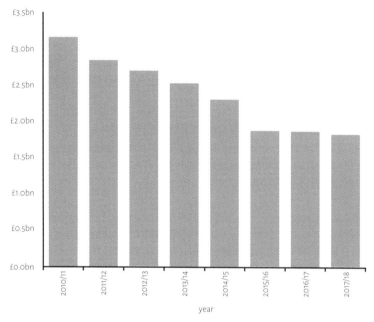

year

Source: Dromey and McNeil (2017)

Schools are judged by the government in terms of the proportion of their pupils taking so-called EBacc subjects (all academic subjects) and these are embedded in the main measure of secondary school success – Progress 8. Vocational qualifications have been stripped out of school curricula in recent years.

The size of the post-18 vocational education sector is small by international standards – under 10% of the cohort – compared to other OECD countries where sometimes up to one-third of the entire cohort have post-18 vocational qualifications as their highest qualification.

2 Central government sometimes gets it wrong

As chapter 5 suggests, there have been repeated cycles of policy failure, each starting with the newly available data suggesting there is a problem; the rapid imposition of a poorly evidenced programme to tackle it; and then mounting evidence of unintended outcomes. One recent example has been the requirement that all FE students with a grade D/3 in English or maths GCSEs should resit the exam. The problem had been identified correctly (too many students with weak literacy or numeracy), but the solution was wrong (resitting a GCSE has been an inadequate way of improving the situation).

Central government control has often meant there has been failure to consult with employers or those in colleges – too much has been decided in darkened rooms. Because ministers are too often in a hurry to make an impact they have introduced new qualifications without a pilot.

The frequency of change in funding rules and inspection requirements has had a very unfortunate consequence. College leaders have had to prioritise the tactical skills needed for their institution to survive from day to day, rather than the strategic thinking demanded to take the sector forward in the national interest. There has been inadequate focus on the things that matter most.

Mick Fletcher, Julian Gravatt and David Sherlock conclude:

> The way in which policy levers have been used in FE has proved to be an effective method of ensuring compliance with government instructions and of delivering a rapid response to changes in policy. The outcomes for users of FE, however, have seldom been as planned or expected and occasionally were resoundingly negative. Furthermore, one clear consequence of a nationally managed system is that when problems emerge they are usually widespread. Ubiquity of problems leads, in a perverse way, to greater pressure for central intervention and an ever-repeating cycle. (Hodgson, 2015)

3 Too little involvement by employers

Employer investment in continuing vocational training per employee in the UK is half the EU average; investment in training and learning per employee fell by 13.6% per employee in real terms between 2007 and 2015 (Dromey and McNeil, 2017). A recent Employer Skills Survey (ESS) shows that in 2015 less than half of employers in the UK had a training plan and less than a third had a training budget (Vivian *et al*, 2016).

The UKCES Employer Perspectives Survey of 18,000 employers found that, across England, the proportion of employers offering work experience was only 44%. Only 20% engaged with schools and 12% with FE colleges, and such involvement is heavily weighted towards larger companies (Shury *et al*, 2014).

What is more, much of the training that does happen is low quality, confined in many companies to health and safety courses.

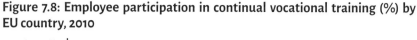

Figure 7.8: Employee participation in continual vocational training (%) by EU country, 2010

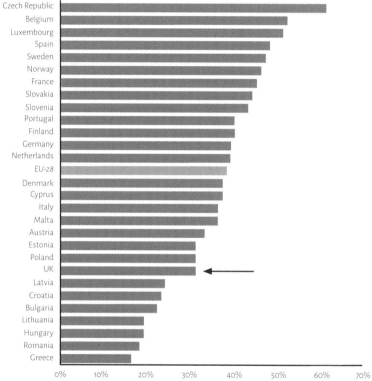

Source: Dromey and McNeil, 2017

There are many reasons why employers in England do little training of their employees:

- The state delivers much of the training.

- It is expensive. Training is especially weak in smaller firms who have limited resources.

- There is always a danger that if you train someone well they will leave to seek a better job elsewhere and your training will have been wasted.

- Our management is weak: managers do not have the skill to identify cases where investment in training would produce good returns. Nor is there, in England, a strong tradition of support for businesses to help them think in these terms. The country lacks institutional knowledge of the ways in which training could help a company increase its profits.

- There is too little long-term thinking in many firms. This is because they have found it hard to get long-term loans that would enable them to invest for the future and because the governance of many companies encourages quick profits for shareholders. Also it is easy to hire and fire staff as demand fluctuates and this discourages investment in workers.

- Too many firms have contented themselves with a low-skills-low-pay model of production, especially in retail, hotels, food and administrative sectors. They do not see continuous improvement of their staff as part of their strategy.

- England has a large number of self-employed workers and they are less likely to arrange training.

- England has a large number of small businesses and fewer large employers.

- Many immigrants have entered the labour market, often with specific vocational skills.

The links between employers and education were weakened with the conversion of polytechnics to universities in 1992. Polytechnics had been established to provide higher-level technical and business diplomas with strong links to employers; this was lost once they became academic degree-awarding universities.

We know that work experience with employers is an essential aspect of vocational training for young people. But many employers find that providing work experience is difficult, not least because of growing health and safety and chid protection constraints. Employers like to employ staff who have had work experience, but they are reluctant to offer it themselves.

In England, post-secondary vocational training programmes make much less use of workplace training than in other countries. In Denmark, post-secondary two-year programmes include three months of workplace training. In Sweden, all two-year higher post-secondary vocational programmes have a considerable amount of work-based learning – at least 25% of total programme hours.

Yet workplace training is valuable for many reasons. It enables students to learn both hard and soft skills (punctuality, working in a team etc). It allows students access to the latest technology, which is hard to replicate in colleges. Working in a real firm is a better way of picking up skills than sitting in a classroom.

There have been several attempts to involve employers more in designing vocational qualifications, but good intentions often lead to disappointing results. Training and Enterprise Councils, Sector Skills Councils and Local

Enterprise Partnerships have all been examples of attempts to get employers to define the training they needed, but with limited success: these intermediary bodies have been too remote from employers. What is more, employer bodies, awarding organisations and regulators have all had a role in the production of qualifications, but when there was a problem it was unclear which one of these was responsible for solving it.

Reformed apprenticeships and T levels may now become means by which there can be greater employer engagement in training.

4 Poor-quality workplace training

Not only is the amount of workplace training limited but there is evidence that the quality of such training is often poor. In England, there is no general framework for the placement of students in workplaces, and quality-assurance mechanisms are discretionary. In some countries, like Germany and Austria, workplace-training supervisors are required to have some form of workplace teaching qualification.

Yorke (2010) quotes a survey of 41 foundation degree students that found that in most cases the students themselves had negotiated the conditions and goals of the placements with the employer, with little involvement from the educational institution responsible for their degree. Another survey of students that had completed a placement in industry found that one-quarter of the respondents observed that they had never been clear about what they had been supposed to do, and the same proportion of students said they had received no feedback about their work during the placement (Yorke, 2010).

So in England we make less use of workplace training than other countries and much is low quality.

5 Failure to offer courses that employers value

The system in England has assumed that young people will gain a qualification and then try to find a job. There has been less attempt to align the supply of skills to the needs of employers. As a result many courses on offer do not lead to a particular career. The close partnership between employers and further education colleges seen in many countries is harder to discern in England. In many ways, vocational training in England is little more than state-led basic skills training for disadvantaged groups in society – as opposed to being a vehicle for engaging employers to improve productivity and pay.

The Sainsbury Review (Sainsbury, 2016) noted:

> It is striking how in many countries with high-performing technical education systems – including Norway, the Netherlands and Switzerland – there is widespread integration across the two modes of technical education learning: employment-based, such as an apprenticeship; and college-based, such as a full-time study programme at a college. In England these two modes of learning already overlap to a significant degree: all apprenticeships, for example, are required to include at least 20% 'off-the-job' (college-based) training. **However the two systems have largely been designed to operate separately** [emphasis added].

When employers have been involved in designing courses the emphasis has been on big companies, even though they employ fewer people in total than smaller firms. The Frontier Economics report (2017) found that:

> Both our quantitative and qualitative findings indicate that smaller employers are less likely to be involved in designing qualifications than larger employers. This means that the qualifications provided may be less suited to their skills needs, where these are systematically different from the needs of larger employers.

In the past, employers were more closely involved in designing qualifications than they have been recently. Central government has taken over the qualifications system and has vested control in national-level bodies. There used to be far more direct links between employers and qualification awarding bodies (and also between employers and local colleges) than there is now.

So it is not surprising that there is a mismatch between vocational qualifications and what employers want. The system of vocational qualifications has been set up by exam boards centrally and delivered by colleges. Neither ensures that the qualifications are what employers want – they have other motives. There are too many students doing low-level courses in subjects that do not lead to jobs, while there are many employers who cannot find employees with the skills they need.

In 2017, the top three most popular subject areas for Applied General students in England were business, administration, finance and law; leisure, travel and tourism; and arts, media and publishing. Relatively few took science and maths. The most popular subject for tech level students was arts, media and publishing.

Participation by subject area in applied general, tech level qualifications, England 2017

Ofqual sector subject area	Applied general		Tech level		Tech certificate	
	Number of qualifications available	% Applied general students	Number of qualifications available	% Tech level students	Number of qualifications available	% Tech certificate students
Health, public services and care	9	17.5	18	6.0	9	3.3
Science and mathematics	8	13.4	–	–	–	–
Agriculture, horticulture and animal care	4	0.1	70	10.2	32	12.7
Engineering and manufacturing technologies	3	0.4	59	17.2	25	12.6
Construction, planning and the built environment	3	0.0	33	4.6	33	22.8
Information and communication technology (ICT)	5	12.8	14	13.8	5	11.4
Retail and commercial enterprise	3	0.1	40	3.7	33	25.2
Leisure, travel and tourism	21	22.3	14	8.9	7	4.3
Arts, media and publishing	29	19.8	30	30.2	6	3.0
Social sciences	1	0.3	–	–	–	–
Preparation for life and work	1	0.1	–	–	–	–
Business, administration, finance and law	20	26.6	6	6.9	12	6.0

6 Low status accorded to vocational qualifications

There is a culture of inequality between vocational and academic routes to work. In England, the system focuses on academic achievement of a particular kind: eight or more good GCSEs, then A levels, then a university degree.

Government policies, funding, and incentives support this focus. Performance tables incentivise the promotion of academic routes that help meet targets. As a result, few young people see vocational routes as a positive option when in fact many, including those who achieve well at GCSE, could benefit more from a good vocational course than a university degree.

The Sainsbury Review (2016) commented: 'Parents, teachers and the general public have long regarded technical qualifications as inferior to academic qualifications and tend to believe that they are most suited to less-able learners'. A OnePoll survey in 2014 found that able children were labelled 'too clever' for vocational education. In 2017 the Select Committee report on Apprenticeships 'heard that many parents were hostile to non-university routes, even when their child was more suited to an apprenticeship'.

7 Low quality of vocational courses

Many of the courses on offer have limited teaching. Further education students currently receive fewer than 17 hours per week of tuition over a 36-week teaching year, compared with over 27 hours a week within schools up to the age of 16. High-performing countries often have bigger and broader programmes, some with nearly twice as many FE hours: at least 30 hours a week in Shanghai, 27 in Singapore, 26 in Canada and 28 in Norway (Department for Business, Energy & Industrial Strategy, 2017).

In 2017 Ofqual looked at a sample of externally marked exams across 27 vocational qualifications, all of which counted or will count in 16-19 performance tables. Out of the 49 exams Ofqual scrutinised, 14 were not 'functioning' as a trustworthy reflection of pupil performance. The 14 exams were either too easy or too hard, though some also had too many or too few questions for the time limit (Ofqual, 2017).

There are a number of reasons why low-quality courses have thrived.

The first is that the awarding bodies are private companies seeking to make a profit or, at least, break even. They need to attract customers. One way they have done that is to offer courses that are easier than those of the competition: shorter syllabuses; assessments divided into units (called 'modules'), which mean the student never has to master the whole syllabus; opportunities for multiple resits, which mean that a student's final grade may not reflect their true ability; easier question papers; a greater emphasis of teacher-assessed coursework; and more generous grading.

In my interview with Alison Wolf she commented:

> The government made a big mistake when, believing that market forces would drive up standards, it encouraged multiple awarding bodies to offer vocational qualifications. This resulting in a confusing array of such qualifications and, as happened with GCSEs, they competed with each other by dumbing down.

Yes, dumbing down happened at GCSE and A level; but since 2011, Ofqual have been clamping down successfully on grade inflation and exam boards racing to the bottom. The Department for Education has gripped standards in GCSEs and A levels. This same degree of control has not happened so far with vocational qualifications. Some functional skills qualifications, for example, are marked by the teacher who has seen the paper in advance and is under pressure to ensure that all pass.

Another reason that low-level courses have thrived is that colleges need successful results to enhance their achievement data, so it is in the interest of the college to push students towards the easy routes. There is 'payment by results'. Colleges are rewarded for attracting students onto short courses that they are most likely to complete.

There has been dishonesty in the system. Students have been offered attractive-looking courses with no information given about their value in the jobs market.

Another problem that has faced vocational qualifications is lack of clarity about what a qualification should look like. At times we have created 'certificates of competency' – 'I have done these 12 things' – with no pass or fail, which lacks the rigour of a course with assessment at the end and a pass-or-fail grade.

Another reason for the low quality of the qualifications was that the job of regulating them was left to Ofqual and its predecessors. But they were unable to do the job properly because there are thousands of qualifications, so they tended to confine themselves to a paper-based audit: they were not given the resources to do the job properly. The Frontier Economics report, 2017, found that: 'The regulation of general vocational qualifications, which does not include regulation of curriculum content and assessment strategies, appears insufficient to prevent a race to the bottom in terms of rigour'.

And, as the Wolf Report notes, 'scrutiny of individual vocational qualifications requires sector and subject expertise. There is no way that a national regulator such as Ofqual can possess knowledge relevant to the thousands of qualifications, reflecting myriad occupations, which are currently being put across its desks.'

Ofqual can check that an assessment looks coherent and fair but it cannot control the level of course content or the quality of teaching. For vocational courses the latter was the responsibility of the Sector Skills Councils and the awarding bodies, but too often they have been concerned with satisfying Ofqual and each other without fully focusing on the quality of the course.

What is needed, for vocational qualifications and apprenticeships, is independent **external quality assurance**; this is what Ofqual does for GCSEs and A levels. They:

- do not write the syllabuses but they DO check that syllabuses can be assessed properly. For example, they will not accredit (approve) a Japanese GCSE syllabus with an oral exam if they know that the exam boards cannot find enough Japanese oral examiners.

- check that the proposed assessment methods are good enough. For example, they will not accept coursework marked by the teacher unless there are rules about the amount of help the teacher can give and external moderation to check the teacher has not been too generous (or too harsh). They will not approve an end-point written exam if the length of the exam is not long enough to cover the syllabus.

- check that the level of knowledge required by the candidates is right for the level of the exam.

- check that the grading of marks is fair and consistent from one year to the next, from one subject to another, and above all is consistent between different exam boards.

- check that the awarding organisations (exam boards) have good procedures for keeping question papers secure, sending out question papers on time, finding and training adequate numbers of markers, and issuing results on time.

Evidence of continuing problems with quality came in 2017 when Ofsted inspected the private company Learndirect, the country's biggest training provider, and failed them. 8211 apprentices out of 19,940 were found to be not getting their off-the-job training entitlement and many were simply not being monitored at all.

At the same time, Ofsted reported on the North Liverpool Regeneration Company Ltd and found that the 'vast majority' of its construction apprentices were not in fact employed, which is a key principle of any apprenticeship. They, too, were graded 'inadequate'.

The organisations who do the external quality assurance need to be competent and well resourced otherwise there will still be a danger of private awarding bodies offering qualifications which are low quality and poorly managed. In a free-market environment there will always be pressure on awarding bodies to dumb down qualifications, which leaves students wasting time and money taking courses that are of little value to employers. At the time of writing, there were 31 external quality agencies for apprenticeships; one leader of an FE college said, 'It's like the Wild West out there'.

8 Failure to offer clear progression routes

The 2017 Frontier Economics report found that: 'particularly at lower levels of FE, a high proportion of learners take multiple qualifications at the same level. This suggests that learners may not face clear routes to progression and/ or sufficient incentives to progress onto higher levels of learning.'

Too many young people take level 1 or 2 courses after their GCSEs and these often lead nowhere. For those with level 3 vocational qualifications, progression to higher education is less straightforward than for those with academic level 3 qualifications. So progression from vocational programmes to higher-level programmes (in both universities and FE colleges) is hard unless there are locally designed progression routes available.

There is substantial 'churn' in the system – switching between course types, dropping back to lower-level learning, or repeating study at the same level. Analysis of learning records for young people between the ages of 16 and 18 showed that nearly a quarter of students entering further education at age 16 – around 125,000 within a single cohort – have subsequent patterns of study that are indicative of some form of churn. This means they waste time and money starting but not finishing qualifications (Department for Business, Innovation & Skills and Department for Education, 2016).

9 The massive expansion of universities and the destruction of level 4-5 courses

In 2016-17 there were 2.32 million students studying at UK higher education institutions:

- Undergraduates: 1.76 million
- Postgraduates: 552,000

Of these:

- Students from the UK: 1.87 million
- Students from the EU: 135,000
- Students from non-EU countries: 308,000

Source: Universities UK (2016)

In 1990 18% of 18- to 19-year-olds in England went to a UK university (HEFCE, 2017). This rose to 32% by 2000 and 43% by 2018, 50% by age 30. This expansion has focused on academic courses and has inevitably sucked the life out of vocational alternatives, especially at sub-degree level (courses which are between the standard of A levels and a university degree).

Wolf *et al* (2016) argue for a big increase in level 4 and 5 vocational courses – what they call intermediate tertiary qualifications or sub-degree courses, such as Higher National Diplomas and Higher National Certificates. Such qualifications make up below 1% of university courses and an even smaller proportion of non-university adult skills provision, and their number is declining. Other countries make much more of this sector. In England we focus on getting as many as possible into university degree courses (level 6) while FE colleges concentrate on low-level 1-2 courses. So the cliff-edge is too steep: those who get good GCSEs end up going to university; those who don't often end up doing low-level courses at college.

The graph below is from Wolf *et al* (2016) and shows the distribution of qualifications achieved by those aged 19 and above who were enrolled in further education. The proportion getting a level 4 or above qualification is so small the figure can hardly be read on the graph.

Figure 7.9: Adults achieving qualifications: education and training budget, England (thousands)

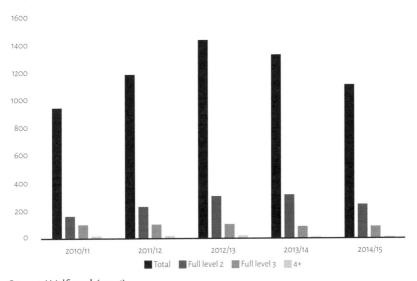

Source: Wolf et al (2016)

In the past we had many more taking these sub-degree courses, both at FE colleges and at universities, but these have almost disappeared. In 2015/16, 332,000 UK students obtained a first degree in UK universities (HESA, 2017) compared to 6000 obtaining an HND or HNC. HNDs and HNCs are valuable and have been used to train people to become hospital administrators, hospital technicians and nursing assistants. The other sub-degree qualification available at universities is a two-year Foundation Degree and here the numbers for UK students fell to 14,000 in 2015/16. What is more, the sub-degree courses include only a small number of STEM qualifications, having a heavy concentration on business qualifications.

Foundation degrees were originally for people *in work* as a higher-level route to improving their skills. Over time these were taken over by universities so they are no longer work-based, which undermines their real purpose.

There is plenty of evidence that England is desperately short of people with higher-level technical qualifications, partly because courses offering such qualifications simply don't exist. The Farmer Review (Farmer, 2016) showed that the huge construction sector, for example, lacks progression routes for ambitious construction workers: the level 4-6 qualifications which exist are limited in scope and very few places offer them.

Why do colleges offer so few level 4 and 5 courses?

1. No one knows about level 4 and 5 courses. They are invisible, unlike A levels and degree courses. A degree seems like a better bet for students simply because the currency is known.

2. Governments have prioritised those needing very basic level 1 and 2 courses – the unemployed and migrants needing English courses.

3. Setting up level 4 and 5 technical courses is expensive and there has been little financial assistance to make it seem worthwhile. It is safer to offer low-level courses.

4. The funding system for level 4 and 5 courses at FE colleges has been subject to constant change and this makes the establishment of such courses a high-risk venture.

5. Advanced Learner Loans started in 2013 and were extended to those aged 19+ from 2016 for courses that are level 3 and above. But the introduction of these loans has reduced the number of enrolments at level 4 or above. Whereas university students accept that their tuition and maintenance loans are a price they pay for higher salaries in the

future, FE students do not see this connection with the same degree of confidence.

6. In other countries level 4 and 5 qualifications are most successful when there exists a clear set of institutions to champion them – for example, the community colleges in Canada and the United States. In England the awkward location of high-quality post-secondary vocational courses between further and higher education leaves them in no man's land. FE colleges are in a weak position to play the necessary role of champions for this type of provision, partly because much of their energy is now devoted to mainstream academic teaching at upper secondary level, and partly because ownership of the relevant qualifications is vested either in awarding organisations or (in the case of foundation degrees) in universities (Musset and Field, 2013).

University numbers have grown fast but in many ways FE can be the best place to run vocational courses. The McLoughlin Commission (2013) that the four key characteristics of effective workplace training were:

1. Clear routes to work from the training course

2. Teachers who combine teaching skill with experience in the profession

3. Access to industry-standard facilities and resources

4. Clear routes to higher-level vocational training

An FE college is more likely to provide these than a university. However, universities are increasingly offering vocational courses in order to boost their numbers. Many are starting to offer degree apprenticeships and some will offer level 4-5 courses as a stepping stone to a full level 6 degree course. Some are making this process easier by merging with or forming a partnership with an FE college. The University of Derby, for example, merged with Buxton & Leek College in 2012. Southampton Solent University is looking to merge with City College Southampton.

10 Far too many courses, creating confusion

There are currently 163 organisations offering around 20,000 regulated vocational qualifications in England. There are far too many vocational courses on offer – over 30 just for plumbing, for example.

Why so many?

In recent decades the policy consensus within government has supported the idea of a 'market' in qualifications for adult skills and secondary vocational and technical awards. So anyone could offer a qualification as long as it was accredited by Ofqual.

The system is run by private awarding companies, each of whom has tended to offer their own suite of qualifications. The system of multiple private awarding companies is wholly different from many countries in continental Europe where a national agency works with employers and unions to establish a single set of qualifications. The problem with a 'market' is that it results in huge numbers of little-known qualifications – a qualification is not worth having if no employers have ever heard of it or, at the very least, don't know what standards it represents.

Furthermore, at various points governments have introduced new sets of qualifications, but the old ones they had intended to replace did not go away (page 96).

The consequence of such a huge number of courses is that students find it hard to identify which is the right course for them, and schools, who should be advising their leaving pupils, cannot grasp the information they need: it is too complex.

Such a huge number of courses means that it is also harder for any regulatory process to ensure rigour and quality is maintained or that qualifications are genuinely comparable to others with similar titles.

Because there are so many courses and careers advice is poor, too many students embark on the wrong vocational course. Those who study further education courses are 12 times less likely to complete their course than those who study A levels (Social Mobility Commission, 2016). The cost of post-16 learning courses which were not completed was about £814 million in 2012/13, representing around 12% of the funding allocated to provision for 16- to 18-year-olds (House of Lords Select Committee on Social Mobility, 2016).

Having multiple courses and awarding bodies might, in theory, create competition which drives prices down and quality up. But there is little evidence this happens. Colleges do not choose qualifications on the basis of the fees they will have to pay, so price competition is weak. The main effect of competition is to encourage awarding bodies to offer easier courses with high pass rates, and it is this which creates the race to the bottom.

11 Far too many changes over time, creating confusion

A City & Guilds report in 2014 showed that since 1981, skills and employment policy had been subject to 28 Acts of Parliament, 10 transfers of responsibility between government departments, and had been overseen by 61 Secretaries of State.

National agencies have come and gone. The Manpower Services Commission lasted up until 1987 before being scrapped. Since then, the UK has had the Training Commission (TC), Training Agency (TA), Further Education Funding Council (FEFC), Learning and Skills Council (LSC), Young People's Learning Agency (YPLA), Skills Funding Agency (SFA), the UK Commission on Employment and Skills (UKCES), the Education Funding Agency (EFA), the Education and Skills Funding Agency (ESFA) and the Institute for Apprenticeships (IfA).

In terms of vocational qualifications there have been NVQs, GNVQs, AVCEs, Applied A levels, Diplomas, Technical Awards, Applied Generals, Tech Levels, Technical Certificates and now T levels.

In terms of local organisations, there were 72 Training Enterprise Councils – abolished in 2000 to be replaced by 47 Local Learning and Skills Councils. A network of nine Regional Development Agencies was also introduced in 1998. These were scrapped in 2011 and replaced with Local Enterprise Partnerships (LEPs).

Policy fashions change. In the early 1990s the focus was on efficiency and cost savings. In the late 1990s there was a strong drive on widening participation. In recent years there has been a focus on safeguarding, British values and Prevent. Since the Brexit vote the emphasis has been on substituting for skills provided by EU workers in Britain. At various times governments have tried to bring academic and vocational qualifications into a single framework; at other times they have been separate. The role of employers has undergone constant reassessment, as has the relative importance of apprenticeships.

A levels have retained status - despite many changes to content and format - because the name doesn't change. Vocational qualifications have changed names endlessly to the point where employers just don't understand the qualifications applicants put forward on their CVs.

The average government minister is only in post for two years and the easiest way he or she can make a mark is by changing a qualifications system. But it takes decades for employers and the public to understand and value a qualification, which is why the most readily understood are A levels, university degrees and City & Guilds vocational qualifications: they have been around for a long time. Employers recognise and value familiarity.

Government attempts to reform vocational qualifications have been well-meaning. Some have been an attempt to simplify the complex mass of vocational qualifications. Having a tidy structure of qualifications seems tempting but, as the Wolf Report says, 'because a complex modern economy has a correspondingly complex occupational structure, central attempts to impose a neat, uniform and "logical" structure on it always fail' (Wolf, 2011).

Looking at the long history of vocational qualification reforms suggests that there has been a failure to learn lessons from the past, coupled with a temptation to adopt a 'clean-sheet' approach to reform, when in fact many existing qualifications were popular and effective.

12 Poor careers advice from schools

There are a number of reasons why schools do not give their pupils good information about vocational courses. Most teachers are university graduates who know nothing about these qualifications. Schools will not wish to lose pupils at age 14 because they get £5000 a year or so for each of them, so they will not promote university technical colleges. The school is not that interested in pupils leaving at the age of 16 to go to FE colleges – their priority is to obtain good university entry statistics for those leaving at age 18; they will not wish to lose academically able pupils at age 16 because they need them in their sixth forms.

Schools sometimes take weak pupils onto A level courses because the school needs the money. However, they also need good A level results, which is why many schools 'persuade' 17-year-olds who are less strong academically to leave at end of Year 12. These students might then go on to FE colleges, but they have wasted a year.

The Careers and Enterprise Company, which was started with government funding in 2015, has 2000 advisers working with over half of the schools and colleges in England, providing support to develop a careers programme. We need it to succeed.

13 Qualifications which are much too specific or too broad

Some qualifications cover a very specific range of narrowly defined skills reflecting specific job roles for particular firms; unless the perfect job happens to come up, the qualification is of limited value to the student.

Equally some are too broad, with awarding organisations trying to produce a qualification which meets the needs of every student but which satisfies no one.

14 Finding good teachers

It is hard to find teachers for vocational courses. They need to have up-to-date knowledge of the job sector they are teaching as well as good subject knowledge and teaching ability. Traditionally they are career changers who move from industry into a college, but the number of such people is limited. There is a constant tension between the desirability of requiring staff to have been trained as teachers and the fact that the time and cost of such training will deter good people from abandoning their current job to move into teaching.

There is a particular need to recruit part-time teachers because, if they can continue to work part-time in industry, they are able to remain in close touch with the changing needs of the modern workplace – they are 'dual professionals'.

The relative underfunding of the FE sector has led to the average pay in FE falling below that of school teachers and is often lower than the wages they could earn in their own technical and professional sphere. Recruitment is obviously going to be challenging when you require staff to be dual professionals but then pay them less than they could earn in either profession on its own.

15 Finding good governors

Governors of FE colleges are responsible for the strategic direction of the colleges, their finances and for overseeing the work of the senior management team. As with schools, colleges have difficulty finding governors who have the time and skills to do this huge job properly and who also represent the locality and employers of the area.

Conclusions

Technical and vocational education in England is quite weak compared to many other countries. Further Education colleges do a good job but they are underfunded and often focus on low-level courses for those who have underachieved at school. Universities have grown rapidly and this has undermined higher-level technical education somewhat. The vocational qualifications system is complex, lacks good regulation, has been subject to constant change, and standards are highly variable. Financial cuts have led to an FE workforce with worse pay and conditions than in our schools and universities.

In 1993 control of FE colleges passed from local authorities to central government. Government has exercised control through the funding mechanisms, performance indicators and inspection. Despite this, FE colleges have lacked a clear national strategic role, something that reflects the diverse nature of local needs. There is a tension between the high degree of central control of FE and the need for colleges to be flexible and responsive to local needs.

Parity of esteem between academic and vocational routes has proved impossible to achieve while A levels remain the gold standard in the minds of many parents and politicians. There is too much snobbery about vocational education amongst parents. The best way of changing this culture is to publish the lifetime earnings premium of every qualification, something that has recently become possible with the availability of so-called longitudinal data (page 291).

There has been a steady drive to get employers to be more involved with the design and funding of further education, but this has been largely unsuccessful. Since the 1960s, Industry Training Boards, followed by Occupational Standards Councils and Sector Skills Councils, have been employed to do this, but in the end much has had to depend on the initiative of individual colleges and independent training providers to make the system work.

Very frequent funding reforms imposed by governments, allied to performance measures and inspection requirements, have forced FE college leaders to prioritise the tactical skills needed to survive – at the expense of other more worthwhile things like strategic planning or developing links with employers. Meanwhile many government reforms have failed or simply been superseded by other reforms. Governments can make changes quite easily by reforming qualifications or by using the levers of funding and inspections, but they are much less good at correctly foreseeing the outcomes of those changes. Too much attention has been paid to qualification reform at the expense of other elements of the system.

Chapter 8

Low-tariff universities

In 2017, there were 34 million people aged between 21 and 64 in the UK who were not on an educational course (ONS, 2017). Breaking these people down by the highest qualification they held:

- 14 million, or 42%, were graduates
- 7 million, or 21%, had qualifications equivalent to an A level
- 7 million, or 21%, had qualifications equivalent to an A^* to C grade GCSE
- 3 million, or 9%, had qualifications not offered in the UK
- 3 million, or 8%, had no qualifications

This 'highest qualification achieved' profile reflects the structure of British society.

In 1989 Ken Baker, Secretary of State for Education and Science, made a speech in which he proposed expansion of the proportion of young people attending university from 15% to 30% by early in the 21st century. In the subsequent years this target was easily achieved because of the opening up of universities to women and the academic success of girls at school – universities expanded by taking large numbers of middle-class young women.

Twenty years ago Tony Blair announced a new target – half of all young people should go to university. Progress towards this target has been steady but less rapid because by 1998 most middle-class school leavers were already going to university. Further expansion had to come from families with no prior experience of higher education.

Progress was also slowed because the government could not afford the cost. Even after tuition fees were introduced in 1998 and tripled to £3000 a year in 2006, there was still a big taxpayer subsidy for educating each student.

But this barrier to expansion was removed when tuition fees were pushed up to £9000 in 2012, transferring most of the cost from the tax payer to the students themselves and enabling George Osborne to announce the abolition of student number controls from 2015. Nick Hillman, Director of the Higher Education Policy Institute, sees no reason why 'a target of around 70 per cent participation by 2035 should not be unachievable' (Hillman, 2017).

Figure 8.1: Percentage participation in higher education by the age of 30 in UK

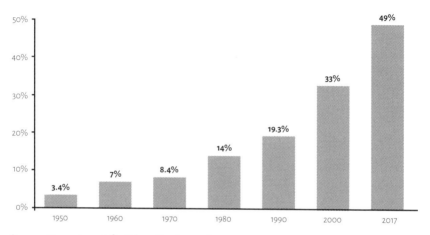

Source: Department for Education (2017g)

Numbers obtaining first degrees in UK, thousands *per annum*			
	Male	Female	Total
1950	13	4	17
1970	35	16	51
1990	43	33	77
Includes degrees awarded at former polytechnics from 1994			
2000	110	133	243
2016	158	210	368

Source: HESA (2017)

How does the government justify this expansion? The Minister of State for Universities spelt it out in 2017: a university degree (he claimed) increases average lifetime earnings by £168,000 for men and £252,000 for women, and a 1% increase in the share of the workforce with a degree raises national economic growth by 0.2% to 0.5%.

There has been a big increase in the past ten years in the number of pupils from disadvantaged homes going to university full-time in the UK, but mainly to the low-tariff universities ('tariff' simply means the grades required). The increase has occurred for several reasons. Universities have spent huge sums on outreach activities, persuading school-age pupils to apply (Oxford, for example, spent £5.6 million in 2017). All universities have set themselves the target of taking more pupils from disadvantaged homes, and these targets are monitored by the Office for Students. Universities are taking more students and this makes it easier for those from the bottom 14% economically (those on free school meals) to find a place. Schools get credit in the performance tables for the proportion of their students going to university, so pupils are encouraged to apply. Finally, more disadvantaged pupils are taking the A levels and level 3 BTECs necessary to win a university place.

Removal of the places cap did not affect the majority of student applicants with good quality entrance qualifications since they would have been able to enter university in any case. It is the weaker students who now fill the extra places.

Data from the Higher Education Statistics Agency shows how the proportion going to university full-time from lower socioeconomic groups has grown:

Figure 8.2: Percentage of young full-time first degree entrants from lower socioeconomic groups, by academic year

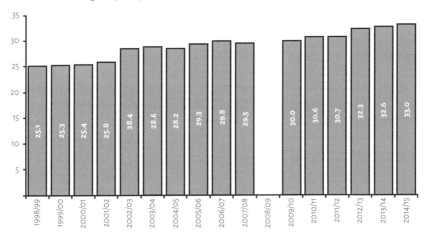

NS-SEC data for 2008/09 is not comparable with the other years and has been excluded

Source: HESA (2017)

However, the loans system has put off **part-time** undergraduates because they often cannot afford debt. Thanks to a 47% decrease in part-time undergraduate entrants from low-participation areas between 2011-12 and 2015-16, unpicking the figures for England show that there's actually been a 16% decrease in undergraduate entrants from low-participation areas over this period. So there

213

has been an increase in the numbers of full-time students from disadvantaged areas entering university, but not in overall numbers from disadvantaged areas.

The relatively poor GCSE and A level results of those from disadvantaged backgrounds makes it harder for them to find places at high-tariff universities. Critics say that many do degree courses that have a limited market value and lead to what used to be non-graduate jobs; yet whatever course you are doing, in 2018 you leave with a debt of £50,000 attached to high interest rates. A much higher proportion of students from low-income households go to low-tariff universities than high-tariff. They will incur the same level of debt as those who go to a high-tariff university yet they are much less likely to gain a high salary job which will enable them to pay it off.

Claire Crawford *et al* (2017) showed that 38% of university students from the 20% least-deprived backgrounds attend a top 40 university compared to 15% of those from the 20% most-deprived backgrounds. Most of this difference is due to the weaker GCSE and A level results of the lower-income students. But part of the difference is that pupils from lower-income homes with good school results are less likely to apply to the better universities.

Another factor is that students from lower-income homes are less likely to take the A level subjects that universities want. The Russell Group are high-tariff universities, named after the Russell Hotel in London where representatives of these universities used to meet. Looking at pupils taking Russell Group facilitating subjects (the list of A level subjects they describe as 'keeping most options open' – maths, further maths, English literature, physics, biology, chemistry, geography, history, and classical or modern languages) the researchers found that 56% of private school pupils took two or more such subjects while 32% of students in the bottom socioeconomic quintile did so.

This finding was backed by recent research carried out by Catherine Dilnot at the UCL Institute of Education who analysed the data on all 475,000 students in England who entered UK universities with three A levels between 2010 and 2012. She found that those taking facilitating subjects tended to go to more high-status universities. Pupils from disadvantaged homes are more likely to believe that A level subjects with a vocational slant, such as business, law or accountancy are more valuable than academic subjects like maths or history, but they are wrong (Dilnot, 2017).

In a survey in 2016, 6500 young people told UCAS why they didn't apply to the **higher-tariff** group of universities.

- Nearly half thought the entry requirements to these universities were too high – more would have applied if they had known they had a chance of getting in. Some students over-estimate the difficulty of gaining places at top universities.

- Three-quarters said they would have applied to a higher-tariff university if they were offered a travel voucher for an Open Day. Small sums of money can have a big impact.

- A quarter of the least-advantaged students who didn't apply to higher-tariff universities said they felt the cost of living would be too high.

The students from the least advantaged backgrounds were 30% more likely to think the degree **subject studied** was key to employment while more advantaged applicants were 50% more likely to think the **university they went** to was more important for securing a job.

So if you come from a low-income family you are much more likely to attend a low-tariff university. The Higher Education Statistics Agency data showed that the proportion of the student intake at Russell Group universities (high tariff) coming from poor backgrounds went up from 19.5% in 2004/5 to only 20.8% in 2014/5. But over that time, non-Russell Group universities (lower tariff) saw the proportion of their students coming from poor backgrounds increase from 32.5% to 37.5%.

One of the main reasons that disadvantaged students go to less good universities than they could is that they are more inclined to go to their local university regardless of its status or quality so they can live at home rather than live at the university. 42% of university entrants from disadvantaged backgrounds attend a university within half an hour of their home compared to 26% of the more affluent (Willetts, 2017).

To name some examples, in 2015-16 the percentage of UK students from poorer neighbourhoods taking a first degree at selected universities was:

Low-tariff	
Glyndwr, Wales	26 %
Teesside	28 %
Sunderland	30 %
High-tariff	
Cambridge	3 %
Imperial	4 %
Oxford	3 %

Source: UCAS (2017b)

Once at university, some students from low-income backgrounds struggle even though they have the same A level grades as students from more prosperous homes. Claire Crawford looked at 400,000 students going through university and found that those from the highest socioeconomic quintile group are, on average, 3.4% less likely to drop out, 5.3% more likely to complete their degree and 3.7% more likely to graduate with a first or 2:1 than those from the lowest socioeconomic quintile (Crawford, 2014a).

Nevertheless, just because a person goes to a low-tariff university, this does not make it a negative experience. Less prestigious universities take more students from disadvantaged backgrounds and can transform their lives, improving their lifetime earnings significantly and leaving them with what is in many cases a profoundly worthwhile experience.

Today pupils are divided into sheep and goats at the age of 16 – after they have taken their GCSEs. Those with, say, eight GCSE passes (formerly grade C or better, now grade 4) including English and maths normally go on to take level 3 courses – mainly A levels but also BTECs and some other level 3 courses, and most of them end up going to university. But those who have not achieved eight GCSE passes including English and maths typically go to an FE college to continue with English and maths as well as a vocational course, often at level 2 (the same level as a GCSE).

The increase in the proportion going to university has had an adverse effect on the 50% who do not go to university. In the days when only 15% of the population went to university, the 85% felt no stigma. I went to a very selective school where about half of the pupils went to Oxford or Cambridge, but the less academic minority went on to become lawyers and accountants via non-university routes and had smart cars before their school friends had graduated. When I was teaching in schools in the 1980s, those who did not go to university were happy enough about that fact. But now that half go to university, the psychology is different.

Economically the huge growth of universities has damaged the prospects of the bottom 50% because so many of the middle-ground jobs they would have taken in the past are now snapped-up by graduates. Of course, this means that many graduates are now taking what used to be non-graduate jobs, which sounds like a waste of a university education. But it is not a waste from the perspective of the university students themselves because these middle-ground jobs now use possession of a degree as means of selection – without a degree you are unlikely to get an interview.

Does the expansion in the number of graduates lead to a more skilled workforce and thus a stronger economy? It is hard to disentangle cause and effect – more people might go to university because they need a degree to access a growing number of skilled jobs. Or employers might create more skilled jobs because the supply of graduates is so good. But what is clear is that many university graduates cannot find jobs for which a degree is a normal qualification. The Office for National Statistics published the following data in 2017 (non-graduate jobs are defined as 'those which do not normally require the knowledge and skill gained from higher education, such as being a receptionist, sales assistant or care worker'):

Percentage of recent graduates and non-recent graduates working in non-graduate roles in the UK and Scotland, 2011 to 2016

	UK		Scotland	
	Recent graduates (%)	Non-recent graduates (%)	Recent graduates (%)	Non-recent graduates (%)
2011	47.4	32.6	53.8	39.8
2012	48.8	33.3	52.3	39.4
2013	47.2	33.7	49.9	39.3
2014	46.7	34.2	52.0	40.9
2015	45.9	35.5	50.3	41.6
2016	46.4	35.1	51.8	40.8

Source: ONS (2017c)

In Scotland in 2016 over half of recent graduates were working in 'non-graduate' jobs, 46% in the UK as a whole (ONS, 2017c). What is happening is that we are creating more graduates than we need in some areas, and the graduates we do produce often lack the skills or work experience that employers are looking for.

Craig Holmes (2014) looked at this issue and found that comparing the UK with other EU countries, 1996-2008, the UK was one of the countries with the widest gap between the increase in supply and demand for high skills over the period (9% supply compared to 4% demand). In fact, across Europe he found only a very weak correlation between the graduate share of the labour market and growth of high-skill occupations. There is little evidence that having more graduates is a necessary condition for future increases in high-skill employment.

Figure 8.3: Changes in high-skill supply and demand, EU countries, 1996-2008

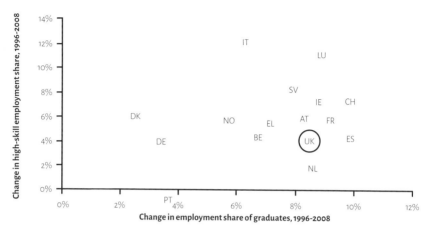

Source: Holmes (2014)

There is also the question of the cost to future taxpayers of unpaid student loans. In 2017 the total value of student loans outstanding was £89 billion, projected to increase to £500 billion in the mid-2030s. About 70% of students who left university in 2016 are expected never to finish repaying their loans according to modelling carried out by the Institute for Fiscal Studies. Instead they will have to make repayments for 30 years and then have the unpaid loan written off. Women are paid less than men and are more likely to take career breaks or stop work, so the growth in the proportion of undergraduates who are women has reduced the amount of student loans that will ever be repaid.

But the great advantage of the university funding system is that current governments contribute relatively little to undergraduate degrees.

Alternative providers

An alternative provider is a provider of higher education courses that does not receive annual funding from the government and is not an FE college. Some students are able to access loans from the Student Loans Company if their course is specifically approved. Some are for-profit; some are charities.

There are 112 private higher education colleges able to offer degrees, always through an established university. Fifty-eight are in London. In 2017 it was revealed a recruitment agent at one of these, Greenwich School of Management, which has a partnership licence with Plymouth University, was fraudulently admitting bogus students who merely wished to access the maintenance loans of up to £11,000 pa. There was little attempt to ensure students were qualified or indeed did any work.

Grafton College in London offers degrees offered in partnership with the Open University. It was found that an associated firm was creating fake A level certificates, and some students taking a level 5 course HND in business management were handing in assignments written for them in Pakistan (*Panorama*, 2017).

So the Office for Students has its work cut out checking the legitimacy and rigour of some colleges.

I've got a BTEC

A research survey by Scott Kelly (2017) for the Higher Education Policy Institute found that students arriving at university with BTECs as opposed to A levels account for much of the growth in students from the lowest participation neighbourhoods and other under-represented groups over the past decade. But those with BTECs face a 'glass ceiling'; for example:

- Only 15 BTEC students were accepted at the four most selective higher education institutions in 2015.

- Under 60% of students with BTECs at Russell Group universities complete their course.

- BTEC students achieve a lower class of degree and have lower average earnings after graduation, compared to those who hold A levels.

Kelly also notes that the subjects taken at BTEC level 3 do not always correspond to the subjects universities want, certainly not the higher-tariff universities. The number of pupils achieving high grades in sports science tripled from 3305 in 2005-06 to 9570 in 2012-13. Kelly commented: 'BTECs engage students that other qualifications do not reach. But, when Sports Science has been growing faster than all other STEM subjects, their rapid growth raises important some questions. Young people need better information on the options they are choosing.'

And Nick Hillman, Director of the Higher Education Policy Institute, concluded: 'There is a yawning gap between how BTEC students think they will fare at university and how they actually fare'.

Going to a low-tariff university might damage you

Education has two different aims. It is there to teach students something. Sometimes that something is obviously beneficial – such as basic numeracy and literacy. Very often the benefits are less obviously useful to the economy and society as a whole but may be important in terms of the personal interests and development of the student.

Secondly, and very differently, education is used to sort children and young people out into a hierarchy of perceived competence – it is a 'positional good'. Most people with a university degree get a job regardless of what they learnt at university. The degree simply allows employers to recognise that they have a certain level of ability. But is it better than obtaining a vocational qualification?

Jack Britton *et al* (2016) showed that men who studied at any of 23 of the lowest-performing British universities went on to *earn less than those who did not enter higher education*. The research, by the Institute for Fiscal Studies and the universities of Cambridge and Harvard, took several years and required permission to access tax data for the first time. This allowed them to track the earnings of 260,000 students up to ten years after they left university. The data set includes cohorts of graduates who started university in the period 1998-2011 and whose earnings (or lack of earnings) were then observed over a number of tax years.

There were 23 universities whose male graduates earned less, on average, ten years later than the median for non-graduates. Female graduates from nine universities earned less than the figure for non-graduates. The names of the 23 and nine universities have not been disclosed.

The study, the first to match tax data with student loan records, also highlighted the big differences in earnings of graduates depending on their choice of degree. Graduates who studied creative arts, such as drama, dance, fine art, design or music, had the lowest earnings and were paid, on average, the same as non-graduates: £17,900 for men and £14,500 for women. Medicine and economics graduates earned most, with big premiums even allowing for higher A level grades.

Using similar data sources, the Department for Education (2017h) correlated salaries five years after graduation with various variables showing:

1. Those with good A level grades tended to earn more regardless of which university they attended. This may not be surprising because A level grades are a good measure of intellectual ability. In the graph opposite, 360 points = AAA, 300 = BBB, 240 = CCC.

Figure 8.4: How A level grades (measured as points) correlate with earnings five years after leaving university

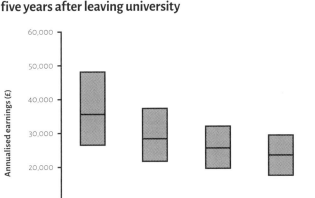

Source: Department for Education (2017h)

2. Those who go to the universities with the highest entry requirements earn more.

3. Those who choose to work in the south-east earn more. In other words, the nature of the regional economy where you are employed can be as important as your university or degree subject.

4. Degree subject matters: there are low returns from creative arts and design courses. Median national earnings after five years for these graduates are the lowest of all subject areas at £20,000, with a bottom quartile of only £13,300. A noticeable number of courses in agriculture, mass communication and documentation, psychology, and English studies also generated median salary outcomes below the median salary for all 25- to 29-year-olds in work in 2014-5, graduates and non-graduates.

    The earnings potential is higher for STEM courses and economics than for arts and humanities.

Figure 8.5: Distribution of median annualised earnings across HEIs for each subject area five years after graduation (minimum, lower quartile, median, upper quartile, maximum), graduating cohort 2008/09

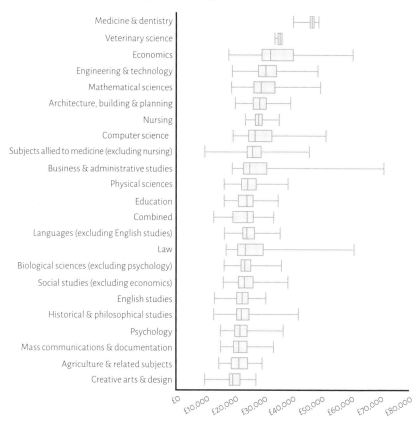

Median earnings across HEIs by subject studied
five years after graduation, female + male

HEI = Higher education institution

Source: Department of Education (2017h)

How to read the boxplots

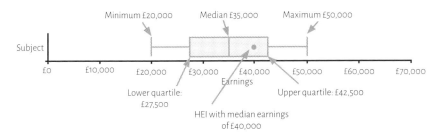

Looking at the boxplots you can see not only the AVERAGE difference between subjects but also the huge RANGE of salaries commanded by those who studied certain subjects – such as law. Lawyers who went to top universities earn far more than those who went to low-tariff universities because of a massive oversupply of law graduates.

5. Gender: for all university subjects except English men earn more than women five years after graduation. The gender pay gap starts immediately after graduation. The situation is especially poor for Pakistani, Bangladeshi, and Black Caribbean women.

Some of the highest pay gaps are in subject areas dominated by men, such as Engineering and Computer Science (see table on page 224).

The gender pay gap

University subject	Number		%	Difference between genders' median pay, five years from graduation
	women	men	women	
Engineering & technology	2125	11780	15.3%	−£4300
Computer science	1930	9350	17.1%	−£4400
Architecture	1970	5210	27.4%	−£3700
Mathematical sciences	1127	2930	27.8%	−£3200
Economics	1200	3015	28.5%	−£3000
Physical sciences	5190	7035	42.5%	−£2600
Business and administrative studies	15310	15855	49.1%	-£2800
Biological sciences	8255	8165	50.3%	−£700
Historical and philosophical studies	8160	7090	53.5%	−£800
Mass communications & documentation	4650	3680	55.8%	+£300
Medicine & dentistry	4805	3205	60.0%	−£2600
Creative arts & design	18735	11990	61.0%	−£500
Law	7730	4660	62.4%	−£3200
Agriculture	1210	645	65.2%	−£3200
Languages (excluding English)	5715	2555	69.1%	−£1500
Social studies (excluding economics)	16255	7255	69.1%	−£2800
Subjects allied to medicine (excluding nursing)	11085	4360	71.2%	−£3600
English studies	7700	2765	73.6%	+£800
Veterinary Science	580	155	78.9%	−£1500
Psychology	9425	2025	82.3%	−£2000
Education	12225	1900	86.5%	−£2500
Nursing	11270	1060	91.4%	−£3300

Figure 8.6: Average gross pay for graduates according to their degree subject

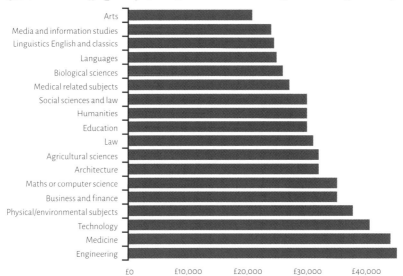

Source: ONS (2017d)

For most it is still worth going to university. Blundell *et al* (2016) found that in 1993, 13% of 25- to 29-year-olds were graduates, rising to 41% by 2015. Despite this big increase, the wage differential between graduates and non-graduates did not vary much over time. Real wages fell significantly among all education groups after 2008 but the median wage among 25- to 29-year-old non-graduates fell by a similar percentage as graduates – so that the wage difference between graduates and school-leavers has stayed flat.

But there are now signs that this graduate advantage might be reaching a natural end, with some small falls in the wages of graduates in the private sector relative to school leavers in recent years. The authors conclude that further increases in the number of graduates could start to erode the graduate wage premium in the future. According to the Taylor Review (Taylor, 2017) 18% of those who are inactive but would like to work hold a degree or equivalent qualification.

There is also some evidence that weaker university students would be better-off financially and in career terms if there were good quality two-year courses geared to local market conditions. We should reinvigorate good level 4-5 courses, such as the HNC and HND, which used to provide such an attractive route to employment for those in the middle ground academically.

Are too many weak students going to university?

It could be a mistake to think that the population is more educated simply because more go to university. The increasing number of places at university, and the decrease in the number of 18-year-olds, is making it easier and easier to find a place at university. Many higher-tariff universities now advertise places on UCAS clearing (*ie* they have places going begging shortly before the course begins).

The OECD Adult Skills Survey (2013) found that one in ten young university graduates in England have numeracy or literacy levels below level 2. 'Below level 2' means struggling with simple quantitative information, such as a petrol gauge in a car, or inability to read and understand the instructions one might see on a bottle of aspirin.

Figure 8.7: Literacy and numeracy skills of university graduates by aged 20-34

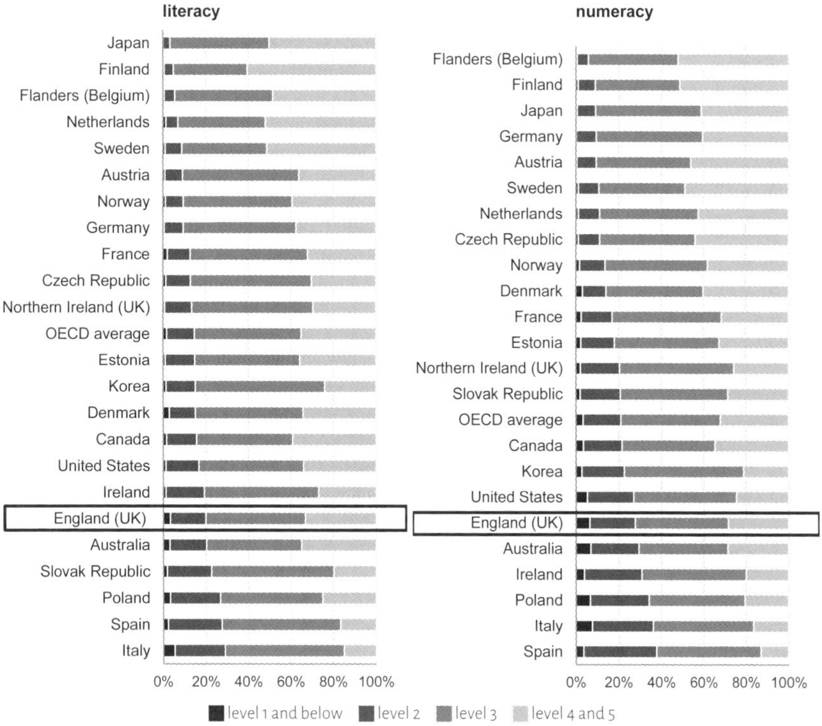

Source: *Kuczera* et al (2016)

Figure 8.8: Low literacy and numeracy skills among 20- to 34-year-old graduates

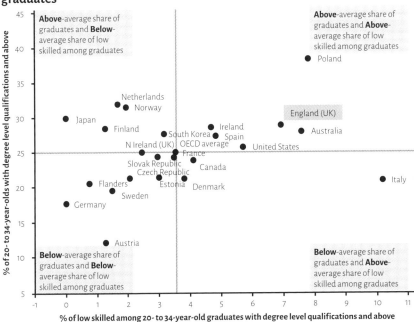

Source: Kuczera et al *(2016)*

This graph shows that England has more students going to university than many countries but more of those students have a low level of numeracy and/or literacy.

Kuczera *et al* (2016) in their OECD report recommend that:

> Those with low basic skills should not normally enter three-year undergraduate programmes, which are both costly and unsuited to the educational needs of those involved, while graduates with poor basic skills undermine the currency of an English university degree. These potential entrants should be diverted into more suitable provision that meets their needs.

The 2017 *Times* Higher Education Teaching Survey confirmed the OECD findings that universities are admitting students who have poor English skills and are unprepared for degree courses. A survey of more than 1000 university staff found that only 28% of academics believed that students had a 'good grounding for higher study'.

Who needs a degree?

Figure 8.9: Percentage of graduates and non-graduates employed in each main occupational area, UK, 2017

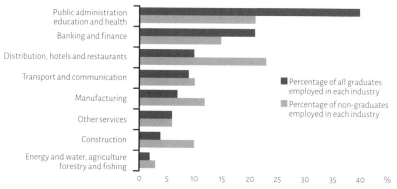

Source: ONS (2017d)

This graph shows that of all employed graduates in the UK 40% are working in just three areas: public administration, education and health. They are also over-represented in banking and finance. But non-graduates are far more numerous in distribution, hotels and restaurants, manufacturing and construction.

Where do university students come from?

The table below shows that in 2016 over 37,000 university students came from FE colleges where they took A levels, BTECs or successful Access courses. So it is wrong to assume that FE Colleges are set against universities – the one supplies the other.

Centre type	Number of Acceptances by Cycle Year									
	2007	2008	2009	2010	2011	2012	2013	2014	2015	2016
Academy	56,015	61,465	64,560	66,470	70,300	66,540	73,210	75,000	79,855	81,740
Further education	31,830	34,585	37,755	37,625	35,875	32,795	36,120	37,730	37,810	37,415
Grammar	10,640	11,010	11,010	10,610	10,730	10,095	10,660	10,455	10,235	10,775
Independent	28,550	30,325	30,720	30,685	30,190	29,255	29,210	29,405	30,445	30,615
Sixth form college	46,740	52,015	55,850	56,405	57,745	53,745	55,975	57,365	60,185	60,005
Maintained schools	63,715	69,105	71,315	69,075	69,110	64,940	67,375	69,125	71,675	72,175
Other	18,760	15,525	15,960	21,880	28,150	24,710	27,205	28,290	28,860	30,200
Total	256,245	274,030	287,165	292,755	302,100	282,080	299,750	307,365	319,060	322,930

Source: UCAS (2017b)

Universities v FE Colleges

Half the population of England now go to university. In some successful countries the proportion is higher than that – over 75% in Finland, Sweden and South Korea for example – but now the cap has been taken off university numbers in England there is no reason why the proportion here should not carry on growing. Further expansion of universities is attractive to those who want to see social mobility because most of the extra students will be from lower-income families. For the individuals concerned, going to university gives them an advantage in the labour market over non-graduates, even if not all end up with well-paid jobs.

Universities are trying to attract more and more students with poor qualifications. Some are offering Foundation courses – one-year courses that lead into a three-year degree. Such a trend is damaging recruitment to FE colleges.

So the main issues are whether, from the point of view of the country as a whole, it is good to have so many university students studying courses that do not in themselves lead to good jobs, and whether, in terms of skills shortages in England, universities are the best places to provide vocational training.

Universities have one big advantage and that is prestige. If we want to create thousands more coders, for example, then arguably we are more likely to succeed if we incentivise universities to offer such courses. Universities are better funded than colleges and with 109 public universities in England they are almost as well placed as FE colleges to forge links with the local community and local employers. On the other hand, universities are residential – they provide accommodation – so they take students from all over the country and all over the world, reducing their allegiance to the local area in which they sit.

The presence of a good university in a city can transform it economically, as has happened in Exeter, Lincoln, Newcastle and Manchester. Our universities are amongst the best in the world and can drive economic growth simply through the jobs they create and the spending power of students.

Comparing people who went to university with those who could have gone (given their academic record) but chose not to shows that university graduates are more likely to earn more, to generate higher tax revenues for the country, to have better health, to have longer life expectancy (Willetts, 2017). University graduates are more likely to be in a job than non-graduates:

Figure 8.10: Employment level by highest qualification held, UK, 2017

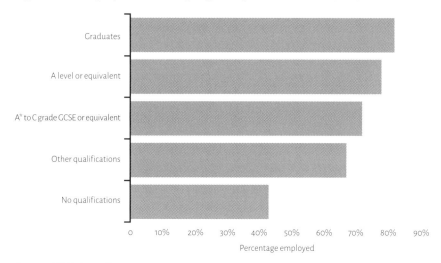

Source: ONS (2017d)

Universities and vocational courses

40% of university students are doing vocational courses. Over 12% are on courses allied to medicine, 7% teacher training, 6% engineering. To these one can add nurses, architects and lawyers. The 40% figure excludes the most popular subject of all, business studies (14% of undergraduates), but many doing this course go into a business career.

Some whole universities are vocational, notably the medical schools. The College of Law was set up by the Law Society to provide vocational training for future solicitors and this recently became the University of Law – the first private profit-making university.

Other examples of 'vocational universities' include Sunderland University and Teesside University in the north-east of England. Sunderland offers automotive engineering degrees in association with the local Nissan car plant. Teesside University offers an engineering degree with a year of work experience in a wide range of industries such as aerospace, robotics, automotive, marine, renewable energy, oil and gas, and process industries. Many universities offer courses in law, accountancy, nursing, teaching and agriculture. Ravensbourne is a university college in Greenwich that specialises in digital media, fashion, television and broadcasting, interactive product design, architecture and environment design, graphic design, animation, music production and sound design.

Another example is Brunel, which became a university in 1966 having previously been a College of Advanced Technology. Many undergraduate courses are vocational including aerospace engineering, civil engineering, computer science, electronic and computer engineering, film and television studies, physiotherapy and nursing. Brunel offers sandwich courses where students undertake paid work placements as part of the degree.

The removal of the places cap means that higher-tariff universities have been able to poach students who would previously have gone to lower-tariff universities, forcing the latter to find new sources of students. Level 4-5 courses that lead on to a degree course are one way of doing that, as are Foundation courses and degree apprenticeships. University income from apprenticeships, traineeships and the adult education budget more than doubled from £12.6 million in 2014/15 to £31.9 million in 2016/17. Over the same period the number of universities in receipt of funding for FE provision (that is, apprenticeships and vocational courses below level 6) has trebled from 21 to 62. Over 100 universities are now registered to deliver higher and degree apprenticeships.

But FE colleges are the experts at offering non-degree level vocational courses, they offer shorter courses than universities and they are more flexible and quicker to respond to local markets than universities. This is why colleges can be better at providing the training element of apprenticeships than universities. Universities always tend to veer towards academic courses, paper-based examinations and research, when what may be needed is more practical hands-on training with assessment methods that reflect that.

One of the reasons why high-tariff universities may not wish to offer more and more vocational courses is that many will only attract students with weaker academic records, and the conventional rankings of universities are based in part on the grades possessed by the students on admission. So it is always better to run degree courses for doctors (high A level grades) than nurses (lower A level grades); 26 English universities have medical schools training doctors but only 12 of these (high-tariff universities) have a nursing school out of the 56 universities offering nursing (mostly lower tariff).

Universities are judged on the volume and quality of their research through the Research Excellence Framework (REF). This, too, tends to dampen their enthusiasm for vocational courses because the lecturers are less likely to be involved in research. Business courses comprise a fifth of the undergraduate student population. One would think that a good business course would involve close links with employers and some work experience, but the REF encourages an academic approach, with a focus on research.

Government needs to decide whether we are going to allow universities to carry on expanding. They could start to offer many of the more vocational, sandwich and two-year sub-degree courses that most commentators seem to think are needed, but if that happens the role of FE colleges needs to be clarified. This argues for a 'local ecosystem' approach where colleges, schools and universities are forced to agree who will offer which types of course, rather than operating in competition with each other the whole time. Colleges and universities will increasingly merge or work as partners (page 159).

What universities and FE colleges offer is demand-led: what individual students want determines which courses are offered. Personal choice is a good thing, but arguably the weakness of the English system is that we narrow our curriculum so much at age 16 – down to three or fewer subjects. Really important, life-determining decisions are taken by English pupils when they are only 16 and know almost nothing about the employment consequences of their subject choices. We start to specialise four years younger than most other countries.

Summary

University numbers have grown fast. There has been an increase in the proportion of students from disadvantaged backgrounds going to university, but mainly to low-tariff universities. Many of these end up with a £50,000 debt and a non-graduate job. Many young people feel obliged to apply for a three-year degree course, not because it is necessarily the best thing for them but because the alternatives are either unclear or are less easy to fund.

Experience in recent years shows that different elements of the education system need funding in different ways. Student loans have been a successful way of funding full-time university degrees for school leavers. They have not been a success for adults wishing to take part-time degrees or participate in sub-degree FE adult education – they are not willing to commit to such a loan.

While for most students it is clearly in their interests to go to university, some courses in some universities seem to act as a negative qualification: financially the students would have been better-off not going. The Department for Education should be congratulated for starting to publish this data.

The growth of universities has diverted more students away from vocational training and STEM subjects, of the sort that used to be offered by polytechnics, and into business, arts and social science degrees. It is not clear that the country as a whole has benefited from this.

Universities are facing a number of other criticisms: limited amounts of teaching to non-scientists, the huge increase in numbers of non-EU overseas students simply because they pay massive tuition fees, the use of foundation courses to get weak foreign pupils in through a back door, degree class inflation, an explosion of unconditional offers, vice-chancellors paid over £300,000. The gloss is coming off the university experience and this may be a good time to promote worthwhile alternatives.

On the other hand, the relative prestige of universities, and the fact that some of our top universities are amongst the best in the world, argues for further expansion of the university sector.

Chapter 9

Funding further education

by Maggie Galliers

There is growing evidence that funding – its quantum, its sources and the constraints placed upon it – plays a crucial role in determining the effectiveness and success of any public service.

The further education (FE) sector has had more than its share of funding pressure and has, in the main, been remarkably enterprising, agile and innovative in the face of this. But there are worrying signs that, unless the issue of funding is urgently addressed, the sector will be unable to fulfil its vital role in upskilling the nation and promoting social cohesion.

Compared with schools and universities FE has had a particularly tough set of funding settlements and regimes over the last quarter of a century. Public funding for pre-16 children has risen under successive governments since the mid-1990s, whilst post-16 and college budgets have been much more constrained. Income-contingent adult learner loans and higher education tuition fee rises have compounded the problem so that the English education revenue budget is now 80% schools and 20% everything else, with the former squeezing the latter. This is neither desirable nor sustainable.

FE has been subject to funding rates often much lower and more volatile than other parts of the education sector. It has also been buffeted by massive fluctuations in policy, by changes to the balance between public and private funding and by conflicting views about whether FE funding should be centrally planned and allocated or devolved locally.

The ever-changing landscape of funding and other arms-length bodies and the various attempts to introduce new providers to the sector have added a layer of complexity and confusion which has undermined colleges' and other providers' ability to deliver consistent high-quality, enduring and responsive education and training. Its funding has been less generous, less stable and less coherent than any other sphere of education in England.

Funding policies

Before 1993

Until the 1990s further education, sixth form and tertiary colleges were funded through a block grant system based on expected numbers of students. These grants, which were awarded annually in advance by local education authorities, gave colleges relatively secure and predictable revenue funding irrespective of actual student numbers, institutional performance or learner outcomes.

Some local authorities prioritised colleges as flagship vehicles for delivering a key strand of their activity and they invested heavily in both revenue and capital terms; others had different priorities. Colleges supplemented their income through fees charged to individuals and employers but the bulk of their funding was from the local authority block grants.

Despite the relative consistency in funding over time, the economic downturn from the 1970s onwards impacted on the role of colleges. There was a reduction in part-time day-release as big organisations cut jobs or shut down completely and there was an increase in younger full-time students because of rising unemployment.

Alongside colleges, most local authorities also funded and managed adult education delivered in community settings, while a small number of independent providers and employers offered skills training schemes managed through the Manpower Services Commission (later handled through the Training and Enterprise Councils).

This system had its limitations: there was huge geographical variation in funding for further education, the quality of college and other provider infrastructure varied widely and the sector could coast too easily, with few national benchmarks for finance or quality. But it also had considerable strengths. It positioned colleges, which offered the vast bulk of publicly funded education for 16- to 18-year-olds and adults, as a valued and necessary resource for the local community that complemented the school, polytechnic and other education sectors. The block grant system enabled them to set informed budgets, to take considered risks in terms of programmes offered, to anticipate and respond to the accelerating demand for technical and professional skills and to reach out to the gifted and talented as well as those furthest from the labour market. It also enabled local planning of provision, with duplication of providers kept to a minimum in a local area.

1993-2001

I entered senior management in FE in the early 1990s just as the Further and Higher Education Act (1992) was about to change things fundamentally. This Act was intended to set colleges free from local authority control and encourage institutional autonomy, choice for learners and 'healthy' competition in line with the prevailing political view at the time. My memory is that this was largely welcomed by the sector, which wanted to be freed up from what were often seen as unnecessary bureaucratic constraints imposed by local authorities and from a system which did not distinguish between low- and high-performing institutions.

Funding streams after 1992, whether from the Further Education Funding Council (FEFC) and Training and Enterprise Councils (TECs) or their successor body the Learning and Skills Council (LSC), were complex and increasingly output based. This encouraged better providers to innovate, to tailor provision according to local need, to recruit more students and maximise success. But poorer providers tried to game the system, which sometimes resulted in too much low-level provision and did not equip students with the skills that would give them lifelong employability (Felstead and Unwin, 2001). With each change to the funding system there was an incentive for colleges and other providers to respond by tweaking their programmes to 'follow the money'.

2001-2010

The following decade was characterised by volatility. The FEFC and TECs were abolished and replaced by the LSC. The remit of the LSC included planning and regulation of FE. This was exemplified by three-year funding agreements for 16-19 education linked to meeting local needs, quality improvement and performance. In parallel, Individual Learning Accounts for adults were set up to put purchasing power into the hands of individuals and employers which, because the scheme was seriously flawed, quickly descended into disrepute (page 94). The closure of this scheme after only 18 months caused further instability for the sector.

Train to Gain (a programme which provided government-funded work-based training to adults), which followed in 2006, was also relatively short-lived and there was much criticism of private providers for offering poor-quality training which was not relevant to employer needs. The impact of these changing initiatives for colleges was to further exacerbate the volatility of revenue funding. In a perverse consequence of the attempt to be market-led, rather than encourage individuals and employers to value and pay for training, Train to Gain resulted in a culture where there was an expectation that provision should be 'free' and a government responsibility.

Capital funding was another source of turmoil for the sector. For colleges, this strand of funding was distributed through a competitive bidding system led by the LSC. Independent providers relied on their own resources for capital investment and adult education capital funding was at the discretion of the relevant local authority. On the upside, this funding for colleges was relatively generous and the general fabric of college estates improved markedly, turning underinvested and often outdated buildings and equipment into state-of-the-art facilities that compete with some of the best in the world. On the downside, colleges were expected to contribute a substantial percentage of building costs themselves (unlike the school sector). Many colleges were encouraged to take out loans predicated on growth in income, funding rates and student numbers which did not always materialise and which threatened individual college financial sustainability. Other colleges had not made a successful bid for funding by the time the money ran out (another story entirely) and capital investment amongst other providers was very variable; so the quality of some estates and equipment continued to be poor.

In 2007, under Machinery of Government changes, the Department for Education and Skills became the Department of Children, Schools and Families and the responsibility for FE passed to the Department of Business, Innovation and Skills. This was not the only change to the funding landscape. The LSC was replaced in 2009 by the Young Peoples' Learning Agency (YPLA) and the Skills Funding Agency (SFA). More schizophrenia ensued. The YPLA was charged with commissioning 16-19 education in association with local authorities, essentially a 'plan-led' funding approach, and the SFA allocated post-19 funding through a 'demand-led' approach tied to learner and employer decisions about what they wanted to buy. Colleges were no longer able to smooth out their budgets by compensating across income lines according to actual rather than forecast delivery.

The FE sector also experienced reductions in higher education funding when universities, responding to a numbers cap, engaged in widespread withdrawal from franchising provision to colleges. A marked reluctance by the colleges' traditional higher education market – part-time adult learners from diverse backgrounds – to take out loans for their education was another factor in the reduction of HE courses taken at FE colleges.

2011-2018

Since 2011 funding and income for many colleges and other providers have been in decline in cash terms. Increased competition for 16- to 18-year-old students from school sixth form expansion, coinciding with a demographic downturn in this age group, has been another factor. Increasing proportions of the adult education budget were switched to apprenticeships, where FE colleges have to compete with private providers, so this has also been a factor in reducing college budgets. Added to this, sluggish economic growth and a strategy of deficit reduction have prolonged the period of austerity.

And, if a funding squeeze was not difficult enough for the sector, the funding methodology had become extraordinarily complex and did not always support programmes that could meet all the needs of the learners. The influential *Review of Vocational Education* by Alison Wolf in 2011 concluded:

> The current funding regime for 16- to 19-year-olds (and indeed post-19) is unique to this country in tying funding overwhelmingly to qualifications rather than to the individuals who take them. The system is completely opaque to the vast majority of the people working within the system, let alone to the public at large. It imposes very large administrative costs on institutions and, as basic economic and management theory tells us, opaque systems are intrinsically inefficient and subject to extensive gaming.

> It is hard to believe that we alone need to maintain a system of such complexity that senior college staff need to attend annual courses so that they can understand – partially – how they are being funded and how they can game the system.

This led in 2013 to a new 16-18 funding formula administered by the replacement body for the YPLA, the Education Funding Agency (EFA), based in a reformulated Department for Education (DfE). The new funding formula related to individual study programmes rather than qualifications. Different formulae for adults and for apprenticeships were applied through the Skills Funding Agency.

Advanced Learner Loans were introduced in 2013 for adults studying courses at level 3 or above and aged 24 and older. Their introduction led to a fall in adults studying at levels 3 and 4+, from 273,400 in 2012/13 to 195,200 in 2013/14 (Department for Education and Education and Skills Funding Agency, 2017b). By 2015/16, that number had fallen further still. Despite this persistent under-delivery, loan eligibility was expanded in 2016 to include 19- to 23-year-olds, and courses at levels 5 and 6. Loans must be paid back when a student earns over £21,000 *pa*.

But there was marked reluctance by learners to take out loans for further education. A massive 58% of FE loans funding – amounting to almost £1 billion – was not spent from 2013 to 2017 (Burke, 2017). The Student Loans Company, which processes Advanced Learner Loans on behalf of the Education and Skills

Funding Agency, revealed that just £652 million in loan-funded provision had actually been delivered since 2013, against £1.56 billion in allocations. And aside from maintenance loans for students on higher-level courses at national colleges, there is no help for living costs after the age of 19.

After the 2015 election there was a widespread fear that the college sector was not sustainable. Funding rates were fixed in cash terms to provide stability while college mergers took place through a process of Area Reviews.

The latest developments in this already complex landscape have been the combination of the two funding agencies to create the single Education and Skills Funding Agency, the creation of the Institute for Apprenticeships and the Register of Approved Apprenticeship Providers which has opened up the market to a plethora of new companies. The introduction of an apprenticeship levy is expected to raise £2 billion for apprenticeships in England and is intended to remove pressures to make savings elsewhere.

At Croydon College we were told that 16- to 17-year-olds are funded by the taxpayer for 540 hours a year of teaching, while 18-year-olds are funded by the taxpayer for 450 hours a year. Those aged above 18 take out a loan. But members of these three groups might be sitting together in the same class! The complexity of the funding is still a problem in itself, made worse by ESFA changes to the funding methodology after a new college year has started.

Scandals continue. In a bid to boost loans-funded provision, the SFA handed out huge sums of loans cash to untested providers. These include John Frank Training, which went bust under mysterious circumstances in November 2016. While £6.4 million had been paid for around 2200 adults to complete their training, a further £464,000 was thought to be effectively missing – leaving around 500 people with large debts but no courses.

No other part of the education system has been so buffeted by the changing winds of policy, and whilst this has created an enterprising and adaptive sector the volatility it has created has done little to support the development of sustainable and valued vocational, technical and professional routes for learners and employers alike. FE finds itself squeezed between the politically dominant school and university agendas.

Funding: the quantum

Spending per 16-18 FE student has evolved in three distinct phases. In 1990, spending per student stood at just over £5000 (in 2016-17 prices). It then fell by over 20% in real terms over the course of the 1990s to reach a low of £4000 per student in 1998-99. Over the 2000s, spending per student rose significantly, to reach a level of around £6000 in 2010-11. Since then, further education spending per student has again fallen in real terms due to cuts in public spending (Belfield *et al*, 2017a). **Spending per student in further education is now about 10% lower than spending per pupil in secondary schools, having been about 45% greater at the start of the 1990s.**

The FE sector is underfunded in relation to the massive task that it is undertaking and in relation to the investment made by government and employers in many other parts of the world. Brexit has raised the profile of skills and productivity in a way which makes the FE sector a vital component of national plans to upskill and retrain our existing population, and we are now beginning to see a demographic upturn at 16+. There may not be enough funding to meet these dual challenges unless things change rapidly.

Amongst others, the Chartered Institute of Personnel and Development is critical of the country's under-investment in vocational skills and the lack of a meaningful long-term policy in this area. Our employers spend less on training than other big economy countries in the European Union and the gap is getting worse as the graph below shows:

Figure 9.1: Investment in vocational training across EU

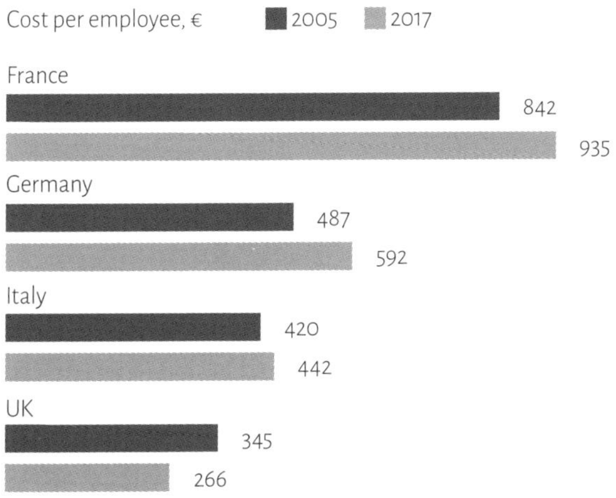

Cost per employee, € ■ 2005 ▓ 2017

France
842
935
Germany
487
592
Italy
420
442
UK
345
266

Source: Eurostat

FE colleges receive money from several different sources, including government funding for 16-18 students, funds for adult education, funds for students with high needs, the European Social Fund, funds for apprenticeship training, funds from students over 19 who have taken out loans, and fees for courses paid directly by the adults taking them.

The adult skills budget has been declining as a proportion of total public education spending since 2010. In absolute terms, less is now spent on it than on either pre-primary education or on taxpayer contributions to university teaching costs. Devolution has also had a part to play, with the recent devolution of the adult education budget to mayoral areas.

Adult Learner Loans are intended to provide another route for funding certain types of provision but they lack flexibility and there is market resistance to incurring debts to pay for training below higher education level. Providers have been fighting an uphill battle to increase revenue from this source.

FE is underfunded, not just compared with schools, not just compared with many other countries, and not just compared with the past. It is also underfunded compared with higher education. Baroness Wolf compared the resources available to further and higher education in *Heading for the precipice* (2015), which concludes:

> The current situation is financially unsustainable. It is deeply inegalitarian in its allocation of resources. It is also inefficient and bad for the 'human capital development', which increasingly drives and justifies education policy. In post-19 education, we are producing vanishingly small numbers of higher technician level qualifications, while massively increasing the output of generalist bachelor's degrees and low-level vocational qualifications. We are doing so because of the financial incentives and administrative structures that governments themselves have created, not because of labour market demand, and the imbalance looks set to worsen yet further. We therefore need, as a matter of urgency, to start thinking about post-19 funding and provision in a far more integrated way.

The impact of this is that the FE sector faces some steep financial challenges – funding rates well below that for pupils aged 11-16 and which dip again at 19, rising staff costs as national insurance and other contributions increase, flat cash funding on many income lines, poorly controlled pension funds, the loss of students to universities and constant uncertainly about future funding which makes planning difficult. Many colleges are merging; some are trying to diversify by taking foreign students; little is being spent on capital projects; and there is growing interest in online courses, which offer the potential for staff savings.

Inevitably all this has led to a lack of financial stability in the sector, to increased intervention by the FE Commissioner, to college mergers and to independent providers having contracts stopped and/or going out of business. This is not a context in which it is easy to sustain excellence in the post-16 vocational and technical sector, which learners, society and the economy so badly need.

To quote Julian Gravatt from the Association of Colleges, 'Funding is political, not a technocratic exercise'. Decisions about the quantum of funding for upskilling the nation post-16 are political. Levels of funding for FE, where it comes from and the constraints placed upon it must be addressed in the round if we are to have the kind of inclusive, skilled and prosperous economy and society to which the country aspires.

Chapter 10

The geography of waste

Success and failure are not distributed evenly.

Geographical inequalities are mainly related to social class (poorer areas do less well) and ethnicity (areas with a higher proportion of white working-class pupils do less well) but cannot be solely ascribed to these factors. Some regions simply have less successful schools than others. In the late 1990s, London schools were the worst in the country. Today they outperform schools in the rest of England, achieving the highest proportion of students obtaining good GCSEs, the highest percentage of schools rated 'outstanding' by Ofsted and the highest GCSE attainment for pupils from poorer backgrounds.

If a school gets bad GCSE results, this could be because the teaching there is bad, or it could be that most of its pupils come from a white working-class background (the group that does less well in almost all schools). So the relative success of children at school can be ascribed to 'between-school factors' (how well a school does compared to other schools with similar children) or 'within-school factors' (the background and ability of the children). Most research shows that in secondary schools only 12% of the variation in GCSE results is due to between-school factors. *Differences in pupils' backgrounds do more to determine their achievement and progress than the school they attend.*

Why do pupils in the north do less well at GCSE than pupils in London? According to Mike Treadaway's research (Treadaway, 2018a) it has little to do with schools. 58.5% of the gap is due to differences in ethnicity and the proportion on free school meals long-term; lower Key Stage 2 attainment in the north accounts for 26.2% of the difference; and 12.3% of the gap is due to the fact that pupils in the north take fewer GCSEs. He concludes that differences in school effectiveness between London and the north are quite small and attainment gaps are more a reflection of the areas they serve than the effectiveness of schools in each region.

Nevertheless, and starting with childcare, the Social Mobility Commission (2016) quoted an Ofsted report saying that 'the more prosperous an area, the more likely it is that good and outstanding childcare options are available. In the most deprived areas, double the percentage of children are in childcare provision that is not good enough, compared with the most prosperous areas.'

Looking at the Early Years Foundation Stage Profile (which measures how ready children are for school at the age of five) in places like Newham in London, free school meal pupils do as well as those not on FSMs. In other areas, such as Wigan, the gap is over the equivalent of six months of development on this measure. Local authorities are responsible for the sufficiency of childcare and reducing inequality. There is very little consistency in the degree to which each council focuses on early years outcomes for the disadvantaged.

The *Commission on Inequality in Education* report in 2017 (Clegg *et al*, 2017) looked at the age 11 verbal reasoning scores of children born in 2000. They found that Yorkshire and Humberside and the West Midlands had a disproportionately large number of low-scoring pupils while the North West and London had proportionately many more high-scoring.

What is more, they found that the impact of where you live seems to be getting stronger. Comparing the performance of 11-year-olds born at different times showed that the area a child comes from was a more powerful influence on Key Stage 2 verbal reasoning results for those born in 2000 than it was for those born in 1970. Some areas, such as the North East, Yorkshire and Humberside and the East Midlands, are falling further behind.

Another interesting finding was that schools serving poorer communities are more likely to have weak teachers – more who do not have a formal teaching qualification, teachers with less experience of teaching, more without a degree in the subject they are teaching, and higher teacher turnover (especially in secondary schools). While many inexperienced teachers are keen to work in schools that serve poor communities, they find not only that such teaching is tough but also that the schools are less likely to provide good support for new teachers. They are more likely to leave.

The largest expertise gaps in schools serving deprived communities occur in technical subjects like maths and physics, but these are the very subjects for which teachers having a relevant degree is most important.

The map opposite shows age 11 attainment in reading, writing and maths by local authority. The highest-performing local authorities are concentrated in London. The poorest-performing areas are in the West Midlands, East of England, Yorkshire and Humberside, and parts of the South East.

Figure 10.1: Percentage of pupils reaching the expected standard in reading, writing and mathematics at age 11

England, 2017 (state-funded schools only)

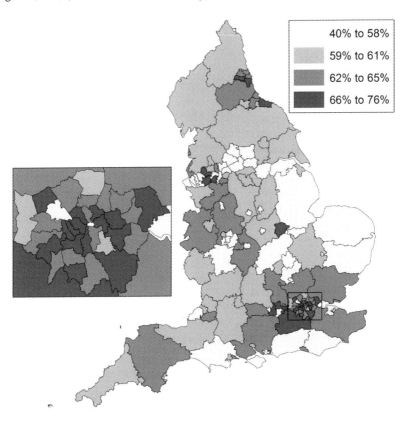

Source: Department for Education (2017a)

Turning to GCSE results, performance at age 16 across England shows some differences between regions, with over 60% of pupils in London achieving five good GCSEs including English and maths, compared to 55% in the West and East Midlands:

Figure 10.2: Percentage achieving 5+ A*-C GCSEs or equivalent including English and Maths by region, 2015-16

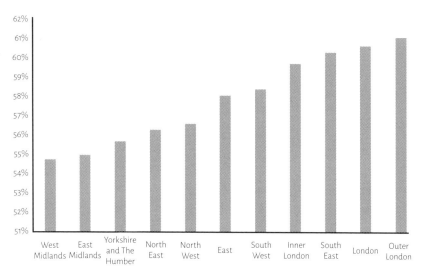

Source: Clegg et al *(2017)*

Andrews *et al* (2017) found that the gap in 2016 GCSE results between disadvantaged pupils and their peers was smaller in London, the South and the East (the gap being the equivalent of 16-18 months of teaching); while in the East Midlands and the Humber, the North and the South West, the gap was significantly larger: at 22 months by the end of Key Stage 4. In the Isle of Wight, disadvantaged pupils were well over two years (29 months) behind their peers by the end of secondary school. 51% of London children on free school meals achieve A* to C/9 to 4 in English and maths GCSE, compared with an average of 36% in all other English regions. In Westminster, 63% get good English and maths GCSEs; but in the Isle of Wight, only 27% do.

They also find that the gap becomes more prominent in rural areas by the end of secondary school. In areas such as Cumbria and Northumberland, the gap is 9 months at the end of Key Stage 2 but widens significantly to over 25 months by the end of Key Stage 4.

The Northern Powerhouse report (2018) found that, on average, pupils in the North are a third of a grade below the national standard across all subjects, and almost half a grade lower in mathematics.

Pupils from disadvantaged areas in the North achieved an average GCSE score of 39.9 across the main eight subjects – 13 below the national average, and roughly equivalent to achieving Cs at GCSE instead of Bs. This is partly linked to the class and ethnicity of pupils. Treadaway (2018b) found that while progress made by minority ethnic pupils is certainly much better in London than in all other areas of the UK, this is much less true of White British pupils (who form most of the pupils in the North). White working-class pupils in the North East do little worse than those in London at GCSE. The low attainment of white working-class British pupils is not simply due to where they live.

Another factor is the uneven distribution of good schools as measured by Ofsted inspections. The graph below shows the percentage of pupils on free school meals attending 'outstanding' or 'good' secondary schools by region (three-year average, 2015-17):

Figure 10.3: FSM pupils attending 'good' or 'outstanding' secondary schools

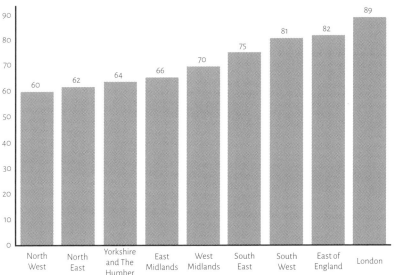

% FSM pupils attending a secondary school rated 'outstanding' or 'good'

Source: Social Mobility Commission (2017a)

A **Social Mobility Index** was devised by the Social Mobility Commission using two sets of measures:

- The educational attainment of those from poorer backgrounds in each local area – from the early years, through primary and secondary school, to post-16 outcomes and higher education participation.

- Outcomes achieved by adults in the area – average income, prevalence of low-paid work, availability of professional jobs, home ownership and the affordability of housing. This measures the prospects that people have of converting good educational attainment into good adulthood outcomes.

Some areas of the South East, where educational outcomes for young people from disadvantaged backgrounds are relatively poor, have strong job markets that provide more opportunities for young people from disadvantaged backgrounds to do well as adults, even if they don't do so well at school. By contrast, some parts of the North East have good educational outcomes for young people from disadvantaged backgrounds but progress is hampered by relatively weak local job markets, making it difficult for these young people to translate good performance at school into a decent job and good standard of living as adults.

The Department for Education in 2018 is focusing extra investment on schools in 12 Opportunity Areas, all social mobility coldspots identified by the Social Mobility Index.

Social mobility coldspots are concentrated in remote rural or coastal areas and in former industrial areas, especially in the Midlands, where young people from disadvantaged backgrounds face far higher barriers to improved social mobility than those who grow up in cities and their surrounding hinterland. Only 13% of disadvantaged young people in former industrial areas and 14% in remote rural coldspots progress to university compared with 27% of disadvantaged young people in the most successful areas in terms of social mobility, most of which are in London. Many coldspots combine poor educational outcomes with weak labour markets that have a greater share of low-skilled, low-paid employment than elsewhere in England.

The graph below uses the Social Mobility Commission's Social Mobility Index to divide areas into coldspots (which do badly) and hotspots (which do well in terms of results for pupils from low-income homes). It highlights the problem of remote rural and coastal areas and declining industrial areas:

Figure 10.4: What proportion of the social mobility hot and cold spots are found where?

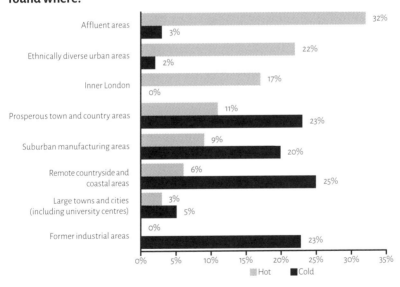

Source: Social Mobility Commission (2017a)

Remote rural and coastal areas suffer from poor transport links, both in terms of public transport and roads, which makes it harder to access good schools, colleges and jobs. Many isolated areas have no school sixth forms. Schools in deprived coastal and rural areas have a higher proportion of unqualified secondary school teachers than do those in affluent inland rural areas (7% compared with 4.6%). Schools in deprived or remote areas often struggle to recruit teachers, and where they do manage, they often lack the highest-quality applicants (Social Mobility Commission, 2017a). Remote areas find it harder to form meaningful school partnerships, including multi-academy trusts, than cities – where clusters of schools are physically closer together.

As well as looking at raw results, one can measure the progress a child makes from one point in their schooling to another. For example, Shaw *et al* (2017) looked at progress from age 11 to 16 (GCSEs). FSM pupil progress compared to non-FSM pupils is lowest in rural areas and highest in urban areas. There are a number of possible reasons for this, including the greater concentration of non-white pupils in urban areas (they tend to make more progress), and the impact of greater employment opportunities in cities (versus the countryside) on the motivation of pupils.

This graph shows the progress made between the ages of 11 and 16 in different regions using the 2016 Progress 8 scores.

Figure 10.5: Progress made between ages 11-16, 2016

-0.16	North-east
-0.15	North-west
-0.04	Yorkshire and the Humber
-0.14	East Midlands
-0.07	West Midlands
East of England	0.03
London	0.16
Inner London	0.17
Outer London	0.16
South-east	0.02
-0.05	South-west

Source: Pidd (2017)

Inner London moved from being the worst-performing area to the best-performing in the 2000s. This was due to a combination of factors – the London Challenge project to drive up standards in schools, the higher concentration of recent immigrants who tend to place a great emphasis on the education of their children, more Teach First teachers, better-qualified teachers, better job opportunities, and better funding. In 2012, Tower Hamlets in London received approximately £8000 per pupil through the dedicated schools grant allocation; this compares with Leicestershire, which received almost half as much. By 2017, this disparity had reduced but London still received more money than other areas. Sponsored academies were initiated in London and the capital has larger and higher-attaining multi-academy trusts, like Harris and Ark, than other parts of England. London primary schools have also developed strong system leadership and positive school cultures to a greater extent than other areas.

The Social Mobility Commission (2016) also looked at Ofsted inspection reports across the country and concluded:

> A child living in England's most disadvantaged areas is 27 times more likely to go to an inadequate school than a child in the most advantaged. The widely acknowledged success of London schools has mainly been driven by improvements in results for poorer children. In 2015, children in London eligible for FSMs were 52 per cent more likely to get five good GCSEs than their peers in other parts of England.

> The Government's failure to take responsibility for delivering a high-quality and fairly distributed teaching workforce continues to be the most significant weakness in its approach to schools. For poor children, the difference between a good and poor teacher is equivalent to one year of learning. But schools in poorer areas are more likely to have more unqualified teachers, less likely to have teachers with an academic degree in a relevant subject and they have higher turnover.

The graph on the next page shows that students in London are much more likely to go on to a school sixth form after GCSEs and much less likely to go on to FE college than other areas. Dave Thomson (2015) showed that staying on at a school sixth form meant you were much more likely to choose academic subjects and go to a good university. In some parts of the country students have little choice – there may be no school sixth forms and the sixth form colleges are very selective academically. This drives a higher proportion of post-GCSE students into the arms of FE colleges.

Figure 10.6: Sustained destinations after Key Stage 4 by region

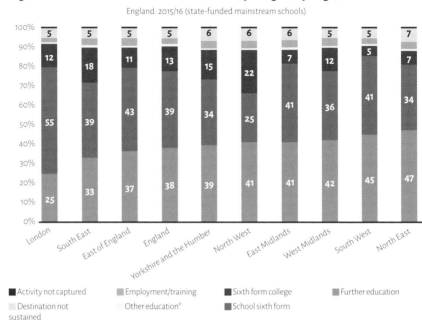

England: 2015/16 (state-funded mainstream schools)

Legend:
- ■ Activity not captured
- ▨ Employment/training
- ■ Sixth form college
- ▨ Further education
- ░ Destination not sustained
- ⬚ Other education*
- ▨ School sixth form

Source: Department for Education (2017i)

Data for August 2017 showed that in the West Midlands, the North East and Yorkshire and Humberside the proportion of 16- to 24-year-olds who were not in education, training or employment was between 13.5% and 14.7%, whilst in both London and the South it was between 9.0% and 10.1%. The figures are worse for young women than men, despite their better qualifications.

In terms of university entrance, the East Midlands fares worst at university participation, while the North East has the worst youth unemployment and selective university entry rates. In isolated rural and coastal areas, disadvantaged young people can find themselves trapped as they have limited access to education and employment opportunities and lack the means to move home or travel to access them (Social Mobility Commission, 2017a).

There are more-limited employment opportunities outside London. The two regions with the lowest youth social mobility – the North East and the East Midlands – have the fewest employers. The North East has 70,000 employers and the East Midlands 177,000, compared with 506,000 in London (ONS, 2017e). More than one in five of all jobs in England are in London, as are nearly one in three of England's high-skilled jobs (NOMIS, 2017).

Regional economies

London and the South East of England have a stronger economy than the rest of the UK. The reason is that they have a higher proportion of those jobs that have grown significantly in the past 50 years (high-level services such as finance and law) and a lower proportion of those that have declined (manufacturing, mining). They also have a more diversified economy, so when individual sectors decline the impact is less serious.

Other regions have had a greater dependence on other types of jobs. The north-east, for example, was dominated by coal mining, steel manufacture and ship building up to 1980, all of which have declined rapidly. The north-west depended on textile manufacturing up to the 1970s. The Midlands had a strong background in car manufacturing and specialist engineering; the South West relied on agriculture, mining, quarrying and tourism.

Regions relying on manufacturing have suffered. Manufacturing as a proportion of output has fallen from 18% of GDP in 1997 to 10% today. In Germany, by contrast, manufacturing has fallen from 25% of GDP to 22% today (Wiseman, 2017). Jobs in manufacturing in the north of England have halved during this period.

An ONS report (2017e) found that London, the South East and East of England were the only parts of the UK generating a fiscal surplus – that is, they generated more in tax revenues per head than was spent in public expenditure. These three regions support the rest of the UK. London generated £3070 per head more in tax revenue than was spent per head in public expenditure. Scotland consumed £2824 more per head than it generated, the North East £3825, Wales £4545, and Northern Ireland an astonishing £5437.

The report came to two conclusions. First, we need to do all we can to look after the economy of London. If it is the goose that laid the golden egg, we should be careful before we assume that the best way forward is to reduce London's productivity as a way of boosting other regions. If that doesn't work, we are all going to suffer greatly. The challenge is not to cut London down to size but to make other regions a bit more like it.

Secondly, we need to rebalance regional economies. Other countries have succeeded in doing this. Since Germany reunified in 1991, billions of euros have been poured into former East Germany, lifting GDP per capita in the East from 43% to 72.5% of West German levels over 25 years.

In the 1960s and 1970s we tried to do this in the UK with the creation of Development Areas in the depressed regions, using grants to attract employers. This had some success – think of the foreign car plants that were seduced to come to areas of high unemployment, like the Nissan factory near Sunderland in the North East. But the problem was that as fast as new employers came in, other, huge and long-standing employers – such as coal mining, steel and ship building – fell away in the face of international competition and, in the 1980s, the removal of government subsidies for loss-making nationalised industries.

The Midlands is especially interesting because it is the region with the highest density of population outside the south-east. The area is responsible for over a fifth of the UK's total manufacturing capability, while the services sector in the Midlands accounts for over four million jobs and is worth around £160 billion a year. It has well-known strengths, such as the cluster of car firms around Coventry and Warwickshire and the ceramics industry in Stoke and Staffordshire. The science and research base is also strong: the region has 20 universities, with research ranging from civil engineering to space technology.

But according to a Department for Communities and Local Government 2017 review, the Midlands economy has been falling behind over recent years. In 1997, the productivity gap between the Midlands and the UK average was about 10%. By 2015, it had grown to about 15%.

There is a shortage of skilled workers in the Midlands. The proportion of highly skilled people is about 15% below the England average. One in every eight people in the West Midlands has no qualifications. Many skilled graduates leave the region after completing their studies.

The region's economy is fragmented into small, poorly connected areas. This means that the whole sometimes adds up to less than the sum of its parts and the Midlands isn't making the most of its position at the centre of the country.

There is also a lack of entrepreneurship and economic dynamism. In 2015, the number of businesses created for every 100,000 people in London was more than double the rate in the Midlands.

Summary

1. Pupils in much of the south of England achieve better exam results than those in other areas. However, it was not always thus. London went from being the least successful region to being the most successful in only a few years.

2. A high proportion of the difference in educational attainment between different parts of the UK reflects their different social class and ethnic make-up. So the trick is to focus on the impact of social class and ethnicity, not geography per se.

3. But part of the difference reflects the difficulty some regions have in recruiting and keeping good teachers, and the fact that some areas have more powerful school sixth forms than others.

4. Rural areas, coastal zones and declining industrial/mining areas with higher unemployment are struggling compared to those regions with a more dynamic economy.

Chapter 11

International comparisons

How does the UK differ from other OECD countries?

The regular OECD analyses of vocational training in the UK compared to other OECD countries allows us to draw some conclusions:

1. We are unusual in that we allow students to drop English, maths and science at age 16. The Nuffield Foundation published a report (Hodgen *et al*, 2010) showing that England, Wales and Northern Ireland were alone among 24 economies (mostly OECD members) in having fewer than 20% of upper secondary students studying some mathematics.

    It is argued that the weakness of the English system is that we narrow our curriculum so much at age 16 – typically down to three or fewer subjects. Decisions that are taken in other countries at the age of 20 are effectively taken by English pupils at age 16, when they know little about the employment consequences of the decisions they are taking. We start to specialise four years younger than other countries and as a result we have some of the youngest graduates in the world (Willetts, 2017).

2. We have a higher proportion with bad literacy and numeracy (page 122). The OECD (2016a) placed England 22nd of 29 OECD countries for numeracy of 16- to 24-year-olds. There are 9 million working-age adults in England (more than a quarter of adults aged 16-65) with low literacy or numeracy skills or both.

3. The relationship between social class and educational outcomes is closer in the UK than in other countries (OECD, 2016a).

4. The duration of our upper secondary education is shorter. In Europe the most common pattern of official participation is four years (15-19) or three years (15-18 or 16-19). There are a few instances of a longer phase of 14-19, but only two cases of a short duration (16 to 18) – the UK and Spain (Spours *et al*, 2017).

    England divides the educational system into three main periods: 5- to 11-year-olds, 11- to 16-year-olds and 16- to 18-year-olds. This structure determines much of what we do. Sweden and Switzerland, for example, have upper secondary courses that last three or four years compared to the two in England. This is why Sweden and Switzerland have more level 4 courses – they have more time. Indeed the dominant system in Europe is the extension of secondary education up to age 19.

5.   In England our students have less contact time than is the case in other countries. We pay for 600 hours in FE which has to include work experience, remedial English and remedial maths. This compares to 1200 hours in Sweden, for example. It is perfectly possible that the new T levels would be better taught over three years, but the structure of our education system does not permit that.

6.   We have a smaller proportion taking a vocational/technical qualification as their main post-16 qualification. In Germany, France, Denmark, the Netherlands and Norway, between 40 and 50% of every youth cohort enrol on upper secondary (age 16-19) vocational programmes. In England the figure is no more than 20%, including apprenticeships, level 2 and level 3 vocational qualifications.

7.   We have a smaller proportion taking level 4 and 5 courses and a higher proportion going to university. Most young people now either go to university (a degree is a level 6 qualification) or they do a low-level qualification (Entry level, level 1 or 2). As we saw in Chapter 7, 332,000 UK students obtained a first degree in UK universities in 2015/16 (HESA, 2017) compared to 6000 obtaining an HND or HNC (level 4 and 5 courses). The numbers taking a two-year Foundation Degree fell to 14,000 in 2015/16.

In many other OECD countries, the picture is wholly different. In the United States for example, around 12% of the labour force have a post-secondary level 4/5 certificate as their highest qualification. In Canada, around one-quarter of the cohort gains an associate degree (below degree level) as their highest qualification. In South Korea, one-third of the youth cohort enters junior college or polytechnic programmes, which are dominated by two-year programmes in post-secondary vocational training.

8.   The UK has low participation in adult learning that is linked to their work. According to a European comparison study of 2010, 31% of UK employees attended vocational training courses at work, compared with a European Union average of 38% (Eurostat, 2016).

9.   We spend less money per head on technical and vocational education. Greatbatch and Tate (2017) compared the vocational education and training (VET) on offer in Denmark, France, Germany, the Netherlands and Norway. These countries spend more per student following

vocational tracks than for those following academic routes; Germany spends over £3000 more, for example.

Why so much money? Vocational costs are higher due to smaller class sizes and costs of equipment, among other things. Students undertaking vocational education and training in these countries receive almost double the number of direct teacher-supervised hours than students in the UK. And there is significant investment taking place in the professional development of the teachers.

In Norway upper secondary vocational education and training at both vocational colleges and workplaces is mainly supported by state funding. In Germany, Denmark, the Netherlands and France, the state finances training at vocational schools, while employers mainly finance on-the-job training. In Denmark, the Netherlands and France employers are required to pay apprenticeship taxes/levies, regardless of whether they employ apprentices. All of these countries offer financial incentives for employers to participate in the training of pupils in vocational education and training programmes (Greatbatch and Tate, 2017).

10. We have weaker links with employers. Around 90% of the students who follow the vocational tracks in Germany, Denmark and Norway have a training agreement with an employer.

11. We have a system of multiple private qualification providers, which leads to vast numbers of competing qualifications.

12. Our awarding organisations have historically not involved employers in the design of vocational qualifications in the way that is common outside the UK. In some countries, the process has been top-down, with qualifications designed with employers at national level. In others, such as Canadian colleges, the colleges can establish their own qualifications, allowing them to design curricula in partnership with local employers.

13. We have a more complex system for regulating qualifications.

14. We have a smaller proportion of students doing apprenticeships.

15. We have much weaker systems for facilitating progression from one level to the next.

How are we similar to other OECD countries?

1. A rising proportion of students are staying in education or training until they are 18 and a decreasing proportion are going into employment when they are 16.

2. Most parents and students aspire to academic as opposed to vocational qualifications because academic qualifications are the passport to higher education.

3. We do few vocational courses before the age of 16.

4. Growing centralization of accountability and assessment.

5. The influence of PISA and other international assessments on educational policy.

France

In France, when students leave their junior high school at age 15 (unless they repeat a year, which 28% of students do), they can either:

1. attend a general education and technological high school called a *lycée d'enseignement général et technologique* (LEGT) (60% of students)

2. attend a *lycée professionnel* (LP), a vocational high school (27% of students). There are around 1600 LPs in France.

3. start an apprenticeship or pre-apprenticeship (11%).

4. start training contracts other than apprenticeships (2%).

In France, 43% of students aged 16-19 are in vocational training. Vocational qualifications are achieved either through programmes in vocational high schools or an apprenticeship. Within the vocational high schools there are two main pathways:

- The first one is *Certificat d'Aptitude Professionnelle* – CAP (professional aptitude certificate). This prepares students for a definite career path, such as hairdresser or electrician, over a two-year period. More than 50% of the training is related to professional skills. The rest covers core subjects such as maths, French, history and geography, and English. After completing the CAP, students can move into employment or further training. The CAP comprises 2300 hours of learning over two years, of which 420 to 560 hours are spent in work placements.

- The second option is *baccalauréat professionnel* – Bac Pro (professional baccalaureate). This offers a professional training in an employment field wider than in the case of CAP, such as agriculture or building. This training takes place over three years. The main purpose of the professional baccalaureate is entry to the job market but it also enables students to move on to higher education, particularly University Technical Colleges.

The taught curriculum includes knowledge and techniques related to the vocational area and general studies such as French, history, geography, moral and civic education, mathematics, applied arts, a modern language, environmental health, sciences, economics and law. The Bac Pro consists of 3400 to 3500 hours over three years, of which 770 hours are spent in work experience.

The Ministry of Education in France has the responsibility for quality assurance of vocational education and training, defining strategies, policies, and teaching programmes and ensuring staff recruitment.

Laws governing apprenticeships are framed and passed at national level; regional authorities are responsible for their implementation and have wide discretion over training activities including apprenticeships. Employers and employees are represented at national and regional level and on the sector-based bodies (*Commissions Consultatives*) which determine training content. The *Commissions Consultatives* operate at national level.

In addition to the state qualifications, since the mid-1980s employer organisations and unions have been developing and promoting competence-based *Certificats de Qualification Professionelle* (CQPs). CQPs are occupational qualifications based on standards set by the relevant sector. They are common in construction and vehicle repair and tend to be narrower than the CAP or Bac Pro – they prepare you for a specific job. Organisations that can provide training for CQPs include *les groupements d'établissements de l'education nationale* (Greta). The Gretas are taught by state schools: *collèges, lycées technologiques* and *lycées professionnels* which pool their skills and are grouped together depending on their geographical proximity. Present in all regions, Gretas located in 6500 sites train some 450,000 young people and adults every year.

Netherlands

About 43% of 16- to 19-year-olds in the Netherlands enrol in vocational programmes. This group have two options open to them, both leading to the same qualifications:

1. a school-based course with short intermittent periods with companies which take up 20-60% of the study time. Two-thirds of vocational students take this route. There are 1000 direct teaching hours a year for the course.

Or

2. an apprenticeship which involves study at a vocational school and work for a firm, the latter occupying at least 60% of the time. One-third take

this route. Students are required to have a contract with a firm if they wish to follow this route.

A key feature of the system is the coherence of the different pathways. Irrespective of the pathway taken, students must have a work placement that is quality-assured and accredited. Students also take the same qualification regardless of which pathway they are on.

In contrast to Britain, there have been no new universities in the Netherlands since 1976. They have chosen to concentrate on vocational education.

There are 65 colleges offering vocational courses, all drawing students from a particular region. The courses on offer range from Entry level to level 4. There are three types of college: those who offer courses in technology, economics, personal/social services, or health care, agricultural colleges, and specialised colleges offering programmes for one branch of industry only, such as graphic art and design, butchery, house painting, furniture making, fishing or shipping and transport.

Colleges are incentivised by their funding agreement with the Ministry of Education to have good course completion rates, quality of workplace learning and staff development. The college system is also completely interlocked with employers, which allows a greater number of high-quality work experience placements.

The Netherlands has created strong 'sector bodies', which have taken responsibility for designing qualifications, setting standards, and coordinating employers, so that they become more likely to engage in the training and apprenticeship programmes. At the same time, companies and colleges are allowed to develop course modules in response to changing employment needs in their area.

Germany

Germany pursues a dual-track system that involves the state providing theoretical training in state-funded vocational schools and employers providing the competence elements through work-based training.

16- to 19-year-olds seeking vocational training have three possible routes:

1. Apprenticeship training, which lasts three years and is split between on-the-job training and vocational school-based education. The occupational competencies to be acquired in the work-based training are specified in training regulations that are binding and guarantee a uniform national standard.

Apprentices typically take an intermediate and final examination. The latter consists of written exams, an oral exam and a practical test. Responsibilities for apprentice training are shared by the federal government, Länder (regional authorities), employers, unions, and self-governing industry sector expert bodies ('Chambers'). The apprenticeship system is monitored by the Chambers or by autonomous trade and industry associations.

The federal government has a legal framework for governance of apprenticeship training, administered through the Federal Institute for Vocational Education and Training (BiBB) that also conducts labour market research to underpin vocational education decision-making. BiBB prepares a single national standard for each apprenticeship occupation.

Apprenticeships survive in Germany because access to many jobs depends on obtaining a licence to practise, which can only be gained by doing an apprenticeship. Much manufacturing is protected by government intervention. This model is very different from the systems used in the UK and USA with their flexible labour markets. There is no possibility of us adopting the German system in the UK and little point in assuming that we could create a similar apprenticeships system.

2. Full-time 16-19 school-based vocational courses, which often include work placements and take two to three years. The regional authorities (*Länder*) are responsible for these. There are three types of school offering these courses:

- *Berufsschulen*, vocational schools that lead to employment or to a technical school. They cover commercial, languages, craft, household, caring and artistic sectors.

- Senior technical schools, which cover welfare, financial and commercial and technical courses. They lead to employment or to a university of applied science.

- *Gymnasium*, grammar schools with a vocational bias offering courses in business, technical, nutrition, agronomy, health care, welfare, ICT. They lead to universities of applied science.

The *Länder* governments are responsible for education provided by schools and universities in their region.

3. A transition system for those who do not fulfil the entrance requirements for full-time vocational schools or failed to obtain an apprenticeship position.

Almost half of Germans take one of these three routes.

Every company providing training is required to prove its suitability as a training place, develop a training plan for each apprentice based on the training regulations for that occupation, employ an in-company trainer with required professional qualifications and ensure the apprentice keeps a record book. These requirements are monitored by the chamber in charge. The final exams are set by an independent committee of the chamber and this maintains quality assurance.

Funding is provided mainly by public sources (around four-fifths of the total), with large contributions from the employers who train apprentices (the remaining fifth). The state finances the vocational schools, whilst the on-the-job training component of apprenticeships is mainly financed by the employer.

In Britain our tertiary education system only recognises one type of institution – the university. But the German tertiary education system has two types of institutions: the *Universitäten*, which have the right to confer doctorates; and *Fachhochschulen* (Universities of Applied Sciences), which offer the same degrees as *Universitäten*, but often concentrate on applied science. Subjects taught at *Fachhochschulen* include engineering, computer science, business and management, arts and design, communication studies. The *Fachhochschulen* focus on employability and have a close relationship with employers. They are geared to applied research instead of fundamental research.

Norway

In Norway about 40% of 16- to 19-year-olds are enrolled in vocational study courses. Most attend two years of training in a vocational school followed by two years of practical training apprenticeship in a firm. Most courses lead to a level 4 certificate.

The teaching time for the two years at school is set at 980 guided learning hours for each of the two years – 24 hours of tutor-led contact time a week. This high level of contact time is why Norway spends 60% more on upper secondary education than the OECD average.

The vocational courses are monitored by trade-specific vocational training councils. They make adjustments every year based on the changing demand for skills. They set the content of the training, exams, approval of apprenticeship providers and teacher competencies.

The figure shows the structure of the four-year programme. The common core subjects are Norwegian, English, maths, gymnastics, natural sciences and social sciences and are the same for all students. The common programme subject is a course specific to the employment type the student has chosen. The study project includes hands-on training in workshops in the schools and short work experience placements with firms.

Figure 11.1: The 2+2 model in Norway

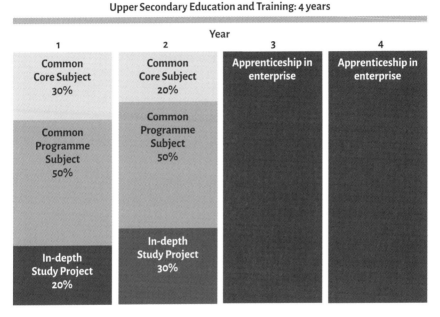

Source: Greatbatch and Tate (2017)

After two years in the vocational school, 25% of this group of students transfer to a third-year course that qualifies them for entry to higher education. In this third year they study Norwegian, English, maths, natural science, social sciences and history.

Norway spends large sums on special needs and specially adapted tuition too – 8% of the total spend on upper secondary education and training. This includes new programmes for recent immigrants needing language tuition. For weaker students there is a special 'training candidate scheme', which leads to certificates at level 3.

Vocational education and training is a paid for by the state. Employers are given a grant to cover all the costs of training an apprentice for the two years.

Conclusion

In England additional funding will be needed to increase the quality of our vocational education, improve recruitment and retention, streamline and improve the transparency of vocational pathways and ensure that vocational training is continuously adapted to meet evolving skills needs and changes in the labour market. Compared to other countries we are relatively weak. Too few of our young people engage in high-quality vocational training.

Chapter 12

What are the bottom 50% going to do now?

Until August 1914 a sensible, law-abiding Englishman could pass through life and hardly notice the existence of the state, beyond the post office and the policeman.

A J P Taylor, *English History, 1914-1945*.

Government reforms 2012-18

The recent Coalition and Conservative governments have made several reforms designed to improve the quality of vocational courses in England. It is hard to assess how successful these will be because no such changes can be honestly appraised for some years. Nevertheless, this is what is happening:

National Colleges

National Colleges are intended to be expert training centres focusing on key areas of the economy. First announced in April 2014, they are designed to fill high-skill vocational gaps. The National Colleges focus on delivering high-level technical skills at levels 4 to 6. They combine academic study with practical application and will collaborate with schools, employers and universities.

Each college is led by employers, with 50% of initial investment to establish a college coming from these employers. Examples include:

- National College for High Speed Rail (hubs located in Birmingham and Doncaster)
- National College for Digital Skills (hub located in London: Tottenham Hale and Whitechapel)
- National College for the Creative and Cultural Industries (hub located in Purfleet, Essex)

Post-16 Skills Plan based on the recommendations of the Sainsbury Review (2016):

1 – Post-16, in the 2020s all students will have two options: an academic route or a technical route, with opportunities to move between them. The technical education option (employment-based and college-based) will be designed to meet the needs of employers and will be managed by the new Institute for Apprenticeships. The academic option is designed to meet the entry requirements of university undergraduate degree courses. So universities will take the lead in specifying the standards to be met by the academic option, while the needs of employers will drive the design of the technical education option.

The term 'vocational' has been replaced by the word 'technical'. The view was that the word 'vocational' was too vague. 'Technical education' means something that leads to skilled employment and requires the acquisition of both a substantial body of technical knowledge and a set of practical skills valued by industry.

Figure 12.1: How the academic and technical options would work

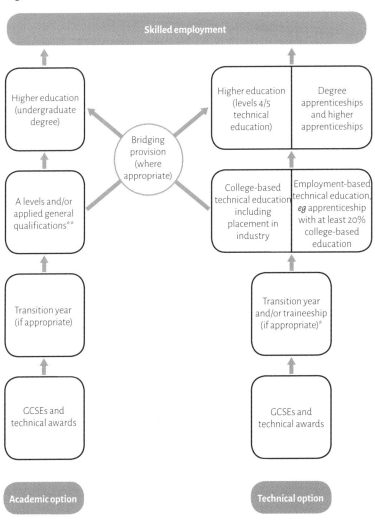

* Where a student does both, the traineeship will follow the transition year. Students doing both the transition year and a traineeship may progress directly to employment.

** Some students will move directly from A level and/or applied general qualifications to degree and higher apprenticeships.

Source: Department for Business, Innovation & Skills and Department for Education (2016)

2 – There will be a common framework of 15 routes across all technical education (T levels and apprenticeships) based on 15 occupational sectors. The 15 technical education routes just cover occupations where there is a 'substantial requirement' for technical knowledge and practical skills. The 15 are based on existing labour market information; as the labour market changes, the 15 routes may change:

Agriculture, Environmental and Animal Care

Number currently employed: 454,726

Typical job roles: Conservationist, park ranger, farmer, horticulturalist, agricultural manager, agricultural technician

Business and Administrative

Number employed: 2,204,478

Typical job roles: Human resources officer, office manager, administrative officer, housing officer

Catering and Hospitality

Number employed: 568,998

Typical job roles: Chef, butcher, baker, catering manager, events manager

Childcare and Education

Number employed: 1,060,804

Typical job roles: Nursery assistant, early years officer, teaching assistant, youth worker

Construction

Number employed: 1,625,448

Typical job roles: Bricklayer/mason, electrician, building/civil engineering technician, carpenter/joiner, construction supervisor

Creative and Design

Number employed: 529,573

Typical job roles: Arts producer, graphic designer, audio-visual technician, journalist, product/clothing designer, upholsterer, tailor, furniture maker

Digital

Number employed: 351,649

Typical job roles: IT business analyst/systems designer, programmer, software developer, IT technician, web designer, network administrator

Engineering and Manufacturing

Number employed: 1,319,645

Typical job roles: Engineering technician, vehicle mechanic, aircraft fitter, printer, process technician, energy plant operative

Hair and Beauty

Number employed: 293,004

Typical job roles: Hairdresser, barber, beauty therapist

Health and Science

Number employed: 915,979

Typical job roles: Nursing assistant, pharmaceutical technician, sports therapist, laboratory technician, dental nurse, food technician

Legal, Finance and Accounting

Number employed: 1,325,482

Typical job roles: Accounting technician, paralegal, financial account manager, payroll manager, finance officer, legal secretary

Protective Services

Number employed: 398,400

Typical job roles: Police officer, fire service officer, non-commissioned officer (NCO), maritime operations officer (coastguard)

Sales, Marketing and Procurement

Number employed: 957,185

Typical job roles: Buyer, procurement officer, sales account manager, market research analyst, estate agent

Social Care

Number employed: 865,941

Typical job roles: Care worker, residential warden, home carer, probation officer, welfare counsellor

Transport and Logistics

Number employed: 589,509

Typical job roles: Ship's officer, railway signalling technician, HGV driver

Source: Department for Business, Innovation & Skills and Department for Education (2016)

There are some obvious areas of employment such as retail missing from the list, but this was because, according to Lord Sainsbury, the skills and knowledge of the retail industry are 'almost all company-specific'. In such cases there is no need for an external technical course – the employers can do the training. The areas where you need technical education are where there are transferable skills applicable to many employers.

These 15 routes cover both apprenticeships and T levels. There is some trade-off between the two. When the economy is booming and employers need more staff, apprenticeships might grow. In a recession they would shrink and college-based technical courses might grow to compensate.

A single, common framework of content will cover both apprenticeship standards and T levels. The Institute for Apprenticeships is responsible and has convened panels of professionals to advise on the knowledge, skills and behaviours to be acquired for the standards in each route and on suitable assessment strategies.

3 – T levels

Two-year level 3 T levels will be offered to students aged 16+, phased in after 2020. The T levels will be offered for 11 of the 15 routes – 4 of the 15 technical education routes will be delivered through apprenticeships.

The 11 routes are broad so they will each be broken down into separate 'occupational specialisms', each of which can be a T level. In other words, there will be many more than 11 T levels – probably 40-60. For example, the 'Digital' route could be broken down into three: IT support and services; software and applications; data and digital business services.

A T level is a level 3 qualification, like an A level. But that it doesn't mean it has the same academic demand as an A level. Which 'level' a qualification is set at depends on the purpose of the qualification and several other things.

Each T level will have several elements:

- a common core of useful knowledge, skills and behaviours that may be examined on paper
- a specific vocational course (called a Technical Qualification) which assesses the ability to do things – called 'competences'
- employability skills such as computer literacy, reliability, attitude
- a 45- to 60-day work placement
- maths, English and digital requirements
- any other occupation-specific requirements/qualifications, as set out by the relevant T level panel within the Institute for Apprenticeships

The aim of the Technical Qualification is to achieve 'threshold competence' in the occupational specialism, which means that a student is well placed to develop full occupational competence, with further support and development, once in employment. Threshold competence is as close to full occupational competence as can be reasonably expected of student studying the qualification in a classroom, workshops and simulated working environments.

The Sainsbury Review acknowledged the difficulty with work placements: 'We recognise that delivering this recommendation in practice is far from trivial. We are suggesting that up to 250,000 17-year-olds could require work placements.' Finding employers willing to offer work placements on this scale may be impossible – and where it is impossible then it is hard to see how colleges can offer the courses.

Each route will be offered by just one organisation to prevent the 'race-to-the bottom' that can happen if exam boards are in competition with each other.

There are at least four elements to the creation of T levels:

1. Writing the content – the syllabus. This will be managed by the Institute for Apprenticeships and Technical Education, who will also need to define what 'good' looks like for each element of the syllabus.

2. Managing the process of selecting just one awarding organisation per route.

3. Deciding how each element of the T level is to be assessed and graded, and how Ofqual is going to regulate this, including the maintenance of grade standards from one year to the next.

4. Finding employers willing to offer work experience.

The idea is that for college-based technical education at level 3 the system of qualifications will be simplified dramatically, with only one tech level qualification approved for each occupation or cluster of occupations.

The aim is to achieve parity of esteem with A levels. In theory, students taking T levels will be able to enter an apprenticeship or employment, move to a level 4 course or enter higher education.

The intention is that the hours spent on the courses will increase by 50% more than current courses, to 900 hours a year or more.

At the end of the T level course each student will receive a certificate, which might include:

- a grade for the occupational specialism
- a grade for the common core
- grades for maths and English qualifications (whether these were completed prior to the start of a route or not)
- any additional professional qualification/registration which has been taken and the grade achieved, if applicable
- confirmation of successful completion of the work placement

4 – Level 4 and 5 qualifications

For each of the 15 routes, **the Institute for Apprenticeships will maintain a register of technical qualifications at levels 4 and 5** that are eligible for public subsidy through government-backed student loans. To begin with, this register will be drawn from those **existing** technical qualifications that are considered to be valuable. Again, the number of competing qualifications will be greatly reduced.

At university level the new Office for Students (OfS) will determine which academic qualifications at levels 4 and 5 could be part of a wider programme of study leading to a full bachelor's degree.

5 – Progression routes

The Government will ensure that clear progression routes are developed – from level 2 and 3 to 4 and 5, from levels 4 and 5 to apprenticeships and higher education.

6 – They will establish a transition year for students not yet ready for further education – those with low prior attainment, some of whom will have special educational needs and/or disabilities or who missed school due to illness. The

transition year will focus on developing basic skills, with the aim of progression to academic or technical education, or to employment with training, by the end of the year. At present 20% of each cohort (of whom only a small proportion have severe physiologically based learning difficulties) finish GCSEs at too low a level to start even level 2 courses.

The 2017 Industrial Strategy

1 – Picking winners

Despite the failure of all previous government attempts to 'pick winners', the industrial strategy intends to do just that:

> Technologies which the new Industrial Strategy Challenge Fund could support [include]: smart and clean energy technologies (such as storage and demand response grid technologies); robotics and artificial intelligence (including connected and autonomous vehicles and drones); satellites and space technologies; leading edge healthcare and medicine; manufacturing processes and materials of the future; biotechnology and synthetic biology quantum technologies, and transformative digital technologies including supercomputing, advanced modelling, and 5G mobile networks. (Department for Business, Energy & Industrial Strategy, 2017)

They just can't resist it! It is reminiscent of the National Enterprise Board of the 1970s that started as a project to match the best firms with the most advanced technology and ended up helping failing businesses stay afloat.

2 – New Institutes of Technology will be created to increase the provision of higher-level technical education. These may be new or linked to existing colleges or universities and will focus on technical education in STEM subjects at levels 4 and 5, but will extend to level 6 and above. They will receive a grant for extra equipment and buildings from a capital fund of a mere £170 million. The IoTs will in every case be a collaboration between local employers, at least one FE College or independent training provider and a university. The first IoTs are expected to open in 2019.

Much like the 400 Centres of Vocational Excellence scheme instituted for FE colleges after 2001, which achieved little, the Institutes of Technology will get IoT plaques and kite-marks for websites.

3 – A UCAS-type online application process for technical qualifications will be created – a good idea.

These reforms look good on paper. How could they fail?

The reforms look radical but are little different from very similar reforms attempted by previous governments. Many times we have tried to create specialist institutions, many times governments have tried to rebrand qualifications – for example the GNVQs and the Qualifications and Credit Framework. Transferable skills have long been on the agenda, as has 'putting employers at the heart of vocational education'. The 14-19 Diplomas, which were announced in 2005 and scrapped in 2010, were similar to T levels – they covered 14 sectors such as construction or hair and beauty, and they were an attempt to mix specialist skills with transferable skills plus work experience.

How might we fail this time?

1 – Very few will want to take T levels. In England, what universities and FE colleges offer is demand-led. What individual students want determines which courses are offered. So we can offer courses, but they fail if demand is not there.

T levels could fail because most 16-year-olds will not be willing to opt for one particular career (a T level pathway) at that age. They will prefer to keep their options open by taking A levels or Applied Generals. At present only about 15% of 16- to 18-year-olds studying at level 3 take a technical qualification, whether alone or in combination with other types. There are twice as many taking an Applied General qualification. Applied Generals have been the route to university for many disadvantaged pupils so no government is going to be quick to promote T levels ahead of them.

Remember – if you choose three A levels and then have to drop one, it is not a disaster. But you only take one T level subject, so the risk in increased. How many 16-year-olds will opt for (or know anything about) Transport and Logistics T levels, one wonders? In order to make T levels attractive to students, it is desirable that there should be ways in which a student who embarks on one specialism but later regrets that choice can change to a different specialism and, indeed, that students should have the opportunity to experience different specialisms before making a firm choice. For example, if there were separate courses for hairdressing and beauty therapy, it is reasonable to think that a student should have some experience of both before choosing between them.

Schools and colleges are sceptical about T levels and may hold off promoting them until they feel sure that the qualification is valued by employers.

2 – The new qualifications may be inappropriate for many students. Past attempts to create parity of esteem have added more and more academic content and written exams to vocational qualifications in order to gain respectability. This is a mistake. T levels will be most attractive to the third quartile of students who arc reasonably able but who find academic learning and written exams a trial.

Around 10% of those aged 16 and 17 are not engaged in full-time education or apprenticeships and many of them are not ready to join level 2 let alone level 3 technical education programmes.

The Skills Plan assumes young people aged 16 will either acquire the basic skills necessary to undertake a level 3 programme or move directly to work. But there are many occupations, for example in the construction sector, that recruit those with skills at level 2, and there are many students who are miles off being able to embark on a level 3 course successfully. **We need to be clearer about the provision being made for those whose aim is level 1 or 2 vocational skills. It might have been better to have had a level 2 T level as a stepping stone to level 3, in the same way as AS levels were a stepping stone to A levels.**

As for adults, even where courses are funded by the government, they are still put off by loss of earnings or by childcare costs. Arguably we should offer maintenance loans to 19- to 23-year-olds seeking a first level 3 technical qualification who are unable to access support from an employer.

3 – However hard the government tries to persuade students and parents of 'parity of esteem', it will not wash. Now that 50% of young people go to university, and most good jobs go to people who have gone to university (whether a degree is needed to do that job or not), young people understand that there is a hierarchy of qualifications. A degree is high in the pecking order. All previous government attempts to sell 'parity of esteem' have failed. T levels may deserve parity of esteem with A levels but they will not have it. Indeed, taking a T level will be seen as signalling that you are 'unacademic'. So students may continue to strive to go to university.

Trying to achieve parity between all 'vocational' and 'academic' options is not the ultimate aim in any case. In the end some vocational and some academic qualifications will have more prestige than others, as they have always done. The ultimate aim is ensuring that all young people have access to better, sustainable routes, and that a qualification is not deemed to be of lesser value simply because it is labelled as 'vocational'.

4 – The sums of money being invested are not great enough. The apprenticeship levy does not bring spending back to the levels of a decade ago or close to the EU average. The low take-up of full-time technical courses at levels 4, 5 and 6 compared with undergraduate university degrees is probably associated with the more favourable arrangements for maintenance loans at universities. The low take-up of full-time level 3 courses after the age of 19 is due to inadequate funding.

5 – It is hard for the FE sector to make up for teaching young people have received at school. This is especially true of literacy and numeracy. The only effective way of making most of our population literate and numerate is to raise the bar for 5- to 16-year-olds (as the Government has done) and to improve the level of teaching.

To put it another way, policy makers underestimate how long it can take for students who have underperformed at school to catch up.

School subject choices also matter. It is hard to generate engineers if so few take physics A level.

6 – The standards being set for the new qualifications will be low. Some assessment organisations are backing out because of the costs and uncertainty involved. This suggests that money is short, and shortage of resources could easily reduce the quality of the qualifications.

Training providers will continue to compete on the basis of price. Having a target of '3 million new apprenticeship starts by 2020' prioritises quantity over quality.

If the work done by students taking T levels is assessed by the teachers themselves – desirable as such assessment might be – then we will be faced with the problem of centres inflating scores in order to boost pass rates. It is not possible for awarding bodies and Ofqual to monitor centres all the time. When you are scoring competence at practical tasks it is hard to question a centre's decision – you would need to film every student throughout the course and have thousands of qualified examiners to watch these films. Yet T levels need to be of high quality if they are to be used for students to go onto higher-level courses, including university, and if they are to be used to hold FE colleges to account in performance measures.

The proposal to teach 'transferable skills' as part of T levels sounds like a repeat of the same mistake made many times in the past (page 99).

7 – The current emphasis is on 'putting employers in the driving seat', but what if they don't want to drive or cannot drive skilfully? It is unclear if employers have the desire or capacity to take control of the apprenticeship and T levels system. Real reform requires employers to believe that it is in their interests to upskill their workforce. At present, too few seem willing to accept this, preferring to compete by using a low-skill low-pay model. In any case, employers are not homogenous: they usually speak for their own business rather than 'the industry'. Small and medium-sized firms lack the time to develop and run successful apprenticeship schemes.

Employer groups are playing a leading role in defining the technical qualification part of T levels. Although they may have a strong grasp of what should be needed in a particular occupational role, their expectations of 16- to 18-year-olds may be unrealistic.

At present most FE colleges find it very hard to persuade employers to offer 1-2 weeks of work experience. T levels may require 45-60 days of work experience, a seemingly impossible ask. After all, employers are also being asked to provide work experience related to apprenticeships, traineeships, schools and higher education. Making sure that we have the right number of placements in the right place at the right time will be a challenge, particularly in rural areas – matching the supply of work placements in each sector to the demand from learners.

8 – The issue of progression from one level to another is still unclear. Those doing a level 3 T level may want to progress to level 4 and 5 courses, but these are thin on the ground.

9 – It will be impossible to find enough good teachers. This is one reason why we have been so bad at developing maths skills amongst students aged 16-19: there are not enough maths teachers. There are not enough maths teachers because most people drop the subject when they are 16 – so this is a vicious circle.

The FE Advice website says:

Teaching qualifications for the FE & Skills sector

There are no two ways about it: this bit can be confusing. There is a suite of teaching qualifications approved for the sector and offered by Universities, Colleges and other providers but they have various names. There are also in circulation qualifications from previous approved series.

FE needs 'dual professionals' who are experts in their profession and also good teachers – a rare combination.

10 – Inadequate leadership – 'There are concerns that there is not enough leadership capacity within the FE sector. In 2016 the effectiveness of leadership and management was judged to be "good" or "outstanding" in only 52% of general FE colleges' (Ofsted, 2016).

11 – The task of simplifying the system is almost impossible. Technical education requires many, many different courses and levels. It cannot easily be reduced to simple structures, like GCSEs and A levels.

Both civil servants and Ofqual tend to be 'tidy-minded'. They prefer qualifications of any type (such as T levels) to be standardised and comparable. They find it hard to cope with the fact that in the vocational sphere different industries need qualifications with different standards. Engineering will be more demanding and more complex than hairdressing. Construction is not the same as the health service.

In my interview with Alison Wolf, she commented: 'The problem with high levels of central government involvement is the civil servants who run things. They have no understanding of the vocational sector and tend to produce schemes which are unworkable.'

12 – The new vocational qualifications will be too bureaucratic. At the same time the history of NVQs (page 96) tells us that because vocational courses can be complex there has been a tendency to make them too bureaucratic – dozens of 'standards' that have to be taught and assessed, for example. T levels include many elements – the occupational specialism, core knowledge, literacy and numeracy, employability skills etc. Once the level of bureaucracy or box-ticking becomes too great, colleges and employers look for alternatives.

13 – Confused roles. New organisations to co-ordinate stakeholders, like the Institute of Apprenticeships, could too easily become part of the tangled confusion of overlapping roles. At the time of writing there are already signs of disagreement between the Department for Education, the Institute of Apprenticeships and Ofqual over the management of apprenticeships and T levels. There is a lack of clarity about the role of the Institute for Apprenticeships in relation to the Office for Students, which controls universities. There is confusion about the respective roles of the Sector Skills Councils, the Local Enterprise Partnerships and the Trailblazers – who does what? Power over adult skills provision is included in each of the 30 or so devolution deals that are at various stages of development across England, adding yet another layer.

In terms of funding, there are many other bodies involved, all of whom can influence what happens. The Education Funding Agency is responsible for all 16-18 education up to level 3, including technical. The devolved authorities are becoming responsible for some of the Adult Education budget, as is the Skills Funding Agency where the Adult Education budget is not devolved. The Student Loans Company and the Skills Funding Agency manage fee-loans for 19+ technical education at level 3 and 18+ technical education at levels 4-5. Most of the education and training funding goes to colleges but much of the funding for work-based learning and apprenticeships goes to private companies.

This is one of the big differences between England and Germany. The Germans have a longstanding focus on system structures and know what works. In England we are always creating new bodies – like the Institute for Apprenticeships.

14 – Awarding Organisations. The 2017 Frontier Economics report was concerned that awarding the contract for T levels to just one organisation per route was fraught with danger. It would reduce the drive to compete on quality. It would expose the qualifications to peril if a provider was to fail. What is more, if an organisation failed to gain a contract first time round, it may be unlikely that they will retain sufficient expertise to bid for the contract when it comes up for renewal – so the system will not benefit from market competition in the way the government would wish. The first successful tenderer could be the only bidder when it is time to re-bid after 5 years.

On the other hand, our system of multiple private qualification-awarding companies is wholly different from many countries in continental Europe where national agencies work with employers to establish a single set of qualifications. T levels take us part way to a more simplified system, but the plethora of private awarders remains.

15 – Reforms are hurried and there is a failure to consult the colleges. There is already deep concern that the introduction of T levels is being rushed and without adequate consultation. Raffe (2013), reflecting on decades of vocational reform, argued for an approach to reform that places as much emphasis on the processes of change as the content of reforms and gives due consideration to the importance of colleges – because they are the ones who have to translate the reforms into courses and assessments for students.

It is easy for governments to revise the content of qualifications – it allows politicians to see quick results. But what takes longer is reform of the providers underpinning skills development in any local area – the schools, colleges and local employers.

16 – Staying power. Too often, governments lose interest, or a new Minister is keen to add further initiatives, or plans are simply abandoned when the going gets tough. What is needed is persistence and stability.

So what else do we need to do?

Schools

We need to do more to improve the performance at GCSE of the bottom 40%, especially boys. At present, many 16-year-olds fail to achieve a pass in five GCSEs including English and maths. This means that they go onto FE college with a sense of failure and spend time resitting their English and maths, often without success.

It could be argued that exams and selection at 16 has depressed post-16 participation and attainment because it forces young people to reach a certain level of attainment in one type of education (academic) at a particular age (16) rather than when they are ready. Those with special needs or from weak academic backgrounds often need more time to realise their potential.

FE colleges are torn between the priority of providing remedial English and maths for students who failed the GCSEs at school and the priority of teaching high-quality vocational courses. At present only 40% of those going to FE colleges have passed both English and maths GCSEs. These students are massively time-consuming. FE gets sucked into saving people rather than progressing more advanced skills. It would be much easier for the colleges if there were less focus on English and maths. We need to aim for a situation where all 11-year-olds have good literacy and numeracy and most 16-year-olds pass either GCSE English language and maths or a level 2 functional skills course.

The proportion that pass English and maths GCSE is capped by Ofqual because of their 'comparable outcomes' approach to grading – the same proportion who failed a given GCSE last year will fail this year. This policy, designed to stop grade inflation, makes it hard for schools with a lower-ability intake to improve their results. The awarding of maths and English GCSEs – indeed all GCSEs – guarantees a set level of failure every year.

Perhaps we should stop forcing pupils who have failed GCSE English or maths at school to retake these qualifications? Too many fail the resit and it would be far better for them to concentrate on functional skills courses which are focused on the most important skills people need at work (addition, subtraction, fractions *etc*) and drops elements like algebra and geometry. It would be a great mistake to force all those taking T levels into resitting GCSEs. What should happen is that each T level route should define the writing or numeracy skills required by that occupation and these, alone, should be examined.

Research into the attitudes of employers shows that they do not care whether a young person has an English GCSE or a level 2 functional skills qualification. What matters is whether they are literate, and in fact employers are often disappointed by the standard of literacy of those who have passed the GCSE. However, HR departments within those same firms do not always take the same flexible approach. They use possession of an English GCSE as means of shortlisting applicants for jobs (Dawe, 2017); this, too, needs to be addressed.

Putting young people on the right path

Chapter 5 describes the struggle there has always been to put young people onto the 'correct path'. Before 1965 only 20% of children took public exams when they were 16. After that date CSEs broadened the exam system, but still only 60% of children attempted some qualification. The arrival of GCSEs in 1986 allowed the majority to have access to a wide range of subjects, some academic others more vocational. After 2010 the government introduced the notion of EBacc subjects based on the assumption that most children were capable of attempting academic GCSEs, and indeed any insistence that less academic children should take 'vocational' subjects was a source of unfairness. Only quite recently have we moved away from the belief that many young people should leave school at 16 and get a job.

After the Second World War we divided children at age 11 into 'academic', 'technical' and 'the rest' by school type. In 1965 we started to move to a comprehensive school system and began to dismantle this tripartite division. So now we have reached a position where all children follow a very similar curriculum from age 5 to 16. Only at 16 do the paths diverge, the more academic taking A levels, the less academic (probably) taking technical qualifications. The cliff-edge has moved from age 11 to 16.

This structure will continue to be a matter of national debate. It is surely certain that some future government will relax the constraints of the EBacc and Progress 8, reintroducing more vocational alternatives to academic GCSEs and, inevitably, more teacher assessment as opposed to end-of-course exams. In the years to come there will almost certainly be further attempts to make all 16- to 18-year-olds study a broad curriculum including English, maths and science, possibly shifting the cliff-edge to age 18. What the 'correct path' is for any child at any given age will continue to be influenced by prevailing ideas about education, by what we see happening in other countries and by the nature of employment in the 21st century.

It is also important to recognise the value of giving people second chances. FE colleges show that plenty of those who did poorly at school can make it to university if they reboot their lives in their 20s. Intelligence and motivation is not fixed at a young age.

We need to greatly improve the quality of careers advice, ideally following Sir John Holman's advice in his Gatsby Foundation Report (Holman, 2013), which includes personal guidance tailored to each pupil (as opposed to general lectures for whole year groups), work experience, and encounters with employers, further education and higher education.

The problem is that many 16-year-olds going to FE college have failed their GCSEs, have never done a vocational qualification at school and have no idea what job they want. Most do a level 2 course in sport, art and design or something else that does not lead to employment. Many lack line of sight to a job or higher qualification. Very few go on from level 2 courses to an apprenticeship.

We need to make it easier to apply for apprenticeships. For those who are considering a choice between university (just fill in a UCAS form) and apprenticeships (much more complicated), the application process itself makes university look like the default option.

Motivation

We need to find ways of motivating the bottom 50% wherever their post-16 education or training takes place. If students are demotivated and lazy, making qualifications more demanding and rigorous will simply increase the failure rate. Many pupils arriving at FE college have had a disappointing experience at school. It takes a lot to encourage some of them to regard the next stage of their education as a fresh start. Attendance rates for many courses are too low.

The McLoughlin Report (McLoughlin, 2013) recommends the following for motivating students:

> A clear line of sight to work is critical because vocational learners must be able to see why they are learning what they are learning, understand what the development of occupational expertise is all about, and experience the job in its context. The real work context should inform the practice of vocational teaching and learning for learners, teachers and trainers.

There needs to be more effort to increase the proportion of able girls taking A level maths, computing and sciences. We know that their low take-up has less to do with ability or discrimination than the fact that girls who are good at maths/science are more likely to also be good at arts/humanities subjects than science-orientated boys (Jussin, 2017). Girls are better all-rounders, but too few of those who are good at science choose it as their specialism post-16.

Vocational courses are market-driven. We may want more engineers but in fact few young people want to be engineers. So if we are to improve the supply of engineers, schools and colleges need to find ways of motivating students to consider this career.

Rigour and validity

Vocational courses need to be rigorous. For example, it must be unacceptable that for some functional skills courses the test papers are seen by the college well in advance of the test being sat and are marked by the teacher with little oversight.

Every qualification needs to be overseen by someone who is trained to know the correct standard the qualification is designed to assess. Every qualification needs an independent person to have oversight of the quality assurance.

But at the same time we need to get away from the idea that vocational courses have to be assessed by means of end-of-course exams and that coursework is a dangerous means of assessment because teachers can influence the results. It is true that they can of course, but that is the lesser of two evils. Some pupils are very bad at exams but quite good at doing things with their hands. They dislike sitting at desks but they are good when given a vocational task. It is not 'abandoning rigour' to suggest that this type of student has to be assessed in a way which is both more realistic for them and likely to elicit a better response. This is particularly true of craft skills, which are little mentioned in the Sainsbury Report. A plasterer, for example, does not need a written exam to be assessed.

The key issue with assessment of vocational courses is what exam experts call 'validity', a technical examspeak term which means the extent to which a qualification measures what it is supposed to measure. For example, a maths test which requires a good knowledge of English to understand the questions lacks some validity because it measures knowledge of English as well as maths. The validity of vocational qualifications is reduced if there is too much emphasis on end-of-course written exams as opposed to continuous assessment of practical, hands-on tasks. To some degree, vocational qualifications are about ways of achieving other than through writing and exams.

If vocational qualifications are to have real validity, they need to deliver the skills employers want.

Being clear about the purpose of FE colleges

The Government needs to decide what FE colleges are for and the relationship between them and universities. Universities are now starting to offer level 4 and 5 courses as well as higher apprenticeships training (pages 64-65 and 181). What is going to be the distinction between FE and HE for such courses? Are we moving to a situation where most FE colleges and universities are going to work in partnership or even merge? If level 4 and above courses can be offered by both universities and FE college it does not at seem at all sensible for the relevant funding arrangements for universities and FE colleges to be different.

We need clarity.

Universities get much better funding, more freedom from government intervention and more freedom to award qualifications than FE. The reasons why FE and HE are treated so differently needs to be better articulated. Universities have flourished without the same degree of detailed government direction as that faced by FE.

There is a need to appreciate that FE is:

- in some respects less successful at running A level and level 3 Applied General courses than schools and sixth form colleges for 16- to 18-year-olds, although their more adult 'feel' is an advantage and they are good for students who for various reasons disliked school (or the school disliked them).

- often more successful than other settings at running courses which relate directly to employers and are good at employing staff who are dual-professionals – teachers who have worked in industry or are still working part-time in industry. Universities tend to veer towards more academic courses and research while FE colleges veer towards on-the-job training – and it is the latter that is generally regarded as best for developing employment skills.

- as or more successful than other settings in being a hub for the local community, providing lifelong learning opportunities.

- more successful than universities at providing a positive working environment for students who have been unsuccessful at school and need a second chance, including quite a high proportion of those with special needs.

- more flexible than universities. If a student goes to university and cannot cope with a level 4 or 5 course they will probably have to leave. In an FE college there will be alternative routes available.

- more successful than other settings for adults with work or care commitments who can only attend part-time.

We have moved to a situation where the majority of funding for FE comes from payments for full-time, non-employed 16- to 18-year-olds and this has changed the nature of colleges which were once focused on day-release, adults and part-timers. Is this what we want?

Local collaboration

There needs to be less centralisation and more emphasis on local colleges working with local firms to establish local training needs and provision. The

Social Market Foundation talks about FE colleges as 'local champions and engines of social mobility', linked to the growing devolution of powers to city regions and local mayors. Localism is central to solving the skills problem because decisions about education and training should be tailored to each area's particular needs. Local Enterprise Partnerships need to have the budget to assess the supply and demand for skills in their region and work towards balancing the two.

There should be much more collaboration rather than competition between schools, UTCs, colleges, National Colleges and universities in local areas, something which has become harder rather than easier with the reduced role of local authorities in education. Schools in bigger cities know little about the FE colleges that many of their pupils go to when they leave. As universities grow there is a danger of duplication of effort and the creation of further confusion for potential students. Individual courses, sometimes with expensive and specialised equipment, only need to be offered in one place within an area. Those metro mayors that have control over the adult skills education budget need to use this power to help rationalise vocational training in their regions.

The current challenges facing UTCs and Studio Schools suggest that there needs to be a collaborative area-based strategy rather than having individual vocational institutions in open competition with secondary schools.

There needs to be much better, fairer advice given by schools about vocational pathways. To better support young people with below-average academic attainment, we must address the aggressive student recruitment and retention practices of schools and sixth form colleges. Pupils must be made more aware of all the different post-16 pathways available to them, including apprenticeships.

Proper funding

According to the Sixth Form Colleges Association, the average education funding per 11-16 student in 2017 was £5751, but only £4531 per student for 16-18 education. Further education students in England receive just 17 hours tuition a week compared to an average of 27 in school and 30 hours or more in most high-performing countries. We may need to spend more on 16- to 19-year-olds to match the academic and technical training of our competitors and we need to spend more to reverse the decline in adult education. Many lower-skill jobs in England are currently being done by EU migrants; arguably there should be an adult basic skills fund to ease home-grown recruitment problems following Brexit.

The courses and training chosen by young people are not principally influenced by the labour market demand for skills. The main factors are the funding streams, costs and incentives that influence not only students but also the suppliers of education. **So much more attention needs to be paid to using funding systems to increase skills where they are most needed.** The fact that post-19 adult skills courses receive so few resources compared to universities, for example, shifts demand towards university study. Is that in the best interests of the students or the country?

The welfare system only supports part-time students if they are willing to accept full-time work should opportunities arise. This rule forces those individuals to discontinue training and instead take a low-skill job. We need to move to a system where workers can receive at least the equivalent of Job Seekers Allowance for up to six months to enable them to upskill or retrain.

Technical courses for adults at level 3 and below are funded by a mix of grants and loans that depend on age, economic status, the level of qualification, whether it is a full qualification or not and, if it is, whether it is a first taken at that level. All too complex. There also needs to be a much greater awareness of Advanced Learner Loans to support learning at level 3 and 4 amongst potential learners and employers.

At present the government decides which courses it will fund and which it will not. This prevents colleges from devising their own courses appropriate to local needs. Colleges are incentivised to chase student numbers and pay less attention to the requirements of local employers. We need more technicians in England but technical courses require upfront investment in equipment and staff and are more expensive to run than non-technical subjects.

At present a college discovers in late May what its budget will be for September, which is no way to run a huge business. Colleges should have some concept of their budget over the forthcoming three years. What is more, 16- to 18-year-olds, adults, apprentices, community learning and higher education are paid according to different formulae. Colleges need an army of finance staff to manage the process.

Another problem is funding for those who take three years – say, from age 16 to 19 – to complete a course. If after a transition year at 16 a young person is qualified to take a T level they will need two further years' study. But the funding for the final year for these students will be lower than that for 16- and 17-year-olds. More money needs to be directed to those who are likely to take longer than two years post-school to achieve level 3 because this is the group who will otherwise remain low-skilled when they had the potential to do better.

The great advantage of our university funding system is that the government contributes relatively little to undergraduate degrees. This ensures good budgets for universities while leaving more taxpayer money for non-university education. But experience in recent years shows that different elements of the education system need funding in different ways. Student loans may have been successful in the short-term as a means of funding full-time university degrees for school leavers. They have not been a success for adults wishing to take part-time degrees or participate in sub-degree FE adult education – they are not willing to commit to such a loan.

Assessment

All vocational qualifications have two elements – the course content and the assessment methods. The course content should be determined by employers, sector by sector. Every employer knows the knowledge and behaviours required at each of levels 2 to 7 and to a large extent therefore course content is established, subject only to small changes from time to time as technology evolves. There is no need for radical change. Course content is the easy bit.

Assessment methods should not be determined by employers but by experts in assessment. Assessment is a complex and technical issue which has been got wrong in the past.

Governments tinker with assessment before the impact of the last round of changes is known, often without proper piloting or consultation with those who are going to teach the courses. They also make the mistake of thinking that qualification reform is more significant than it really is. The recent GCSE and A level reforms can be seen to have improved the standard of work of the more able but may have a more limited impact on the crucial bottom 50%. The success of a qualification depends as much on the teaching of that course and the response of students as the paper syllabus.

Transparency

The government should progress with plans to make transparent the lifetime earnings impact of every qualification. This data has only recently become available. The Small Business, Employment and Enterprise Act 2015 enabled government, for the first time, to link education and tax data together in order to chart the transition of people from further or higher education into the workplace. This is the Longitudinal Education Outcomes (LEO) dataset.

The LEO dataset links information about students, including:

- personal characteristics such as sex, ethnic group and age
- education, including schools, colleges and education institution attended, courses taken and qualifications achieved
- employment and income

It is created by combining data from the following sources:

- the National Pupil Database
- Higher Education Statistics Agency data on students at UK publicly funded higher education institutions and some alternative providers, held by DfE
- Individual Learner Record data on students at further education colleges, held by DfE
- employment data held by Her Majesty's Revenue and Customs
- the National Benefit Database, Labour Market System and Juvos data, held by the Department for Work and Pensions

By combining these sources, we can look at the progress of further and higher education leavers into the labour market. The publication of this data would allow students to understand the employment value of the courses they are purchasing and may help prevent them taking courses which have a negative value.

Progression: what each course leads on to

There needs to be much better progression from each level to a higher level of training and there needs to be greater recognition of late developers. The Post-16 Skills Plan concentrates primarily on levels 3 to 5, with less attention being paid to issues of progression for those students operating at level 2 and below.

The missing middle

There needs to be more focus on universities, FE colleges, National Colleges and Institutes of Technology offering sub-degree courses – the missing middle. The value of these courses needs to be established and publicised as a good alternative to a full degree course.

Employer involvement

There needs to be more employer involvement in vocational qualifications and workplace learning. Musset and Field (2013) for the OECD say:

> What is striking about international experience is that poorer countries with relatively weak infrastructure (Romania), countries with very little history of employer engagement in the vocational system (Sweden) and countries with very high rates of youth unemployment (Spain) have all been successful in implementing mandatory arrangements for work-based learning in some of their vocational programmes.

The key is to build local partnerships between employers and FE colleges and universities and ensure that workplace learning is carefully planned and subject to quality assurance. Because there has been some reluctance amongst employers and colleges to develop these relationships, the incentives have to be strong.

Notwithstanding the difficulties, it is right that vocational courses should include a reasonable amount of workplace learning. Workplace assignments have to be mandatory. Many colleges already work closely with large employers in their area, but more needs to be done to reach out to small and medium-sized enterprises.

Disabled people

6.9 million people in the UK aged 16-64 have a long-term health condition or disability – one in six of the working age population. However, in 2017, just under half of working-age disabled people were in employment, compared with 81% of working-age non-disabled people (Friedman *et al*, 2017). So action should be taken to improve the employment prospects of disabled people. They need more support and improved funding if they are to overcome the barriers which exist at present. We should simplify the overly complex high needs funding system to provide more clarity and certainty for young people with learning difficulties and disabilities.

Appoint a big hitter to manage policy

There is much to do and there needs to be co-ordination across several government departments – education, business and employment. So the Minister in charge of FE and skills after Brexit needs to be in post for a few years and be a 'big hitter' who is capable of pushing through radical reform.

Stop tinkering

It takes decades for employers and the public to understand and value a qualification, so after the next round of reforms governments need to try and back off. Vocational qualification reform in England has rarely been given time to bed down. GCSEs and A levels are well established and understood because even as the content has changed over time, the overarching 'brand' has remained the same.

What is more, colleges and employers are never going to invest in T levels, level 3 and above apprenticeships or in expensive STEM courses unless they can be confident that there is going to be stability in terms of funding.

The Institute for Apprenticeships must be left alone for a long period. T levels will only attract small numbers to start with. Be patient.

Shout louder

The FE sector has to do more to get itself better known. It is ridiculous that some individual schools appear more often in the newspapers than the entire FE sector. FE needs to work harder at self-promotion.

Appreciate those who work with their hands and heart

Notwithstanding the endless rhetoric about social mobility, half the population will always have below-average cognitive ability and school exam results. But if we are to overcome the divisions in society revealed by recent political events, all need to feel valued. That is why we must get back to a more balanced appreciation of those who perform essential jobs, albeit jobs of the hand or heart. We should stop talking about social mobility as simply a way of 'rescuing' people from working-class backgrounds and place more emphasis on valuing the full range of worthwhile occupations.

Arguments about social mobility are normally based on exam results or incomes, not the value to society of different occupations. School accountability measures give little weight to skills other than exam performance. But we need to find a place where those of below-average cognitive ability can nevertheless earn a good living and feel satisfied with their lives. Only then can we build a more productive, happier and less divided society.

Bibliography

AELP (2017) *The unintended consequences of the Apprenticeship Reforms on the social equality of the young and the most disadvantaged.* Bristol: AELP.

Aldrich, R. (ed) (2002) *A century of education.* Abingdon: RoutledgeFalmer.

AllAboutSchoolLeavers.co.uk and YouGov (2016) *The school & college leaver careers market.* Available at: www.mycareerspringboard.org/articles/article/pdf/19

Allen, R. (2015) *Missing Talent.* London: Sutton Trust.

Allen, R., Parameshwaran, M. and Thomson, D. (2016) *Social and ethnic inequalities in choice available and choices made at age 16.* London: Social Mobility Commission.

All-Party Parliamentary Group for Education (2017) *How well do schools prepare children for their future?* London: The Stationery Office.

Anderson, R. (2014) *Making education work.* London: Pearson.

Anderson, R. (2017) *Educating for our economic future.* London: Pearson/EPI.

Andrews, J., Hutchinson, J. and Johnes, R. (2016) *Grammar schools and social mobility.* London: Education Policy Institute.

Andrews, J., Hutchinson, J. and Robinson, D. (2017) *Closing the gap? Trends in educational attainment and disadvantage.* London: Education Policy Institute.

Atkins, L., Flint, K. and Oldfield, B. (2011) *Practical matters: what young people think about vocational education in England.* London: The City and Guilds of London Institute.

Aubrey, T. and Reed, A. (2016) *Rebalancing the UK economy.* London: Centre for Progressive Capitalism. Available at: progressive-capitalism.net/wp-content/uploads/2016/10/Rebalancing-the-UK-economy-final-online-version.pdf.

The Audit Commission and Ofsted (1993) *Unfinished business: full-time education courses for 16-19 year olds.* London: The Stationery Office.

Autor, D., Dorn, D. and Hanson, G. (2012) 'The China syndrome: local labor market effects of import competition in the United States', *American Economic Review* 103 (6) pp. 2121-68.

Bakhshi, H., Downing, J., Osborne, M. and Schneider, P. (2017) *The future of skills: employment in 2030.* London: Pearson/Nesta.

Beatty, C. and Fothergill, S. (2016) *Jobs, welfare and austerity.* Sheffield: Centre for Regional Economic and Social Research.

Belfield, C., Crawford, C. and Sibieta, L. (2017a) *Long-run comparisons of spending per pupil across different stages of education.* London: IFS.

Belfield, C., Britton, J., Dearden, L. and van der Erve, L. (2017b) *Higher education funding in England: past, present and options for the future.* London: IFS.

Benton, T. and Sutch, T. (2013) *Exploring the value of GCSE prediction matrices based upon attainment at Key Stage 2.* Cambridge: Cambridge Assessment.

Bibby, D., Buscha, F., Cerqua, A., Thomson, D. and Unwin, P. (2014) *Estimation of the labour market returns to qualifications gained in English further education.* Department for Business, Innovation & Skills. London: The Stationery Office.

Bolton, P. (2012) *Education: historical statistics.* House of Commons Library. London: The Stationery Office.

Blundell, R., Green, D. A. and Jin, W. (2016) *Big historical increase in numbers did not reduce graduates' relative wages.* London: IFS.

Bosworth, D., Lyonette, C., Wilson, R., Bayliss, M. and Fathers, S. (2013) *The supply of and demand for high-level STEM skills.* Wath-upon-Dearne: UKCES.

Bradbury, B., Corak, M., Waldfogel, J. and Washbrook, E. (2015) *Too many children left behind: the US achievement gap in comparative perspective.* New York, NY: Russell Sage Foundation.

Britton, J., Dearden, L., Shephard, N. and Vignoles, A. (2016) *What and where you study matter for graduate earnings – but so does parents' income.* London: IFS.

Broadberry, S. and O'Mahony, M. (2004) 'Britain's productivity gap with the United States and Europe: a historical perspective', *National Institute Economic Review* 189 (1) pp. 72-85.

Broughton, N. (2015) *The value of apprenticeships.* London: Social Market Foundation. Available at: www.smf.co.uk/wp-content/uploads/2016/06/Social-Market-Foundation-The-value-of-apprenticeships-beyond-wages-FINAL.pdf

Burgess, S., Crawford, C. and Macmillan, L. (2017) *Assessing the role of grammar schools in promoting social mobility.* London: Department of Quantitative Social Science, UCL Institute of Education.

Burke, J. (2017) 'Massive £1bn FE loans underspend revealed', *FE Week*, 22nd September. Available at: feweek.co.uk/2017/09/22/massive-1bn-fe-loans-underspend-revealed/

CBI (2016a) *The right combination: education and skills survey.* London: Pearson.

CBI (2016b) *Unlocking regional growth: understanding the drivers of productivity across the UK's regions and nations.* Available at: www.cbi.org.uk/index.cfm/_api/render/file/?method=inline&fileID=9AF06398-223D-4214-B96F1AD8A2FE4CC8

The Children's Society (2016) *The Goodchild Report.* London: The Children's Society.

Christodoulou, D. (2014) *Seven myths about education.* Abingdon: Routledge.

City & Guilds (2011) *What young people think about vocational education in England.* London: City & Guilds.

City & Guilds (2014a) *Sense and instability: three decades of skills and employment policy.* London: City & Guilds.

City & Guilds (2014b) *Children labelled 'too clever' for vocational education.* London: City & Guilds.

Clarke, S. and D'Arcy, C. (2016) *Low pay Britain 2016.* London: Resolution Foundation. Available at: www.resolutionfoundation.org/app/uploads/2016/10/Low-Pay-Britain-2016.pdf.

Clegg, N., Allen, R., Fernandes, S., Freedman, S. and Kinnock, S. (2017) *Commission on inequality in education.* London: Social Market Foundation.

Clifton, J. and Cook, W. (2012) *A long division: Closing the attainment gap in England's secondary schools.* London: Institute for Public Policy Research.

Coleman, J., Campbell, E. Q., Hobson, C. J., McPartland, J., Mood, A. M., Weinfeld, F. D. and York, R. L. (1966) *Equality of educational opportunity.* US Department of Health, Education and Welfare. Washington, DC: Government Printing Office.

Commission on Adult Vocational Teaching and Learning (2013) *It's about work... excellent adult vocational teaching and learning.* Available at: cavtl. excellencegateway.org.uk/commission-news/its-about-work

Commission on Inequality in Education (2016) *Educational inequalities in England and Wales*. London: Social Market Foundation. Available at: www.smf.co.uk/wp-content/uploads/2016/01/Publication-Commission-on-Inequality-in-Education-Initial-Findings-Slide-Pack-120116.pdf

Conlon, G. and Patrignani, P. (2013) *A disaggregated analysis of the long run impact of vocational qualifications*. Department for Business, Innovation & Skills. London: The Stationery Office.

Conlon, G., Patrignani, P., Herr, D. and Hedges, S. (2017) *The incidence of publicly funded training in England*. London: Centre for Vocational Education Research.

Cook, C. (2013) 'Grammar school myths', *Financial Times*. Available at: ig-legacy.ft.com/content/cb1e02f4-7461-3fd1-ac5d-9fd9befb20dd.

Cook, C. (2016) 'Why not bring back grammar schools?', *BBC News*. Available at: www.bbc.co.uk/news/education-36662965.

Crawford, C. (2014a) *Socio-economic differences in university outcomes in the UK: drop-out, degree completion and degree class*. London: IFS.

Crawford, C. (2014b) *The link between secondary school characteristics and university participation and outcomes*. Department for Education. London: The Stationery Office.

Crawford, C., Dearden, L., Micklewright, J. and Vignoles, A. (2017) *Family background and university success*. Oxford: Oxford University Press.

Crowther, G. (1959) *A report of the Central Advisory Council for Education (England)*. London: The Stationery Office.

Cullinane, C. and Kirby, P. (2016) *Class differences: ethnicity and disadvantage*. London: Sutton Trust.

Cullinane, C., Andrade, J., Hillary, J. and McNamara, S. (2017) *Selection comprehensives 2017*. London: Sutton Trust.

Dearing, R. (1996) *Review of qualifications for 16-19 year olds*. Hayes: School Curriculum and Assessment Authority.

Deary, I., Strand, S., Smith, P. and Fernandes, C. (2007) 'Intelligence and educational achievement', *ScienceDirect* 35 (1) pp. 13-21.

De Coulon, A., Hedges, S., Nafilyan, V. and Speckesser, S. (2017) *Young people in low-level vocational education: characteristics, trajectories and labour market outcomes.* London: Centre for Vocational Education Research.

De Vries, R. and Rentfrow, J. (2016) *A winning personality: the effects of background on personality and earnings.* London: Sutton Trust.

Del Bono, E. and Ermisch, J. (2010) *Education mobility in England: the link between the education levels of parents and the educational outcomes of teenagers.* London: Sutton Trust.

Department for Business, Energy & Industrial Strategy (2017) *Building our industrial strategy.* London: The Stationery Office.

Department for Business, Innovation & Skills (2012) *The 2011 skills for life survey: a survey of literacy, numeracy and ICT levels in England.* London: The Stationery Office.

Department for Business, Innovation & Skills (2013) *The international survey of adult skills 2012: adult literacy, numeracy and problem solving-skills in England.* London: The Stationery Office.

Department for Business, Innovation & Skills (2015) *Skills funding agency priorities and funding for the 2016-17 financial year.* London: The Stationery Office.

Department for Business, Innovation & Skills (2016) *Mapping investment in adult skills — which individuals, in what learning and with what returns?* London: The Stationery Office.

Department for Business, Innovation & Skills and Department for Education (2013) *Future of apprenticeships in England: implementation plan.* London: The Stationery Office.

Department for Business, Innovation & Skills and Department for Education (2016) *Post-16 skills plan.* London: The Stationery Office.

Department for Communities and Local Government (2017) *Midlands engine strategy.* London: The Stationery Office.

Department for Education (2016a) *Education provision: children under 5 years of age.* London: The Stationery Office.

Department for Education (2016b) *National curriculum assessments at Key Stage 2 in England.* London: The Stationery Office.

Department for Education (2016c) *Outcomes for children looked after by local authorities in England*. London: The Stationery Office.

Department for Education (2016d) *Participation in education, training and employment by 16-18 year olds in England: end 2015*. London: The Stationery Office.

Department for Education (2016e) *Early years foundation stage profile results in England*. London: The Stationery Office.

Department for Education (2017a) *National curriculum assessments at Key Stage 2 in England*. London: The Stationery Office.

Department for Education (2017b) *Revised GCSE and equivalent results in England, 2015 to 2016*. London: The Stationery Office.

Department for Education (2017c) *Children looked after in England (including adoption): 2016-2017*. London: The Stationery Office.

Department for Education (2017d) *Revised destinations of Key Stage 4 and Key Stage 5 students, England, 2014/15*. London: The Stationery Office.

Department for Education (2017e) *Further education and skills in England*. London: The Stationery Office.

Department for Education (2017f) *Permanent and fixed period exclusions in England: 2015 to 2016*. London: The Stationery Office.

Department for Education (2017g) *Participation rates in higher education 2006-2016*. London: The Stationery Office.

Department for Education (2017h) *Employment and earnings outcomes of higher education graduates by subject and institution: experimental statistics using the Longitudinal Education Outcomes (LEO) data*. London: The Stationery Office.

Department for Education (2017i) *Destinations of Key Stage 4 and Key Stage 5 students, England, 2015/16*. London: The Stationery Office.

Department for Education (2017j) *Participation in education, training and employment by 16-18 year olds in England: end 2016*. London: The Stationery Office.

Department for Education (2017k) *Level 2 and 3 attainment in England: attainment by age 19 in 2016*. London: The Stationery Office.

Department for Education (2017l) *Graduate labour market statistics 2016*. London: The Stationery Office.

Department for Education (2017m) *A level and other 16 to 18 results: 2015 to 2016 (revised)*. London: The Stationery Office.

Department for Education (2017n) *FE and skills participation: all ages demographic summary 2015/16*. London: The Stationery Office.

Department for Education and Department for Business, Innovation & Skills (2016) *Apprenticeship evaluation 2015: learner and employer surveys*. London: The Stationery Office.

Department for Education and Education and Skills Funding Agency (2014) *FE and skills participation: all ages demographic summary 2013/14*. Available at: www.gov.uk/government/uploads/system/uploads/attachment_data/file/427064/feandskills-allages-demographics-participation-1314.xls.

Department for Education and Education and Skills Funding Agency (2017a) *FE data library: further education and skills*. Available at: www.gov.uk/government/statistical-data-sets/fe-data-library-further-education-and-skills.

Department for Education and Education and Skills Funding Agency (2017b) *National achievement rates tables 2015 to 2016*, Available at: www.gov.uk/government/statistics/national-achievement-rates-tables-2015-to-2016

Didau, D. (2017) 'Is resilience even a thing?', *The Learning Spy*. Available at: www.learningspy.co.uk/featured/resilience-even-thing/

Dilnot, C. (2017) *The relationship between A-level subject choice and league table score of university attended: the 'facilitating', the 'less suitable' and the counter-intuitive*. London: UCL Centre for Longitudinal Studies.

Dolphin, T. (ed.) (2015) *Technology, globalisation and the future of work in Europe: Essays on employment in a digitised economy*. London: IPPR.

Dromey, J. and McNeil, C. (2017) *Skills 2030: why the adult skills system is failing to build an economy that works for everyone*. London: IPPR. Available at: www.ippr.org/files/publications/pdf/skills-2030_Feb2017.pdf

Education Endowment Foundation (2018) *The attainment gap: 2017*. London: EEF.

EngineeringUK (2016) *Engineering UK 2016: the state of UK engineering*. London: EngineeringUK.

EngineeringUK (2017) *2017 annual report*. Available at: www.engineeringuk.com/media/1355/enguk-report-2017.pdf.

Eurostat (2016) 'Continuous Vocational Training Survey', *Eurostat Database* [Online]. Available at: ec.europa.eu/eurostat/web/microdata/continuing-vocational-training-survey

Evangelou, M. and Sylva, K. (2007) 'Evidence on effective early childhood interventions from the United Kingdom: an evaluation of the Peers Early Education Partnership (PEEP)', *Early Childhood Research & Practice* 9 (1) no pagination.

Evans, G. (2007) *Educational failure and working class white children in Britain.* London: Palgrave Macmillan.

Evans, L. (2014) Avoiding the same old mistakes: lessons for reform of 14-19 education in England. London: IPPR.

Exley, S. and Martin, W. (2017) 'Apprentices from less deprived areas than other FE students, research finds', *TES.* Available at: www.tes.com/news/further-education/breaking-news/apprentices-less-deprived-areas-other-fe-students-research

Farmer, M. (2016) *The Farmer review of the UK construction labour model.* London: Construction Leadership Council.

Felstead, A. and Unwin, L. (2001) 'Funding post compulsory education and training: a retrospective analysis of the TEC and FEFC systems and their impact on skills', *Journal of Education and Work* 14 (1) pp. 91-111.

Fletcher, M. (2017) *Reforming technical and professional education: why should it work this time?* Newcastle: NCFE.

Foster, A. (2005) *Realising the potential: a review of the future role of further education colleges.* Nottingham: DfES Publication.

Frey, C. and Osborne, M. (2013) *The future of employment: how susceptible are jobs to computerisation?.* Oxford Martin School working paper. Available at: www.oxfordmartin.ox.ac.uk/downloads/academic/The_Future_of_Employment.pdf

Frey, C. and Osborne, M. (2015) *From brawn to brains: the impact of technology on jobs in the UK.* London: Deloitte.

Frey, C. B., Osborne, M. A., Holmes, C., Rahbari, E., Curmi, E., Garlick, R., Chua, J., Friedlander, G., Chalif, P., McDonald, G. and Wilkie, M. (2016) *Technology at work 2.0.* Available at: www.oxfordmartin.ox.ac.uk/downloads/reports/Citi_GPS_Technology_Work_2.pdf

Friedman, S., Laurison, D. and Macmillan, L. (2017) *Social mobility, the class pay gap and intergenerational worklessness: new insights from the labour force survey.* London: Social Mobility Commission.

Frontier Economics (2017) *Assessing the vocational qualifications market in England.* Department for Education. London: The Stationery Office.

Fuller, A., Unwin, L., Cavaglia, C., McNally, S. and Ventura, G. (2017) *Better apprenticeships.* London: Sutton Trust.

Gill, T. (2015) *Assessing the equivalencies of the UCAS tariff for different qualifications.* Cambridge: Cambridge Assessment.

Goodhart, D. (2017) *The road to somewhere.* London: Hurst and Company.

Goodman, A. and Gregg, P. (eds) (2010) *Poorer children's educational attainment: how important are attitudes and behaviour?.* York: Joseph Rowntree Foundation.

Gorard, S., See, B. H. and Davies, P. (2012) *The impact of attitudes and aspirations on educational attainment and participation.* York: Joseph Rowntree Foundation.

Greatbatch, D. and Tate, S. (2017) *Funding and expenditure in post-16 education: an international review.* Department for Education. London: The Stationery Office.

Gutman, L. M. and Schoon, I. (2013) *The impact of non-cognitive skills on outcomes for young people.* London: UCL Institute of Education.

Hanushek, E. and Woessmann, L. (2015) *Universal basic skills: what countries stand to gain.* Paris: OECD Publishing.

Harari, D. (2017) *Productivity in the UK,* House of Commons briefing paper. Available at: researchbriefings.files.parliament.uk/documents/SN06492/SN06492.pdf

Hart, B. and Risley, T. (1995) *Meaningful differences in the everyday experiences of young American children.* Baltimore, MD: Brookes Publishing.

Hayward, H., Hunt, E. and Lord, A. (2014) *The economic value of key intermediate qualifications: estimating the returns and lifetime productivity gains to GCSEs, A levels and apprenticeships.* Department for Education. London: The Stationery Office.

HEFCE (2015a) *Young participation in higher education A-levels and similar qualifications.* Bristol: HEFCE.

HEFCE (2015b) *Differences in degree outcomes: the effect of subject and student characteristics*. Bristol: HEFCE.

HEFCE (2017) *HEFCE data & statistics* [Online]. Available at: s.hefce.ac.uk/s/search. html?collection=website-meta&profile=data

HESA (2017) *HESA data and analysis* [Online]. Available at: www.hesa.ac.uk/data-and-analysis

Higher Education Commission (2017) *One size won't fit all: the challenges facing the office for students*. London: Policy Connect.

Hillman, N. (2017) 'We must continue to expand higher education', *ConservativeHome*. Available at: www.conservativehome.com/platform/2017/09/nick-hillman-we-must-continue-to-expand-higher-education.html

Hillman, N. and Robinson, N. (2016) *Boys to men: the underachievement of young men in higher education – and how to start tackling it*. Oxford: Higher Education Policy Institute.

Hodgen, J., Pepper, D., Sturman, L. and Ruddock, G. (2010) *Is the UK an outlier? An international comparison of upper secondary mathematics education*. London: Nuffield Foundation.

Hodgson, A. (ed.) (2015) The coming of age for FE?: reflections on the past and future role of further education colleges in England. London: UCL Institute of Education.

Hodgson, A. and Spours, K. (2016) *Tuition time in upper secondary education (16-19): comparing six national education systems*. London: UCL Institute of Education.

Holmes, C. (2014) *Why is the decline of routine jobs across Europe so uneven?* SKOPE issues paper 33. Available at: www.skope.ox.ac.uk/wp-content/uploads/2014/12/Skope_IssuesPaper33Holmes.pdf.

Holmes, C. and Mayhew, K. (2012) *The changing shape of the UK job market and its implications for the bottom half of earners*. London: Resolution Foundation. Available at: www.resolutionfoundation.org/app/uploads/2014/08/The-Changing-Shape-of-the-UK-Job-Market.pdf

Holman, J. (2013) *Good careers guidance*. London: Gatsby Foundation.

House of Commons Science and Technology Committee (2016) *Digital skills crisis*. London: The Stationery Office.

House of Commons Education Committee (2014) *Underachievement in education by white working class children.* London: The Stationery Office.

House of Lords Select Committee on Social Mobility (2016) *Overlooked and left behind: improving the transition from school to work for the majority of young people.* London: The Stationery Office.

Hughes, D., Adriaanse, K., Barnes, S. (2016) *Adult education: too important to be left to chance.* London: All-Party Parliamentary Group for Adult Education.

Hupkau, C., McNally, S., Ruiz-Valenzuela, J. and Ventura, G. (2016) *Post-compulsory education in England: choices and implications.* London: Centre for Vocational Education Research.

Hupkau, C. and Ventura, G. (2017) *Further education in England: learners and institutions.* London: Centre for Vocational Education Research.

Hutchinson, J. (2017) *How many children have SEND?* London: Education Policy Institute.

Hutchinson, J. and Dunford, J. (2016) *Divergent pathways: the disadvantage gap, accountability and the pupil premium.* London: Education Policy Institute.

Impetus-PEF (2017) *The road most travelled? The 16-19 journey through education and training.* London: Impetus-PEF.

Jerrim, J. (2017) 'What PISA tells us about pupils from ordinary working families', *Education Datalab.* Available at: educationdatalab.org.uk/2017/04/what-pisa-tells-us-about-pupils-from-ordinary-working-families.

Jerrim, J., Perera, N. and Sellen, P. (2017) *English education: world class in primary?* London: Education Policy Institute.

Jones, I. and Schoon, E. (2008) 'Child behaviour and cognitive development' in Hansen, K. and Joshi, H. (eds) *Millennium cohort study third survey: a user's guide to initial findings.* London: Centre for Longitudinal Studies, UCL Institute of Education.

Jussin, L. (2017) 'Why brilliant girls tend to favor non-STEM careers', *Psychology Today.* Available at: www.psychologytoday.com/blog/rabble-rouser/201707/why-brilliant-girls-tend-favor-non-stem-careers.

Kelly, S. (2017) *Reforming BTECs: applied general qualifications as a route to higher education.* Oxford: Higher Education Policy Institute.

Kennedy, H. (1997) *Learning works: widening participation in further education.* Coventry: Further Education Funding Council.

King, A. and Crewe, I. (2013) *The blunders of our governments.* London: OneWorld.

Kuczera, M., Field, S. and Windisch, H. (2016) *Building skills for all: a review of England.* Paris: OECD Publishing.

Lane, M., Conlon, G., Peycheva, V., Mantovani, I. and Chan, S. (2017) *An economic evaluation of the National Careers Service, research report.* Department for Education. London: The Stationery Office.

Learning and Work Institute (2016a) *Skills and poverty: building an anti-poverty learning and skills system.* London: Learning and Work Institute.

Learning and Work Institute (2016b) *Halving the gap: making the Work and Health Programme work for disabled people.* London: Learning and Work Institute.

Leitch, S. (2006) *Prosperity for all in a global economy – world class skills.* London: The Stationery Office.

Lenon, B. (2017) *Much promise: successful schools in England.* Woodbridge: John Catt Educational.

Lindsay, G., Cullen, M. A., Cullen, S., Totsika, V., Bakopoulou, I., Goodlad, S., Brind, R., Pickering, E., Bryson, C., Purdon, S., Conlon, G. and Mantovani, I. (2014) *CANparent trial evaluation: final report, research brief.* Department for Education. London: The Stationery Office.

Luyten, H., Merrell, C. and Tymms, P. (2017) 'The contribution of schooling to learning gains of pupils in Years 1 to 6', *School Effectiveness and School Improvement* 28 (3) pp. 374-405.

McIntosh, S. (2013) *Hollowing out and the future of the labour market.* Department for Business, Innovation & Skills. London: The Stationery Office.

McKnight, A. (2015) *Downward mobility, opportunity hoarding and the glass floor.* London: Social Mobility and Child Poverty Commission.

McLoughlin, F. (2013) *It's about work: excellent adult vocational teaching and learning.* London: Learning and Skills Improvement Service.

Moss, G. and Washbrook, E. (2016a) *The gender gap in language and literacy development.* Bristol: University of Bristol.

Moss, G. and Washbrook, E. (2016b) *The lost boys.* London: Save the Children.

Murray, C. (2012) *Coming apart: the state of white America.* New York, NY: Crown Forum.

Musset, P. and Field, S. (2013) *A skills beyond school review of England.* Paris: OECD Publishing.

National Evaluation of Sure Start (NESS) Team (2012) *The impact of Sure Start local programmes on seven year olds and their families, research report.* Department for Education. London: The Stationery Office.

National Audit Office (2009) *Train to gain: developing the skills of the workforce.* London: The Stationery Office.

Nesta and Tech City UK (2016) *Tech nation 2016: transforming UK industries.* Available at: www.nesta.org.uk/sites/default/files/tech_nation_2016_report.pdf

Newman, J. H. (1959) *The idea of a university.* Garden City, NY: Image Books.

Newsom, J. (1963) *Half our future: a report of the Central Advisory Council for Education (England).* Ministry of Education. London: The Stationery Office.

Niven, J., Faggian, A. and Ruwanpura, K. N. (2013) 'Exploring "underachievement" among highly educated young British-Bangladeshi women', *Feminist Economics* 19 (1) pp. 111-136.

NOMIS (2017) 'Workforce jobs by industry', *Office for National Statistics* [Online]. Available at: www.nomisweb.co.uk/datasets/wfjsa

Northern Powerhouse Partnership (2018) *Educating the North.* Available at: www.northernpowerhousepartnership.co.uk/media/1208/npp-educating-the-north.pdf

Norwood, C. (1943) *Curriculum and examinations in secondary schools: report of the committee of the secondary school examinations council appointed by the president of the Board of Education.* London: The Stationery Office.

OECD (2013) *First results from the survey of adult skills.* Paris: OECD Publishing.

OECD (2015) *Education at a glance 2015: OECD indicators.* Paris: OECD Publishing.

OECD (2016a) *Adult education level.* Paris: OECD Publishing.

OECD (2016b) *Skills for a digital world: policy brief on the future of work*. Paris: OECD Publishing.

OECD (2016c) *The survey of adult skills: reader's companion*. Second Edition. Paris: OECD Publishing.

OECD (2017a) *Skills outlook 2017 – skills and global value chains*. Paris: OECD Publishing.

OECD (2017b) *International productivity data*. Paris: OECD Publishing.

Ofqual (2017) *Vocational and technical qualifications: assessment functioning of external assessments: an overview of the functioning of assessments in 27 qualifications and 49 units*. London: The Stationery Office.

Ofsted (2012) *Mathematics made to measure*. London: The Stationery Office.

Ofsted (2014) *Transforming 16 to 19 education and training – the early implementation of 16 to 19 study programmes*. London: The Stationery Office.

Ofsted (2015) *The annual report of Her Majesty's chief inspector of education, children's services and skills*. London: The Stationery Office.

Ofsted (2016) *Annual report 2015/16*. London: The Stationery Office.

Ofsted (2017) *Annual report 2016/17*. London: The Stationery Office.

ONS (2011) *Earnings by qualification, 2011*. Newport: ONS.

ONS (2013) *170 years of industrial change across England and Wales*. Newport: ONS.

ONS (2015) *Transition from a manufacturing to service led labour market over past 170 years*. Newport: ONS.

ONS (2016a) *International comparisons of productivity for 2015*. Newport: ONS.

ONS (2016b) *Balance of payments pink book*. Newport: ONS.

ONS (2016c) *Annual survey of hours and earnings: 2010-2016, headline indicators for UK regions and countries*. Newport: ONS.

ONS (2016d) *NUTS1 GVA per head indices*. Newport: ONS.

ONS (2017a) *Young people not in education, employment or training (NEET)*. Newport: ONS.

ONS (2017b) *International immigration and the labour market*. Newport: ONS.

ONS (2017c) *Percentage of recent graduates and non-recent graduates working in non-graduate roles, 2011 to 2016, UK, Scotland and London*. Newport: ONS.

ONS (2017d) *Graduates in the labour market*. Newport: ONS.

ONS (2017e) *UK business; activity, size and location: 2017*. Newport: ONS.

ONS (2017f) *Migration statistics quarterly report: November 2017*. Newport: ONS.

Osborne, M. and Frey, C. (2014) *Agiletown: the relentless march of technology and London's response*. London: Deloitte.

Owen, G. (2000) *From empire to Europe*. London: HarperCollins.

Panorama (2017) BBC 1, 13th November.

Pemberton, H. (2001) *The 1964 Industrial Training Act: a failed revolution*. Available at: seis.bris.ac.uk/~hihrp/Seminars/2001%20EHS%201964%20ITA.pdf.

Peters, A. J. (1967) *British further education: a critical textbook*. Oxford: Pergamon.

Pidd, H. (2017) 'Children in northern England being failed by educational divide, study finds', *The Guardian*, 30th March. Available at: www.theguardian.com/uk-news/2017/mar/30/children-in-northern-england-being-failed-by-educational-divide-study-finds

Pillans, J. (1852) *The rationale of discipline*. London: Taylor, Walton and Maberly.

Plomin, R., DeFries, J., Knopik, V. S. and Neiderhiser, J. M. (2013) *Behavioral genetics*. 7th edition. New York, NY: Worth Publishers.

Porter, N. and Simons, J. (2014) '5 reasons why a return to grammar schools is a bad idea', *Policy Exchange*. Available at: policyexchange.org.uk/5-reasons-why-a-return-to-grammar-schools-is-a-bad-idea/

Porter, N. and Simons, J. (2015) 'Higher, further, faster, more: improving higher level professional and technical education', *Policy Exchange*. Available at: policyexchange.org.uk/publication/higher-further-faster-more-improving-higher-level-professional-and-technical-education/

Raffe, D. (2013) 'First count to five: some principles for the reform of vocational qualifications in England', *Journal of Education and Work* 28 (2) pp. 147-164.

Raffe, D. and Spours, K. (2007) *Policymaking and policy learning in 14-19 education.* London: UCL Institute of Education.

Rasbash, J., Leckie, G., Pillinger, R. and Jenkins, J. (2010) 'Children's educational progress: partitioning family, school and area effects', *Statistics in Society* 173 (3) pp. 657-682.

Royal Geographical Society (2015) 'Digital divide in the UK', *21st Century Challenges.* Available at: 21stcenturychallenges.org/what-is-the-digital-divide.

Richard, D. (2012) *Richard review of apprenticeships.* Department for Business, Innovation & Skills. London: The Stationery Office.

Richards, B. (2016) *Passports to progress: how do vocational qualifications help young people in building their careers?* London: Social Market Foundation.

Richards, L., Garratt, E., Heath, A. F., Anderson, L. and Altintaş, E. (2016) *The childhood origins of social mobility: socio-economic inequalities and changing opportunities.* London: Social Mobility Commission.

Richardson, W. (2007) 'In search of the further education of young people in post-war England', *Journal of Vocational Education & Training* 59 (3) pp. 385-418.

Richardson, W. and Wiborg, S. (2010) *English technical and vocational education in historical and comparative perspective.* London: Baker Dearing Educational Trust.

Robertson, A. (2017) '"Patchy" progress with work training for special needs', *FE Week* 210, p. 6.

Robey, C. and Jones, E. (2015) *Engaging learners in GCSE maths and English.* London: Learning and Work Institute.

Rothblatt, S. (1981). *The revolution of the dons: Cambridge and society in Victorian England.* Cambridge: Cambridge University Press.

Royal Academy of Engineering (2016) *The UK STEM education landscape.* Available at: www.raeng.org.uk/publications/reports/uk-stem-education-landscape

Sainsbury, D. (2016) *Report of the independent panel on technical education.* Department for Education. London: The Stationery Office.

Sammons, P., Toth, K. and Sylva, K. (2015) *Subject to background: what promotes better achievement for bright but disadvantaged students?.* London: Sutton Trust.

Sammons, P., Toth, K. and Sylva, K. (2016) *Believing in better: how aspirations and academic self concept shape young people's outcomes*. London: Sutton Trust.

Sanderson, M. (1999) *Education and economic decline in Britain, 1870 to the 1990s*. Cambridge: Cambridge University Press.

Save the Children (2017) *Early development and children's later educational outcomes, research briefing*. London: Save the Chidren.

Sax, L. (2007) *Boys adrift*. New York, NY: Basic Books.

Sax, L. (2017) *Why gender matters*. New York, NY: Potter/Ten Speed/Harmony.

Shakeshaft, N. G., Trzaskowski, M., McMillan, A., Rimfeld, K., Krapohl, E., Haworth, C. M. A., Dale, P. S. and Plomin, R. (2013) 'Strong genetic influence on a UK nationwide test of educational achievement at the end of compulsory education at age 16', *PLoS ONE* 8 (12). Available at: journals.plos.org/plosone/article/file?id=10.1371/journal.pone.0080341&type=printable

Sharp, M. (2011) *A dynamic nucleus: colleges at the heart of local communities*. Leicester: NIACE. Available at: shop.niace.org.uk/media/catalog/product/d/y/dynamic_nucleus_-_full_-final.pdf

Shaw, B., Menzies, L., Bernardes, E., Baars, S., Allen, R. and Nye, P. (2016) *Ethnicity, gender and social mobility*. London: Social Mobility Commission.

Shaw, B., Baars, S., Menzies, L., Parameshwaran, M. and Allen, R. (2017) *Low income pupils' progress at secondary school*. London: Social Mobility Commission.

Shury, J., Vivian, D., Spreadbury, K., Skone James, A. and Tweddle, M. (2014) *UK commission's employer perspectives survey 2014*. Wath-upon-Dearne: UKCES.

Simon, B. (1965) *Education and the labour movement 1870-1920*. London: Lawrence and Wishart.

Skills Commission (2015) *Guide to the skills system*. London: Policy Connect.

Skills Commission (2017) *A spotlight on... young people with below average academic attainment and the skills sector*. London: Policy Connect.

Smithers, A. and Robinson, P. (1992) *Technology in the national curriculum*. London: the Engineering Council.

Social Mobility Commission (2016) *State of the nation 2016: social mobility in Great Britain*. London: The Stationery Office.

Social Mobility Commission (2017a) *State of the nation 2017*. London: The Stationery Office.

Social Mobility Commission (2017b) *Time for change: an assessment of government policies on social mobility 1997-2017*. London: The Stationery Office.

Social Mobility and Child Poverty Commission (2016) *The social mobility index*. London: Social Mobility and Child Poverty Commission.

Spens, W. (1938) *Secondary education with special reference to grammar schools and technical high schools*. London: The Stationery Office.

Spours, K., Hodgson, A. and Rogers, L. (2017) *14-19 education and training in England: the concept of an upper secondary phase revisited*. London: UCL Institute of Education.

Steinberg, L., Cauffman, E., Woolard, J., Graham, S. and Banich, M. (2009) 'Are adolescents less mature than adults?', *American Psychologist* 64 (7) pp. 583-594.

Steinberg, L., Graham, S., O'Brien, L., Woolard, J., Cauffman, E. and Banich, M. (2009) 'Age differences in future orientation and delay discounting', *Child Development* 80 (1) pp. 28-44.

Stephens, W. (1999) *Education in Britain 1750-1914*. London: Palgrave.

Stewart, I., De, D. and Cole, A. (2015) *Technology and people: the great job-creating machine*. London: Deloitte.

Stewart, K. and Waldfogel, J. (2017) *Closing gaps early: the role of early years policy in promoting social mobility in England*. London: Sutton Trust.

Störmer, E., Patscha, C., Prendergast, J., Daheim, C., Rhisiart, M., Glover, P. and Beck, H. (2014) *The future of work: jobs and skills in 2030*. Wath-upon-Dearne: UKCES.

Strachey, L. (2009) *Eminent Victorians*. Oxford: Oxford World's Classics.

Strand, S. (2010) 'Do some schools narrow the gap? Differential school effectiveness by ethnicity, gender, poverty and prior attainment', *School Effectiveness and School Improvement* 21 (3) pp. 289-314.

Strand, S. (2011) 'The limits of social class in explaining ethnic gaps in educational attainment', *British Educational Research Journal* 37 (2) pp. 197-229.

Strand, S. (2015) *Ethnicity, deprivation and educational achievement at age 16 in England: trends over time.* Department for Education. London: The Stationery Office.

Strand, S. (2016) 'Do some schools narrow the gap? Differential school effectiveness revisited', *Review of Education* 4 (2) pp. 107-144.

Sutton Trust (2012) *The social mobility summit: report of the summit held at the Royal Society.* London: Sutton Trust.

Sutton Trust (2014) *Internship or indenture?* London: Sutton Trust.

Sutton Trust (2015) *Levels of success: the potential of UK apprenticeships.* London: Sutton Trust.

Sutton Trust (2017) *The state of social mobility in the UK.* London: Boston Consulting Group/Sutton Trust.

Sylva, K., Melhuish, E., Sammons, P., Siraj-Blatchford, I. and Taggart, B. (2008) *Final report from the primary phase: pre-school, school and family influences on children's development during Key Stage 2.* Nottingham: Department for Children, Schools and Families.

Sylva, K., Melhuish, E., Sammons, P., Siraj-Blatchford, I. and Taggart, B. (2012) *Effective pre-school, primary and secondary education project, final report from the Key Stage 3 phase: influences on students' development from age 11-14.* London: UCL Institute of Education.

Taylor, M. (2017) *Good work: the Taylor review of modern working practices.* Department for Business, Energy & Industrial Strategy. London: The Stationery Office.

Thornley, C. (2017) *Tech transitions: UTCs, studio schools, and technical and vocational education in England's schools.* London: IPPR.

Thomson, D. (2015) 'What you study after your GCSEs depends on where you live', *Education Datalab.* Available at: educationdatalab.org.uk/2015/08/what-you-study-after-your-gcses-depends-on-where-you-live/

Thomson, D. (2017) 'The equivalence of A-Levels and BTECs', *Education Datalab.* Available at: educationdatalab.org.uk/2017/02/the-equivalence-of-a-levels-and-btecs/

Times Higher Education (2017) THE Teaching Survey 2017: results and analysis. Available at: www.timeshighereducation.com/features/the-teaching-survey-2017-results-and-analysis

Tombs, R. (2017) 'The myth of Britain's decline', *Spectator*, 8 July 2017. Available at: www.spectator.co.uk/2017/07/the-myth-of-britains-decline/.

Travers, M. (2017) 'Streaming dampens the aspirations of white working-class boys', *Schools Week*. Available at: schoolsweek.co.uk/streaming-dampens-the-aspirations-of-white-working-class-boys/

Treadaway, M. (2017) 'Long-term disadvantage, part one: challenges and successes', *Education Datalab*. Available at: educationdatalab.org.uk/2017/07/long-term-disadvantage-part-one-challenges-and-successes.

Treadaway, M. (2018a) 'What explains the gap between London and the north?', *Education Datalab*. Available at: educationdatalab.org.uk/2018/02/long-term-disadvantage-part-five-what-explains-the-gap-between-london-and-the-north/

Treadaway, M. (2018b) 'Our friends in the north', *Education Datalab*. Available at: educationdatalab.org.uk/2018/02/our-friends-in-the-north/

Tuijnman, A. (1991) 'Lifelong education: a test of the accumulation hypothesis', *International Journal of Lifelong Education* 10 (4) pp. 275-285.

UCAS (2016) *Through the lens of students: how perceptions of higher education influence applicants' choices.* Cheltenham: UCAS.

UCAS (2017a) *UK application rates by the January deadline, 2017 cycle.* Cheltenham: UCAS.

UCAS (2017b) *UCAS data and analysis.* Available at: www.ucas.com/corporate/data-and-analysis

UCAS (2017c) *Progression pathways 2017: pathways through higher education.* Available at: www.ucas.com/file/110596/download?token=aVG758ND

UKCES (2014a) *The labour market story: the state of UK skills.* Wath-upon-Dearne: UKCES.

UKCES (2014b) *The labour market story: skills for the future.* Wath-upon-Dearne: UKCES.

UKCES (2015a) *UK skill levels and international competitiveness.* Wath-upon-Dearne: UKCES.

UKCES (2015b) *Sector insights reports.* Wath-upon-Dearne: UKCES.

UKCES (2015c) *High level STEM skills requirements in the UK labour market*. Wath-upon-Dearne: UKCES.

UKCES (2016a) *Working futures 2014 to 2024*. Wath-upon-Dearne: UKCES.

Universities UK (2016) *Universities UK*. Available at: www.universitiesuk.ac.uk/

University and College Union (2016) 'Committee report highlights huge funding gap between further and higher education', *ucu.org.uk*. Available at: www.ucu. org.uk/article/8155/Committee-report-highlights-huge-funding-gap-between-further-and-higher-education?list=7872

Unwin, L., Fuller, A., Turbin, J. and Young, M. (2004) *What determines the impact of vocational qualifications? A literature review*. Department for Education and Skills. London: The Stationery Office.

Vivian, D., Winterbotham, M., Shury, J., Skone James, A., Huntley Hewitt, J., Tweddle, M., Downing, C., Thornton, A., Sutton, R., Stanfield, C. and Leach, A. (2016) *The UK commission's employer skills survey 2015: UK results*. Wath-upon-Dearne: UKCES.

Waldfogel, J. and Washbrook, E. (2010) *Low income and early cognitive development in the UK: a report for the Sutton Trust*. London: Sutton Trust.

Waldfogel, J. and Washbrook, E. (2011) 'Early years policy', *Child Development Research* 2011, pp. 1-12.

Wang, M., Eccles, J. and Kenny, S. (2013) 'Not lack of ability but more choice: individual and gender differences in choice of careers in science', *Psychological Science* 24 (5) pp. 770-775.

Washbrook, E. (2010) *Early environments and child outcomes: an analysis commission for the independent review on poverty and life chances*. Available at: www.bristol. ac.uk/media-library/sites/ifssoca/migrated/documents/eeco.pdf

Webster, R. and Blatchford, P. (2017) *The special educational needs in secondary education (SENSE) study: final report*. London: Nuffield Foundation.

Whitehead, N. (2013) *Review of adult vocational qualifications in England*. Wath-upon-Dearne: UKCES.

Wiener, M. (1981) English culture and the decline of the industrial spirit, 1850-1980. Cambridge: Cambridge University Press.

Willetts, D. (2017) *A university education*. Oxford: Oxford University Press.

Wiseman, O. (2017) *How to rebalance the British economy*. London: Politics and Economics Research Trust. Available at: pert.org.uk/wp-content/uploads/2016/10/221-OW-Rebalancing-summary.docx

Wolf, A. (2002) *Does education matter?* London: Penguin.

Wolf, A. (2011) *Review of vocational education: the Wolf report*. Department for Education and Department for Business, Innovation and Skills. London: The Stationery Office.

Wolf, A. (2015) *Heading for the precipice: can further and higher education funding policies be sustained?* London: King's College London.

Wolf, A., Dominguez-Reig, G. and Sellen, P. (2016) *Remaking tertiary education: can we create a system that is fair and fit for purpose?* London: Education Policy Institute.

Wood, C. and Scott, R. (eds) (2014) *A tale of two classrooms*. London: Demos. Available at: www.demos.co.uk/files/Two_classrooms_-_web.pdf

Wright, A. (2017) 'Do we need a labour theory of degree value?', *Wonkhe*. Available at: wonkhe.com/blogs/analysis-labour-theory-of-degree-value/

Yorke, M. (2010) *The placement experience of students on full-time foundation degrees: a pilot study*. Lichfield: Foundation Degree Forward.

Young, T. (2017) 'Parents, not schools, are key to our children's knowledge gap', *The Spectator*. Available at: www.spectator.co.uk/2017/08/parents-not-schools-are-key-to-our-childrens-knowledge-gap.

Zaidi, A., Howat, C. and Caisl, J. (2017) *Initial teacher education provision in further education*. London: Education and Training Foundation.

Index